Resiliency
in Hostile Environments

Resiliency
in Hostile Environments

A *Comunidad Agrícola*
in Chile's Norte Chico

William L. Alexander

Lehigh
University
Press

Bethlehem: Lehigh University Press

Associated University Presses
2010 Eastpark Boulevard
Cranbury, NJ 08512

The paper used in this publication meets the requirements of the American National Standard for Permanence of Paper for Printed Library Materials Z39.48-1984.

Library of Congress Cataloging-in-Publication Data

Alexander, William L., 1963–
    Resiliency in hostile environments : a comunidad agricola in Chile's Norte Chico / William L. Alexander.
        p. cm.
Includes bibliographical references and index.
ISBN 978-0-934223-89-8 (alk. paper)
    1. Commons—Chile—Norte Chico 2. Village communities—Chile—Norte Chico. 3. Norte Chico (Chile)—Rural conditions. I. Title.

HD1289.C52N673   2008
333.2—dc22

                                                                        2007022895

PRINTED IN THE UNITED STATES OF AMERICA

To Tom Weaver for twenty years of mentoring, inspiration, and friendship.

To the late Daniel Nugent for the intellectual spark and the exposure to ideas that changed me.

To my friends in Loma Seca for their uncommon generosity and unwavering good humor and patience.

Finally, to Meghan my love above everyone and everything else.

Contents

Preface   9

Acknowledgments   11

1. Transcending Categories through Ethnography   15
2. Articulating "Articulation" to Approach "the Peasant
   Question"   33
3. *Comunidades Agrícolas* in Chile's "Little North"   51
4. Resiliency in Hostile Natural, Social, and Political
   Environments   73
5. Forms of Mutual Assistance in Loma Seca   101
6. Productive Diversity in One Household   128
7. Economic Strategies in a Peasant Community   154
8. Standardization of Rural Livelihood and Market
   Integration Policies   192
9. Rural Development Beyond the Neoliberal Model   226

Works Cited   243
Index   256

Preface

THE *COMUNIDADES AGRÍCOLAS* OF CHILE'S NORTE CHICO ARE unique community systems of indivisible communal land, inherited land use rights, democratic decision making, and diverse economic strategies that are closely linked to changing environmental conditions. Families reproduce their livelihood in this semiarid region where drought is chronic and poverty is widespread through a combination of pastoralism, dryland farming, and temporary labor migration. As this research is based on fieldwork that spanned three years of extreme climate changes, the reader is presented with an opportunity to observe a full range of flexible risk management strategies and cooperative mutual assistance that these people make use of at both the family and community level. One particular family's story is given as an illustration of the extraordinary resiliency that these communities have shown despite the harsh ecological and, at times, social and political environment in which they are situated. State attention to the problems that the comunidades face has increased during Chile's transition to democracy over the past two decades, but economic development programs sometimes limit the options of people living there and at times conflict with local ideals and practices. This book brings to light the specifics of their livelihood and culture and addresses important questions concerning the persistence and the future of peasant culture and small commodity producers in Latin America.

Acknowledgments

I WOULD LIKE TO THANK THE FOLLOWING FUNDING INSTITUTIONS FOR their support of this research: the Fulbright Commission, the Institute of International Education, and the University of Arizona's Department of Anthropology, Graduate College, and Social and Behavioral Science Research Institute. Parts of this book were presented at the annual meetings of the American Anthropological Association (AAA), the Society for Applied Anthropology (SfAA), the Society for the Anthropology of North America (SANA), and the Canadian Anthropology Society (CASCA). I would like to thank my colleagues in those sessions for their valuable feedback as I work shopped earlier versions of this text.

While in Chile, scholars and technical experts such as Milka Castro, Sergio Avendaño, Fabian Reyes, Bernardo Contreras, Claudio Meneses, Hector Navea, Raul Meneses and Ericka Zuñiga were especially generous with their time and knowledge. Special appreciation goes to my long-time mentor and colleague Tom Weaver at the University of Arizona and to my friend Agapito Santander in Chile for their inestimable guidance and encouragement.

I would like to offer my gratitude to my colleagues at the University of Arizona South for their support during my six years on the faculty there and to my new colleagues in the Anthropology Department at the University of North Carolina Wilmington for the exciting opportunity to work with them.

Finally, I want to thank Meghan Geagan for the artwork, the support, the happiest years of my life, and the wonderful times ahead.

Resiliency
in Hostile Environments

1

Transcending Categories through Ethnography

THE *ANNUS HORRIBILIS:* A YEAR OF CATASTROPHES IN THE NORTE CHICO

AT 10:00 PM ON A TUESDAY NIGHT IN OCTOBER, LOS VILOS WAS quiet. Except for the rumble of the occasional truck passing on the Pan-American Highway, the slow steady cadence of the evening tide played unaccompanied by any other sound. During the high season, tourists and local visitors at the seaside motel where we were staying would find this lulling rhythm and the cool ocean breezes agreeable sleeping companions after a day at the beach. But during the chilly midweek days of early spring, the working-class vacation spot and fishing village was occupied almost exclusively by its own residents, most of them settled in for the evening.

In a split second a familiar rumble became a disconcerting roar. As I opened my mouth to offer a speculation as to the size of the passing truck, the small television hanging in a high corner of the room began to bounce violently, its mounting bolts unscrewing themselves from the wall. Although my wife Julie and I had grown up in Iowa and Mississippi, respectively, and had spent the last few years living in Arizona—all three states free from any noticeable seismic activity— we quickly determined that this was an earthquake and, finding the door with surprising efficiency, exited the motel room. Even the uninitiated could tell that this was a "big one."

Joined in the parking lot by the proprietress of the motel, we huddled together in our pajamas and waited. An earthquake elongates the passing of time, the seconds stretching out to distorted proportions as the ground shakes. The feeling of helplessness during a disaster quickly brings one's religious beliefs, or lack thereof, to the surface. We were an interesting mix. Crying, the elderly *dueña* held her medallion and prayed in Spanish. Julie, an agnostic Reform Jew with sporadic temple attendance, recalled every word of a prayer in Hebrew, while I, normally the cocksure agnostic, felt my own grounds for disbelief becoming as shaky as the ground on which I was now standing. We waited interminably for the earth beneath our feet to stop rolling.

The earthquake that struck north-central Chile on October 14, 1997 was the most powerful in over a decade, but seismologists were quick to point out that registering 6.8 on the Richter scale was minor in magnitude in comparison to others that have devastated a country that accounted for 40 percent of the world's release of seismic energy in the twentieth century. The 1985 earthquake that caused massive destruction and hundreds of deaths in central Chile was thirty-three times stronger. At 9.3 on the Richter scale, the earthquake in Valdívia in 1960 was thirty thousand times stronger and killed more than five thousand people. The worst event occurred in Chillán in 1939 in which nearly thirty thousand lost their lives.

The people of the Norte Chico—the semiarid ecologically transitional region lying between Chile's fertile central valley and the vast rainless Atacama desert to the far north—were thankful that the damage had not been worse, but these statistics were little consolation to an area that had suffered through what was being referred to in the press and in the popular discourse as the "year of catastrophes." (Two days after the earthquake, the national daily *El Mercurio* dramatically called the year the region's *Annus Horribilis* [Oct. 16, 1997, C 3].) The year began as the continuation of a long period of drought and when the winter rains fell at last, the zone had endured the driest of four consecutive years of inadequate rainfall. In April, after persistent pressure from the inhabitants and local politicians, the government declared Region IV (known as "Coquimbo" and occupying the southern half of the Norte Chico) a "disaster zone" and initiated emergency funds when it was estimated that commercial losses attributable to the drought amounted to over one hundred million U.S. dollars. Most of these losses were the result of a one-third reduction in livestock, a drastic decrease in arable land, and low levels of fruit production. Reservoirs were averaging less than one-quarter of their capacity.

The rain finally returned in June, but with a vengeful force. Overall, the winter rainfall was between two to three times above average across the region. The damage was exacerbated because it was concentrated in two intense periods with ruinous results. A recording station near the capital of La Serena reported 110 millimeters of rain for the month of June, nearly six times the area's average. Seven hundred villages were cut off during the flooding as fifteen bridges were disabled and 80 percent of the rural roads were made impassable. Two people drowned in a rural interior sector in major flooding on June 19.

July's precipitation was a little below average. Heavy rains then resumed in August at four times the normal amount of precipitation. Four more died in the flooding and 14,000 families reported serious damage to their property. For dryland cultivators dependent upon rain-fed irrigation and working badly eroded soil desiccated by years of drought, the rain clouds were a cruel Trojan horse, a desperately needed gift that quickly unleashed destruction. The distribution of rain is as important as the quantity. Seventy millimeters of rain spread across the winter months normally ensures a successful harvest of cereal crops, such as wheat and barley, but one event of one hundred millimeters or more coming on the heels of a succession of dry years is disastrous and washes away massive amounts of soil and seeds. This was what many poor farmers experienced in 1997.

As with most weather-related disasters around the world that year, the excessive rains in northern Chile were blamed on the atmospheric changes produced by the El Niño phenomenon, the cyclical warm ocean current identified by Peruvian fishermen two hundred years ago and named in honor of the Christ child. (Later, a wheat-farming friend of mine in the countryside would mock in whimsical sacrilege this popular fixation on the phenomenon by saying that "El Niño is to blame for *everything!*" (El Niño tiene la culpa por *todo!*), continuing the joke by describing the pluvial pattern of no rain followed by too much rain in "the Lord giveth and the Lord taketh away" terms.) On the day before the earthquake, I had been caught in one of El Niño's downpours after visiting a friend in the city of Illapel to make final arrangements for our stay in the little community in which I would be carrying out my fieldwork. Perhaps I would have been less annoyed by this drencher had I known that this would be the last rain that I would see in Chile in my two extended stays over the course of the next two years, for the drought would reappear to make 1998 one of the driest years in the twentieth century.

About sixty kilometers into the craggy interior from Los Vilos, Illapel is the capital of Choapa (the southernmost province of Region IV) and the commercial nucleus for agricultural and livestock production in the valley of the Choapa River. The Choapa and the Elqui and Limarí rivers to the north bisect the region from the Andean *pre-cordillera* to the east to the Pacific Ocean to the west, providing water for the large-scale production of a wide variety of fruits and vegetables. Between these fertile valleys, the terrain is a vast expanse of rugged, sparsely populated desert. The small towns in the interior are linked to one another and to the cities of Illapel and Ovalle (the urban hub serving the rural producers of the Limarí valley) by rough dirt roads that wind their way through rocky hills and negotiate steep precipices. The people who live in and around these communities are among the area's poorest. Many are dependent upon small streams (*quebradas*) and rudimentary irrigation to water their fields and plots. Others rely solely on the sporadic rainfall to irrigate their crops and on the greatly deteriorated natural vegetation to graze their animals. The epicenter of the earthquake was near Illapel, and it was this impoverished interior that was devastated due to the number of antiquated adobe houses. More than 3,600 rural dwellings were completely destroyed and another 10,000 suffered irreparable damage. Of the eight people who were killed, six constituted an entire family who lost their lives when their adobe house collapsed in a sector in the sector of Punitaqui.

In this area there is a specific type of community that I had come to study. Punitaqui and Ovalle are the two *comunas* where most of Chile's comunidades agrícolas are located (figure 1.1). Found only in Region IV, as of 2002 there were about 90,000 people living in 178 of these communities, the total area of which account for about 1 million hectares or roughly one-third of the region (Livenais and Aranda 2003, 278). This land-to-person ratio is high because of the overall low carrying capacity of the dry, degraded land, and by standards of income, poverty levels are the greatest in the region. Due to this scarcity of resources and the uncertainty of rain, these communities have developed particular responses to the environment that have allowed them to survive in this harsh land since colonial times. The comunidades agrícolas are unique entities in Chile. Their system of land tenure, resource use and conservation, and social relations of production are characterized by indivisible communal land, inherited rights to use common land and individual plots; group projects and other forms of mutual assistance; a democratic decision-making political structure; and diverse economic strategies involving a combination of subsistence and market production and dependency upon wage labor and other external sources of income. These characteristics have helped the communities survive changes in the wider economic and political context, as well. From its beginning, the comunidad system has been shaped by and linked with processes of capitalist expansion and regional economic development.

"Survival" was, thus, a keyword in my planned research. It took on a more immediate and personal significance on the night of October 14. But having survived an earthquake just two weeks after arriving in Chile (my second visit to the country and Julie's first), we assured ourselves that after such an inauspicious beginning any subsequent difficulties would be small in comparison and that an earthquake would be the most severe thing that we would have to survive. This

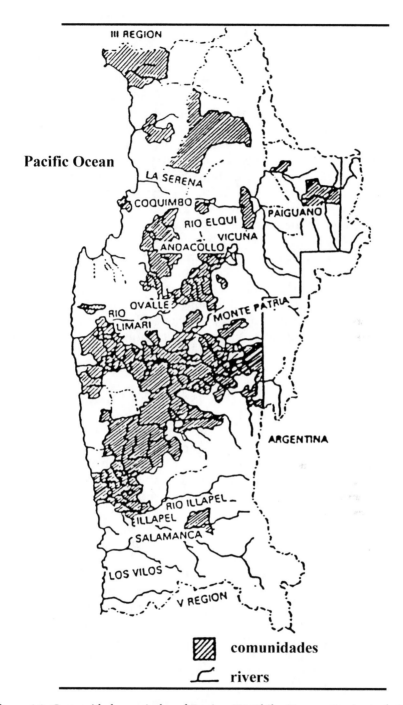

Figure 1.1. Comunidades agrícolas of Region IV, Chile. (Source: Instituto de Investigación de Recursos Naturales para la Corporación de Fomento de la Producción [IREN-CORFO].)

assurance proved to be altogether correct as the people with whom we lived in the *comunidad* of Loma Seca were among the most generous and obligingly helpful we had ever met, and they made any of the problems that we faced there small ones.

The earthquake, however, did delay our discovery of this for a bit. We were stuck in Los Vilos for a few days because the Pan-American Highway, the country's only north–south route, was closed after one-third of the 150-meter-high El Teniente bridge between Los Vilos and Ovalle crashed to the ground. Until an alternate road was constructed, the country was effectively cut in half. When we later bypassed the bridge by bus on the gravel service road, the remains of the towering structure was a sobering sight, made even more so by the gnarled heap of a tractor-trailer rig lying in the rubble below. Shortly after the quake occurred and before barriers could be put up, an unfortunate truck driver descending the steep decline that approaches the bridge from the south was unable to stop his vehicle and hurdled over the missing section like a marble rolling off a table edge. For several months after, the mangled cab remained there as a grim reminder of his death and of the swift and destructive power of Nature.

"Como se existe *esta* comunidad?"

The earthquake was an extreme and, thankfully, rare example of the unpredictability and instability of the environment in which the people of the comunidades agrícolas live. Many people in Chile view the communities from the outside as a kind of rural slum, inhabited only by those too poor, unskilled, uneducated, old, or sick to work and live in the "modern world." Because of the diminishing ability of families to earn a living from the land and the tendency for the younger generations to leave the communities, it is tempting to see their cultural traditions as "dying" and to conclude that the community form of production is merely a means of subsistence for the rural poor and in light of persistent drought, erosion, and desertification, an unsustainable one at that. Though the problems within comunidades and the pressures on their productive resources are great, the above assessments are limited by a misleadingly bounded conception of "community," which cannot account for the ways in which members maintain and reproduce their livelihood and culture through their links with the regional economy.

Most of these communities are far more dynamic than such a static and remote portrait of them renders. They have been described to me by both scholars and *comuneros* themselves as systems of a "human resiliency" tightly linked to climatic conditions. If there is rain many people prefer to stay. When the system is under pressure and when productive resources are scarce, people are driven from the land in search of external sources income. Not all migration is permanent or long-term, and it is common for many of those who leave to maintain their connection to home by sending back remittances and returning at crucial times. For example, migrants will often leave their jobs just for the weekend in order to work a piece of land or pitch in with the harvesting.

Another form of fluidity of movement that community members have at their disposal is transhumant pastoralism. Extreme variability of rainfall demands resourceful and flexible grazing strategies. Based on their understanding of the capacity and limitations of their environment, families who raise goats and sheep often maximize production during times of drought by relocating with their animals during the December to March dry summer season to the Andes where there is water from snowfall runoff. They may also rent privately owned pasture closer to home from commercial farmers in the valley. If the drought persists they may even choose to stay away from the comunidad for years at a time. Such movement is costly, but allows them a certain control over the stability of their herds and maintenance of their productive means.

Within every community there exist three forms of land tenancy and a political body with democratic procedures for controlling resource use. Along with possessions for dwelling, there are tiny possessions (*goces singulares*) irrigated by whatever source of water is available (*bajo riego*). These plots are few and small in size (ranging between 0.5 and 2 hectares) and are used to grow small quantities of vegetables for family consumption and food for their animals. Most families do not have access to these and depend upon their rights as members of the community to the other two forms of land use. Being a comunero entitles one to individual rights (*derechos*) to the sections of land (*lluvias*) located above the water source for rain-fed cereal cultivation and to the community pasture (*campo común*). After the productive capacity of a lluvia has been exhausted, it is reopened to regenerate for a period of years, and the family petitions to enclose another. The title of comunero is inherited and generally passed down to the eldest son or to the widow. There is a limited number and, as with goces singulares, they may only be transferred to or purchased by community members. Along with this land tenure system, comunidades are also unique because of their long history of internal democracy. Officers are elected every three years. Meetings are held throughout the year to arrive at a consensus over land use and apportionment, to set limits to the number of animals and to develop community projects.

Indivisible and sheltered from the open market for land, community possession of the land itself, as poor as it may be, is an important means of security, the constant variable in the changing equation of family subsistence and production. Protecting this land and providing its members with a coherent base that engenders group projects that maximize human resources within the community, the comunidad social organization and the comunero culture of solidarity improve families' chances to make a living from this land. By periodically engaging in wage labor away from the community, by herding their animals in other areas for extended periods of time, and by producing commodities for external markets families improve their life chances by participating in varied economic orbits. The ability to diversify income-generating activities in such ways is crucial in an area of such limited resources. It is crucial to both the reproduction of the family way of life and the community mode of production.

The other important way in which comunidades are articulated with the external economy is through economic development and resource conservation policies and projects. There is a wide array of government agencies, NGOs, and private firms providing assistance in this region of Chile. Their efforts to improve rural economic and ecological conditions include irrigation projects, reforestation and soil reclamation, and promotion of small commercial enterprises. In theory, all of these are attempts to replace environmentally damaging and economically unprofitable local practices such as the overgrazing of animals and the cultivation of wheat on already deteriorated soil with production for regional and national markets that is carried out under sustainable conditions and with stabilized resources. Sometimes these proposals and interventions conflict with community ideals and practices because they are predicated on making drastic changes in the traditional communal structure and productive activities. Sometimes comunidades are excluded altogether because they lack the necessary tools to participate in these programs. Sometimes these policies directly encroach upon community members' ability to make a living. However, there are other more enlightened approaches that understand the communities' particular relationship to the environment and economy and that aim to work with comuneros to determine appropriate forms of development rather than imposing them from above.

My intentions in coming to Loma Seca were to observe the community's particular strategies for survival in this harsh land; to identify to what extent this survival is dependent on outside markets, sources of income, and support; to examine in what ways these external connections serve to help the community reproduce its traditional means of livelihood and social organization and in what ways external relations act as pressures against the traditional structure; to investigate the viability of the comunidad system of flexibility and security in terms of control of natural resources, distribution of risk, and maximization of human resources; and to study the degree to which the organization of land and labor and the associated communitarian ideals accommodate, resist, or work in a complementary fashion with the market-integration ideology of current development goals and policies. Having gathered this empirical information, my goal was to answer larger questions concerning the persistence of the peasantry in Latin America and the articulation of corporate forms of land tenure and communal production with the capitalist economy and to make specific recommendations based on my conclusions, which I hoped would promote appropriate development policy that took into account the comunidades' particular relationship with the regional environment and economy, recommendations useful in other parts of the world where local cultures are striving to maintain their traditions and reproduce their domestic/subsistence economy under similar pressures.

Getting started on the ground in the community in my initial fieldwork phase, I encountered the usual difficulty of translating these somewhat lofty aims and ideas into a simple statement that would answer the comuneros' straightforward questions of why I had chosen Loma Seca, what I was going to study, and why.

"Why are you here?" Surely every anthropologist in the field struggles in abridging his or her thesis into a pithy answer to satisfy this very practical question. I was fortunate. Early on, after fumbling to condense my curiosity about internal relations of production and resource conservation, connections to external markets and development policies, and how all of this is related to unstable environmental conditions, I was provided with a good answer by my interrogator. The man who would become one of my key informants in the community thought a bit and said "Ah. Como se existe *esta* comunidad?" (Literally, "How does *this* community exist?" The implication was: "What does this particular community do to survive and stay together despite the tough challenges that we face?") This became part of his introduction of me to other people in Loma Seca, and it was one that all of them could certainly understand. Considering that my plan was to carry out a study that avoided the limitations of bounded and isolated "case studies," and that I planned to do this by focusing on the larger context of political economy in which the community exists, I could not have said it better myself.

PERSISTENCE IN THE PERIPHERY AND THE UNIT OF ANALYSIS

The comunidades agrícolas of Region IV are often misunderstood by development agents because their members participate in differentiated but connected spheres of domestic or subsistence "internal" production and "external" markets for their goods and labor. In doing so across space and time, communities acquire the means to reproduce themselves in ways that transcend easily drawn community "boundaries." Anthropologists likewise grapple with the analytical problems of such elastic and permeable boundaries. These problems have long been important in the study of peasant culture.

There is a temptation to see the persistence of peasant culture in "all or nothing" terms, according to one's point of view. On the one hand, one might describe peasants as resisting capitalist exploitation in a valiant struggle to go their own way, or existing by some miracle in an idyllic position seemingly out of the grasp of the modern world. On the other hand, one might see "survival" not in the active sense as in "to survive," but as a static and residual form, a vestige from the past, or, if you will, like an atavistic organ that is present in form but no longer serves its original function. In this supposition, the inevitable elimination of the peasantry is an evolution that is irrevocably on course, if not already finished. Peasant production in this case would seem to be relevant only to the point that it subsidizes capitalism in the modern sector by its supply and reproduction of cheap labor and other market commodities.

In their extremes, these interpretations are either valorizing or condescending, conceptualizing the unit of analysis from either the "worm's eye" (from below) or the "God's eye" (from above) point of view. Whether idealized as insulated against and isolated from the wider political economy (perhaps in an ethnographer's attempt of "rescue ethnography" to "save" local culture from the homogenizing penetrations of global capitalism) or represented as diminished if not practically disappeared (perhaps in an economist's attempt to rescue capitalism from the indetermination of its incomplete presence in the countryside), our comprehension of the actual processes of rural culture is left impoverished. In this study, I will construct a framework that takes into account the processual relationship between economy and culture that neither diminishes an understanding of the power of capitalist development and expansion nor ignores the dynamic integrity of communities that are based on other forms of production that do not correspond exactly to the capitalist model.

The study of peasant culture is the study of such boundaries and connections, the problematic nature of which William Roseberry distilled as "the problem of the bounded village" (1989a, 108). Certainly the economy in which peasants participate is increasingly global in nature. Outside of anthropology, most observers of economy and culture today speak of "globalization" not as a process, but as a thing that is with us here, now, everywhere, and forever. One need only watch a half hour of network television news to see the problems and contradictions in this assumption. Within the same broadcast, there may be analyses of "the world economy" and stories of nations improving their position in it by making necessary changes ordered by the logic of this system in the ways that they do business in the world market and in the ways that they conduct their affairs at home. There may also be stories of escalating violent hostilities and struggles for local autonomy based on ethnicity and religion. In many parts of the world over the past decade the "new world order" has been a world of disorder, as people within nation-states fight to divide the globe into increasingly smaller parts. In a recent series of lectures on globalization at the Royal Institute in London (broadcast around the world on the BBC World Service), Anthony Giddens, director of the London School of Economics, remarked upon this dual character as the creation of homogenization and the proliferation of difference, with the weakened nation-state caught in the middle—too small to solve the big problems of economy on its own and too big to solve problems at the local level (1999).

A useful tool, I believe, in addressing the tension between peasant production and external development policy and practice is the concept of "articulation." Developed by Althusser and popularized by many of his neo-Marxist followers in the 1970s, the term was used to look beyond market mechanisms as the sole cause of economic underdevelopment, insisting instead that the concept of "mode of production" is the appropriate unit of analysis. Speaking in general terms, mode of production is the combination or "articulation" of productive forces (the material, tools, and labor needed) and the social relations of production (the relations—whether based on wages or reciprocity—that people establish during this production process). In this introduction I will leave aside the mountain of debate over what exactly constitutes a mode of production, lest we spend all of our time identifying and typologizing articulated modes (or, carrying through the "tool" metaphor, as the expression goes, when you are holding a hammer, everything looks like a nail). I will review this debate (or at least partially scale this mountain) when I make my case for the usefulness of articulation theory in approaching "the Peasant Question" in chapter 2. I take as a given that within the capitalist economy there are distinct and diverse sectors that are linked, but that do not uniformly conform to a singular, monolithic "pure" capitalist ideology and practice. Instead I will focus on the process of "articulation" itself—connection and mutual transformation—as the unit of analysis.

The need for anthropology, particularly the need for anthropological fieldwork at the specific site where local and global histories meet, is obvious. The study of political economy could use the details produced by the anthropological method and perspective. Cultural anthropology would benefit from the framework of political economy. Some have not been so optimistic. In his reflections on the dilemmas of reconciling the concerns of "Marxism and Culture" in his influential book *Anthropologies and Histories* (1989b, 51), Roseberry recounts anthropologist Sherry Ortner's eloquent concern that:

> The problems derived from the capitalism-centered world-view also affect the political economists' view of history. History is often treated as something that arrives, like a ship, from outside the society in question. Thus we do not get a history OF that society, but the impact of (our) history ON that society . . . The political economists, moreover, tend to situate themselves more on the ship of (capitalist) history than on the shore. They say in effect that we can never know what the other system, in its unique, "traditional" aspects, really looked like anyway. (Ortner 1984, 143)

Two decades later, in many ways this is where we still find ourselves today, struggling to find coherence in such concepts as "traditional" and "community," if we are to understand the persistence of local culture in the modern world. Anthropology has had a long history of what Marshall Sahlins calls our "founding contradictions," the theoretical oppositions of evolutionism and particularism, science and history, explanation and interpretation, materialism and idealism, political economy and symbolic anthropology (1976, 55). Roseberry also insists that the tendency in social science to reify oppositional analytic categories like traditional/modern, domestic/capitalist, and developed/developing imposes upon rural peoples of the past the "preoccupations (not to mention the ideological battles) of the present" and marks as disjoined and exotic contemporary people whose means of livelihood seem radically different from those in urban industrial society (1988, 425–26; 1989b, 30–33). These observable differences in livelihood should not eclipse the likewise discernible connections that rural people have historically had and continue to have with states and markets. Analysis based on a long time scale, as Stern suggests, renders a picture of global-local articulation that is more complex than "predictable parochial obsessions with land, subsistence, or autonomy" (1987, 14).

Many critics of "postmodern" ethnography have simplistically pegged that approach as one attempt to do away with once and for all any notions of materialist explanation in cultural anthropology. I believe that in the situations of tension between community and economy that I will describe in this book, we would do better to dispense with the constraints of oppositional thinking and embark upon the methodology Cohn describes as the task of writing anthropological history. Like Ortner, he also uses a ship metaphor, telling us that our task is to navigate between the general and the specific (Cohn 1980). In this book, my own course of navigation will be (1) between national, regional, and community history by exploring the ways in which the comunidades agrícolas were and continue to be articulated with wider economic development and (2) between development policy and ideology conceived externally and encountered locally in a mutually constitutive process that is informed by this history of articulation.

The young subfield of political ecology offers new possibilities for understanding this dialectic between social structure and human agency by situating cultural and political action within a framework of ecological concepts. In conceptualizing limits to individual action as "significant but not always socially constructed" by structures of power, political ecology redresses Marxist political economy's tendency to completely reduce the "productive action of real individuals" to simply class conflict (Greenberg and Park 1994, 1). Marx's concept of production is fundamentally an understanding of the transformation of Nature. It is in particular ecological niches that livings are made, and it is through laboring hands and human minds that Nature is shaped, understood, used, and conserved. Yet the environment also sets certain limits to human behavior, and in an area of extremely scarce resources, such as the Norte Chico, it is important to keep ecological variables as part of the equation.

Natural environment, social environment, and "policy environment" (Weaver 1996) are interconnected components of a common structure from which decisions concerning use and conservation of ecological resources toward productive ends are enacted at the state level and experienced at the local level. Public policy has been shown to be a good place to understand articulation mechanisms when these policies in the process of transferring surplus value from peripheral to core areas seek to tangibly bring under state control local economic practice that has previously operated outside of the reach of the state (Weaver 1996). By analytically isolating specific points of state intervention into the space where distinct spheres of production are connected, we gain insight into exactly how local cultural practice engages capitalism.

In short, it is my contention that peasant studies have fallen out of fashion mainly because of the mistaken belief that peasants no longer exist and because the Marxian-inspired debates about the social-historical position of peasants that were fashionable in the 1970s have seemed to run out of steam. I believe that this is a shame because, as my case study shows, there is much fruitful work to be done in this area. My work questions earlier ideas about peasants from the seemingly opposed modernization and Marxian perspectives that still persist in various guises today. I venture to propose that if peasants seem to have "disappeared," then maybe it is our categories that have failed us. It is obvious that while the political and ecological adaptations of peasants can vary widely, they are always firmly rooted in particular social situations that make sense to the people involved. Suffice it to say, contrary to much development discourse, peasants are not irrational or ignorant in these adaptations, but rather they are seeking to defend local rights to land and livelihood, even if outsiders find their motivations incomprehensible. It is my hope that the light from this work will shine both ways: illuminating both the biases of the observers and the judiciousness of the decision making of the observed.

STYLISTIC AND METHODOLOGICAL CHOICES

There is a similar tendency for those accustomed to ethnographic writing and analysis in which the author's voice is buried in—presumably—neutral and objective observations in which the ethnographer's presence in the field goes remarkably unexamined to dismiss a narrative style in which the author's voice is obviously present as "subjective" or "postmodern." This superficial criticism, I feel, rests upon another example of the misguided oppositions in the social sciences that I am striving to "write against." *Stylistically*, I believe that this book occupies the fertile "middle ground" that I contend articulation analysis achieves *analytically*. I have carefully chosen personal experiences and reflections to draw the reader in to both dramatic and "little" events that act as pieces of a larger mosaic: the communities' overall resiliency in the face of ecological, economic, social, and political crises. If at times these details come across as personal and subjective, it may to a large extent be because mode of production analysis rests on the belief that the relationship between the economic base of society and the social formation is a mutually formative process. The active players in this process as it is described here are the people of Loma Seca themselves, many of whom I got to know quite well.

I have chosen to provide a narrative that integrates theory and ethnographic details while giving the reader a good idea of what daily life is like in the community. In this respect I have elected to chronicle both key events and everyday routines that not only offer descriptions of campesino cultural life in north-central Chile but that are also important illustrations of various aspects of this particular mode of production in this frequently harsh land. For example, as we shall see, celebrations and recreational activities such as the Day of the Dead festivities, Chilean rodeo, horse races, and soccer matches are not only important cultural expressions, they also serve to raise funds for community projects. Collective wheat harvests and other group projects demonstrate work-focused forms of mutual assistance bound up in the bustling social activities of a "year of rain." Descriptions of how goat cheese and other petty commodities are handcrafted and of the arduous duties that migration during times of drought demands will not only give the reader an understanding of one particular family's dedication and sacrifice in maintaining their productive resources, but will translate into an appreciation of the dogged persistence of peasant livelihood in general.

Ethnographic projects entail a special relationship between the ethnographer and the people who are the subjects of study. Through fieldwork, the author engages in a long-term exchange of ideas and insights with the members of his or her host community. What results is, in many ways, a mutually constructed text that imparts knowledge and information produced by particular interactions from "the field." (Some excellent reflections on how one might conceive of "the field" in the globalized world of today where things like free trade, political engagement, human rights issues, and communications make the fieldwork boundaries of the past seem self-serving and, during times of crisis, irresponsible is provided by Lynn Stephen in chapter 1 of her remarkable 2002 book on contemporary Zapatismo in Chiapas and Oaxaca, ¡Zapata Lives!: Histories and Cultural Politics in Southern Mexico.) Also—and perhaps less commented on—there is a third participant in the "end product" of the endeavor of "writing culture": the reader of the text. Every reader brings his or her own particular experiences, interests, and motivations to the book. In an attempt to accommodate this, I have structured this book to anticipate various levels of engagement with this ethnography. For the student of peasant studies and political economy, the following chapter will provide an examination of "the Peasant Question in Latin America"—that is, the debates over the persistence of the peasant mode of production and the applicability of "peasantry" as a valid descriptive and analytical category—as well as a review of what I believe are the strengths of the articulation of modes of production approach to understanding certain aspects of rural culture; it will also succinctly summarize how my study relates to these broader questions and debates. This "reading" will be valuable to those interested in Marxian political economy. A more general reader might choose to proceed to the rest of the book and the beginning of the "meat" of the story and the ethnographic details.

La Guerra Bruta: From the General to the Specific

In chapter 3 I provide a general description of the internal characteristics of land tenancy, political structure, resource use and management, and interfamily productive relations that distinguish the comunidades agrícolas from other rural communities in Chile. This will be followed by an overview of the origins and historical development of the comunidades that pays particular attention to their relation to large-scale commodity production—particularly that of copper mining—in the region. In chapter 4 I will consider the environmental impact of economic development of the region, chronicle key points in Chilean history when changes in land reform and property laws affected the communities, and present the contemporary regional ecological and socioeconomic context in which the communities are situated.

In chapters 5, 6, and 7, I will present ethnographic data from the community of Loma Seca collected during my October 1997 through April 1998 and September 1998 through May 1999 periods of fieldwork. Because the first period followed the abundant winter rains of 1997 and the second was conducted during a time of extreme drought, my data will reflect changing and diverse productive strategies and cultural practices mediated by the comunidad structure across exceptional variation in the availability of environmental, human, and capital resources. I will explore the effectiveness of the comunidad system to flexibly manage, exploit, and maintain these resources during "good" and "bad" years at both the community and individual household level.

My information in chapter 5 is drawn from a combination of my participant-observation experiences, interviews with comuneros, and access to records of community meetings. Living in the community gave me the opportunity to observe day-to-day life and to attend community meetings, shared work projects, and community social activities that raise money for specific objectives. In chapter 6 I will describe the productive strategies of one particular household. In terms of monetary resources and material goods, they might be considered "poor" by outside standards, but within the community they are most certainly not. By any standard, they are among the more successful families, taking advantage of all of the economic activities that are available to them. They have goats and sheep, grow wheat, participate heavily in group projects and in the community organizational structure, and they combine this with a family member who works away from the community during the week and returns to work at home on the weekends. In chapter 7 I will further examine the crucial *mutability* (remarkable versatility in response to changing access to resources) of this household during times of environmental crisis. Through data collected from a household survey, I will compare their activities and resources with those of other families in order to put forward some general statements about prevalent production strategies there.

Political Economy and Rural Development in Chile

This data supports my major argument that flawed understandings of these types of communities have hampered economic development initiatives. In the final two chapters I will proceed from a specific to the general framework. In chapter 8, after an introductory consideration of the implicit themes of nationalism, hegemony, and state formation often present in public policy, I will outline the controversial details swirling around a law that is part of a coordinated economic development program in Region IV. I will argue that along with limiting the options of the "Mutable Mobile Modes of Resource Maximization" (my term for the communal-individual interface in this land of environmental—and previously, political—instability), this program is based on and promotes "Policy-Positioned Ascriptions of Ethnicity, Identity, and History," my term for the arbitrary attributions of racial identification engendered by proscriptive development that reifies images of a "noncapitalist Other" positioned in contrast to ideals of modernization and market integration. In chapter 9 I will locate this law, policy, and controversy within the contemporary social and political context in Chile, in which development specialists generally agree that agropastoral populations that have exceeded the productive capacity of the land under their traditional system need to be more reliant on external markets than they already are. After briefly surveying some key initiatives in order to propose that analysis should recognize the unique histories, ecological adaptations, and social relations of productions in these communities, I will distill the germane elements of the "Subsistence-Stewardship Approach to Productive Diversity" (my term for a perspective that avoids overly centralized, "top-down" decision making) into a series of statements rural development programs will find useful in understanding economic options and environmental resource strategies in places like the Norte Chico. For development specialists, this will help them better understand the previously unconsidered or unseen impact of policies at the local level. For cultural anthropologists interested in the survival and reproduction of peasant culture, this will bring to light the specific mechanisms through which these rural modes are articulated with the external economy via public policy. For these communities specifically, this work is important because there has been no ethnography or anthropological work published in the United States on the comunidades agrícolas of Region IV. Theirs is a story that deserves to be told.

Outside of Chile, in rural areas around the world problems are frequently defined and assistance administered through the rather narrow lens of the ubiquitous export-oriented neoliberal market-integration model. By looking at specific sites of the articulation between local culture and world economy, we can work against the blindly homogenous views and homogenizingly blind actions based on "globalist" assumptions and prescriptions for development. This book will contribute to the formulation of programs that are multi-faceted and flexible, allowing communities to absorb the shocks of the ups and downs of the world market, which at times are no less devastating and no more predictable than an earthquake.

2
Articulating "Articulation" to Approach "the Peasant Question"

INTRODUCTION

THIS BOOK REALLY BEGINS WITH THE PREMISE THAT WHILE MUCH OF the debate over "the Peasant Question" in Latin America has gone away, in many parts of the region, peasant or campesino livelihood and culture simply has not. From this starting point, my fieldwork from north-central Chile contributes to a better understanding of the long debated contradictions that exist between a recognition of "human agency"—the active choices that individuals make in relation to the material resources and opportunities that are available to them—and a structuralist political economy/ecology framework that identifies the parameters of those choices and opportunities. Such "limiting factors" in my study include restricted access to capital and markets, periods of antagonism and engagement with the state, and the shifting variables of environmental and human resources. Focusing on specific cultural practices that reproduce rural livelihoods in the Norte Chico, I seek to understand one community's remarkable resiliency in various "hostile" environments (natural, sociopolitical, and those situated in the economic development milieu). Perhaps this example will reframe "the Peasant Question" (Reinhardt 1988) so as to ask, as Nugent proposed, "how (not why) after all these years, the peasantry refuses to go away" (1994, 302).

The debate concerning "the Peasant Question" in Latin America can be divided into two broad perspectives. The first views the persistence of campesino livelihood in terms of internal stability, a kind of culturally mediated equilibrium between economic opportunity and resource availability at the household level. The second sees persistence in terms of its value to external capitalist forces. Here the inevitable elimination of the peasantry as it is absorbed by capitalism is an evolution that is far along in progress but that has been slowed as production from peasant holdings serves to supplement wage income for the household and to subsidize the regional or national economy through the maintenance of low wages and lowered costs for reproducing wage labor. Both perspectives, taken in their extremes, present unrealistic representations of peasant life and say more about the macrolevel assumptions upon which they are based than about the actual day-to-day activities and aspirations of the people they purport to understand.

"THE PEASANT QUESTION": INTERNAL STABILITY AND EQUILIBRIUM?

In economic anthropology, the homeostasis of peasant life, despite changing pressures on the capacity for maintaining and reproducing production, is usually explained via intrinsic characteristics of the ways in which work is organized and cultural values and meanings are shared in peasant communities (Chayanov 1966; Foster 1965; Shanin 1987). Understanding the decision making behind such "value" and "values" has typically been couched in the familiar "formalist" (cost-benefit decision making based on individual maximization) versus "substantivist" (economic behavior shaped by the culturally specific "rationality" of the particular group) dichotomy. The literature on the formalist-substantivist debate in economic anthropology is seemingly endless. I agree with Wilk's assessment (1996, 13) that "if we judge the winners to be the ones with the most influence on later work, I think we have to call it a draw": although the substantivists wield the most influence in anthropology in general—in that the idea that economic activities are deeply embedded in a variety of social institutions is a "given" in most contemporary work—applied ecological researchers and demographic anthropologists have actively taken up many of the formalist's tools and concepts.

The "persistence" position is usually a modern extension of the work of the Russian economist Chayanov, who believed that family farms outfitted primarily for household consumption are self-regulated by their limited goals of production. The amount of land cultivated, food produced and consumed, and the work involved changes over the course of the family's life cycle as children are born and then themselves grow up to become workers as well as consumers. As each constituent worker in the household must work harder for each non-producing dependent that is added, the enticement of more profit through the expansion of production is offset by the added drudgery of the increased labor needed for this expansion (Chayanov 1966). As the first to systematically analyze the logic of this type of household, his influence is still great today in the field of economic anthropology because, as Wilk observes, "[Chayanov] offered a formalist solution to a substantivist problem" (1996, 21). In other words, he proposed that peasants, like people in all cultures, make rational decisions of maximization based on an understanding of limitations and opportunities in which the end justifies the means ("formalism"), but the logic of this behavior is unique to the household institution and should not be evaluated by historical specificities of a model of Western capitalism ("substantivism"). In comparison to market-oriented businesses in which the measure of production is solely determined by profit considerations, family farms are able to accept lower prices for the products they sell and "superexploit" themselves by receiving a return per hour of labor that is less than the market wage. As a result of these structural advantages, peasant farms would not be displaced in the wake of the rise of capitalist agriculture but would instead be drawn into a complex web of commercial production and distribution.

Shanin presents a similar model of peasant life that is both insulated and connected but with leveling mechanisms that create a kind of Chayanovian equilibrium. He insists that there is a delimiting definition of "peasantry" with four essential facets that can account for the persistence of peasant production. The first tenet in this definition is that the family farm is the basic multifunctional unit of social organization. Like Chayanov, Shanin emphasizes the prominence of the provision of consumption needs and family welfare over the motive of profit maximization and the degree of autonomy that this direct link between consumption and livelihood permits. The second factor is the activity of land husbandry as the primary means of livelihood directly supplying the bulk of consumption needs. The third tenet holds that a specific traditional culture associated with the "way of life" of small communities shapes individual motives and judges potential action by past experience and the collective will of the tightly integrated group. Importantly, as Shanin contends in the fourth part of his definition, peasant communities are always in the "underdog position": politically excluded from external sources of power and economically burdened through things such as tax, rent, and unfair terms of trade with the wider society (Shanin 1987).

From what the reader has encountered so far, it is easy to see that "homeostasis" and "equilibrium" in an ecology of degraded and diminishing resources would be inaccurate in assessing the relationship between people, environment, and economy in this part of the Norte Chico. While land husbandry is the primary means of livelihood for people living in Loma Seca, during nearly all years it alone is not sufficient, and as I will examine in chapter 7, the most successful families utilize diverse income-earning pursuits as they combine farming, herding, and petty commodity production with wage labor income. Additionally, equilibrium (especially when conceived in patronizing terms of "tradition" and quaint rurality) implies inertia, and as will be detailed in the pages to come, there is no lack of entrepreneurial initiative among the most active families of Loma Seca; in fact, I recall an economic development specialist who described the community as a "forward-thinking" comunidad agrícola—in his words one that "has families"—in which potential projects have much viability. Still, as I will discuss in chapter 3, there is something substantively different about the way in which the community structure and ideals mediate the actions of households. My assertion is that while the formalist-substantivist binary is a useful construct for sorting out motivations and choices that differ in style and substance, in practice the logic by which individuals base their actions is not as clear-cut as either the formalists or substantivists would have us believe. The last two elements of Shanin's four-part definition are probably most relevant to what I will present here. The "equalizing" force that inhibits economic growth for some is access to sufficient capital for production: primarily the expense of renting machinery and the costs of renting land during drought. In chapter 5 I will show that the work of community project committees reinvests some of the individual gains of constituent members back into the community into funds for projects with benefits that are shared by all. I argue that one reason that people in Loma Seca continue to produce seemingly low-profit commodities (wheat, artisan cheese, etc.) is because their production costs are low: they utilize family labor, for the most part they use traditional technology, they have access to a maximum amount of land with very little input costs, and they reduce individual family costs by intrafamilial pooling of labor. Also, they can accept lower prices because they do not have to pay rent when living in the community and because they provide a proportion of their own food requirements. In many ways, this supports the Chayanov model of the structural advantage of family production in the marketplace. That they have done so, however, demonstrates that the families are not autonomous and insulated from either each other or the outside economy; in fact they work together at opportune moments contingent upon yearly and seasonal ecological conditions. I offer an alternative model of decision making based on individual and community motives of profit maximization shaped by comunero culture and the cyclical scarcity of resources. One aspect of autonomy is freedom of movement and control over livelihood, and a powerful example of such autonomy is illustrated in chapter 6's description of the "itinerant season of sacrifice" in which one family goes to extraordinary means via migration to maintain its productive resources through lean times. My contention throughout this book is that both "marginality" and "autonomy" are useful concepts with descriptive value, but both can be overdrawn when taken as absolutes. As can easily be seen in this brief summary, some elements of the "internal" position will ring true in my case study while others clearly will not.

As discussed, the problem, of course, with such preoccupations with internal efficiency is that it often tends to gloss over the links between peasant modes and external capitalism and to soft-pedal the subordinate economic position that peasants occupy in a wider economic hierarchy. The benefits of this model is that it lets us see the actual control that people have over their own lives and the actions that they take in pursuing their livelihoods. It is necessary, then, to account for variance within a framework in which capitalism conditions but does not determine courses of action. The problem with an extreme view of this sort is that it presents peasants as living insular, timeless lives, detached from the modern world economy. This perspective overlooks the social disruptions that occur in a peasant culture's relationship with external capitalism. Chayanov's work was important in many ways for economic anthropology, especially as a rejection of explanations based on ethnocentric external assumptions and an insistence upon fieldwork at the local level. Since Chayanov was reacting against orthodox Marxist-Leninist thought, which held that the agrarian class structure will polarize along the same lines as in industrial society with the emergence of rural landowners and wage laborers, he saw peasant economy as largely autonomous and separate from the larger society and the market economy. When they do enter into market relations, Chayanov recommended that peasants form cooperatives in order to provide themselves with a better bargaining position in the marketplace and avoid becoming dependent upon technological inputs, bank loans, and food processing industries that are controlled by owners of capital. As I will detail in chapters 8 and 9, some of the development programs available to the people of Loma Seca and other agricultural communities in the region are predicated on a similar understanding of the nature of peasant life and society. The belief is that because they are isolated, insular, geared toward relatively self-sufficient production, and are generally cash poor, campesino households are required to form small entrepreneurial associations called *sociedades* before they can avail themselves of subsidized government loans and other forms of assistance. Such cooperative arrangements, it is believed, will provide these households with both a larger pool of resources and capital from which to draw and the experience of working together on small-scale capitalist enterprises, such as the cheese factory program described in the final chapters. While it is true that in the past the communal land tenure system has worked against the obtaining of credit through conventional means, as the productive activities in both the community and in an individual family described in chapters 5 and 6 demonstrate, there is neither a lack of cooperative relations nor individual entrepreneurial spirit. In fact, there is a long history of it.

"The Peasant Question": External Domination and Valiant Struggle?

In contrast, the "elimination of the peasantry" perspective entails either adhering to the orthodox Marxist conception of the development of capitalism in agriculture, placing the classical predictions of agrarian transformation within a longer historical trajectory, or reformulating the relationship between capitalism and peasant production in a way that explains the persistence of peasant agriculture in terms of its functional utility to capitalist activity outside its borders. Survival is romanticized as a valiant but ultimately futile struggle. The classical conception of Marx and Lenin held that, as in industry, the agrarian class structure will polarize. Petty commodity producers will disappear and an agrarian bourgeoisie and a rural proletariat will emerge in the development of capitalist relations in the countryside (Djurfeldt 1982, 148–50).

A kind of "antistability elimination" argument for the continued existence of peasant production in Latin America is fully developed in the work of de Janvry. He agrees with the classical argument that the development of large-scale agribusiness in Latin America created direct competition and a wage labor market that negatively impacted the productive capability of the peasantry, but seeks to understand why peasants were not wholly dispossessed by more efficient capitalist production and why they have persisted in being "semiproletarians" rather than full-fledged wage laborers. His answer is not that peasants are internally regulated efficient producers, nor are they simply an externally isolated noncapitalist "traditional" anachronism. Their continuance fills a necessary niche in his "functional-dualist" conception of the development of capitalism in Latin America. Geared toward the production of domestic luxuries and goods for export markets, there is no urgency for industry to open up the mass domestic market by increasing the consumption capacity of wage laborers.

There is no pressure, then, to maintain wages at a certain level that such increased consumption would require. Meanwhile, commercial agricultural production, controlled by a world of economic and political factors, must keep costs as low as possible. So there are real pressures to keep wages low in the agricultural segment. Supplementing the money they earn through wage labor with their small plots, peasants subsidize capitalist production of cheap food with cheap labor (de Janvry 1981, 71–85). Despite the functional capacity of this persistence of peasant production, de Janvry does not say that this is a static situation. The forces that threaten to destroy peasant production are still strong enough to proletarianize them anyway, if it were not for state intervention through rural development programs. Purporting to meet the basic needs of the rural poor, such projects serve to sustain the functional semiproletarian unit as a means of perpetuating low-cost production. These corrective measures are only temporary, according to de Janvry, so that even as it "functions," functional dualism is destroying itself as the growing poverty and environmental deterioration resulting from the contradictions of this process of capital accumulation push more and more peasants into urban areas (de Janvry 1981, 224–54).

While de Janvry sees the inevitable, gradual destruction of the peasantry in Latin America, a related model put forth by Meillassoux (1981) sees the exploitation of a migrant labor force "fed and bred" in rural communities as a foundation of capitalist development in industrialized areas. This process of exploitation is elucidated through his description of three elements of the price of labor power: (1) the cost of maintaining workers during their period of employment; (2) the cost of maintaining workers during times of unemployment; and (3) the cost of replacing workers via their offspring, the "reproduction" of the labor pool. In this model, the first cost is paid in "direct wages" in the "receiving" sector, while the second and third costs are paid via "indirect wages" in the "sending" community of origin. Whereas population growth and concentration in industrialized society eventually requires social and economic institutions that make provisions for the public welfare through social services and "living wage" standards, migrant workers are often excluded from such benefits. While peasant communities absorb the costs of maintaining and reproducing the migrant workforce, the industrial sector benefits from a cheap labor supply and there is incentive for the state to maintain land "reserves" or "marginal" lands as a kind of dumping ground or holding place for nonproducers, such as children, the elderly, the unemployed, and those incapable of working. Although initially writing about the "rural exodus" of West Africans in rotating migration patterns to European cities, Meillassoux extended his analysis to other underdeveloped parts of the world (1981, 94–103).

Viewed critically twenty-plus years on, the model proposed by de Janvry and Meillassoux may sound economistic and one-dimensional at best and conspiratorial at worst. Still, there are elements that resonate with the descriptions and are supported by the analysis that are presented in my case study. As will be shown in the household survey presented in chapter 7, there is a prevalence of families with members working in the mines and at other occupations away from home (11 of 42 households, or 26 percent), households including or headed by retired or semiretired pensioners (12, or 29 percent), and those headed by single individuals with no other working-age members living permanently at home (9, or 21 percent). The popular conception that comunidades are mostly populated with the elderly and other "nonworking" and "nonproductive" members (which I will argue against in my description of Loma Seca) and the sometimes-heard assessment that comunidades are simply where "old miners go home to die" seem to resemble Meillassoux's and de Janvry's thoughts on the role of indirect wages and the costs of reproducing industrial labor in the countryside. Additionally, as I will discuss in chapter 4, it has been recognized that during the grimmest years of the Pinochet era, when the state was indifferent to the plight of rural poverty, the communities' inward orientation worked to their advantage. Finally, the tenacity by which corporate landholdings have been fiercely protected and the recognized value of a comunero's right to use the common land as covered in chapter 3 attests to the part that the community plays as a "safety net" or economic buffer. With questions now looming regarding the solvency of Chile's privatized social security system (*Economist*, 2006), this function may prove more important than ever in the future. While these observations lend some support to the functional dualist conception of a peasant community, something critical is missing. Through short-term and long-term migration, many wage laborers and their families at home supplement or even provide the bulk of their household incomes and at the same time participate in group work projects and contribute to common good efforts for the community as a whole. These positive undertakings to balance such income-generating activities are varied and demanding, requiring much dedication and resourcefulness. Such direct actions to improve the lives of individual families and to make improvements to life in the community defy the passive exploitation that the elimination thesis seems to suggest. A view of articulation in which participants are actively engaged and operating by their own specific motives of self-interest and rationality is needed.

ARTICULATING ARTICULATION

Unlike the functional dualist model, an articulation of modes of production approach contends that a peasant-to-proletarian relationship is not a one-way extraction of value and utility. In entering into wage labor or market relations people find the means to reproduce their domestic/subsistence mode of production, and the rationality of this decision-making process is neither exclusively that of the "isolated household" nor that of the exploitation of wage labor. The specific effects of the relationship between peasant communities and external economic forces cannot be assumed, much less predicted. The modes of production approach arose to fill a void that it perceived was created by global economic models that restricted the notion of underdevelopment to the inequitable circulation of goods and that assumed capitalism had uniformly penetrated all regions of the world. While such macroscale models (such as "Dependency Theory" [Frank 1967] and later "World System Theory" [Wallerstein 1974]) tended to see the modern world as one in which capitalism was pervasive and absolute, articulation theory proposed intricate interrelationships between capitalism and other economic systems in which peasant societies function as distinct modes of production (Kearney 1986a, 341–45). This is a more complex scenario than that of the hungry wolf gobbling up sheep at will as suggested by orthodox Marxist notions of the inevitable disintegration of the peasantry.

Roseberry (1989) refers to a 1981 essay by Martinez that identifies twenty-five different "precapitalist" modes of production being used in studies of Latin America. "When one attempts to 'articulate' these modes with a capitalist mode about the nature of which there is equal disagreement," Roseberry archly comments, "one begins to wonder about one's sanity" (1989b, 145). In a similar vein, a 1978 contribution to a book on the "new economic anthropology" by Foster-Carter (1978) is amusingly titled "Can We 'Articulate' Articulation?" Despite the great proliferation of terminology (which has since fallen out of fashion theorywise), the literature is quite valuable, and its potential remains for the most part, I believe, unrealized. Foster-Carter keenly notes that in both French and English, the term has at least two different levels of meaning: to "join together" and "to give expression to." The expansion of articulation via an anatomical analogy allows for wider consideration of the hierarchical relations of "linkage and effectivity between different levels of all sorts of things" (Foster-Carter 1978, 215–16). The cultural historian Ken Post was the first to use the metaphor of an "articulated limb," that is, the functional connecting of two dissimilar things (1978). Since a mere connection implies a static structure, the inclusion of the second meaning is the key to understanding the active relationship between different spheres of production, as well as the general relationship between economy and culture. The term itself, then, has multiple meanings of both "structure" and "process": capitalist and peasant modes are both linked together —via migration, markets, and, as I contend in chapters 8 and 9, economic development policies and projects—and give efficacy to one another. Economy and culture thus are bound together and find expression in one another at both "material" and "social" levels.

Scholars using "mode of production" as an analytical tool were initially concerned with a macrolevel analysis of world history and the world economic system. Orthodox Marxists conceive of history as the succession of epochs in which one definitive economic system structured social relations, the familiar periods that Marx identified as primitive communism, ancient slave society, feudalism, capitalism, socialism, and communism. Each of these "modes of production" is constituted by specific economic characteristics that are understood in terms of the level of technology within the society ("forces of production") and the relationship between producers and the owners or controllers of the resources required for production (the "relations of production") (Marx 1976). The mode of production is both the unique configuration and the interrelationships of these material forces and social relations. The structures of economic exploitation and differential access to resources and power that these modes engender are likewise historically situated. The ways in which people organize themselves toward goals of production are, in Wolf's words, "specific, historically occurring sets of social relations through which human labor is deployed to wrest energy from nature by means of tools, skills, organization, and knowledge" (1982, 75).

Yet even orthodox Marxists disagree as to the exact transformative effects of capitalism on other forms of production, and as Wolpe (1980) observes, Marx himself suggested different possible evolutionary trajectories. As discussed in the previous section, one interpretation accepts that the expansion of capitalism is a unitary process that beckons the inevitable, the immediate or eventual disintegration of other modes. However, Marx in *Capital* also indicated that the study of capital itself necessitates recognition of the differentiated relationships that may exist between capitalism and other systems and seemed to suggest that the tempo and magnitude of the transformation via the process of capital accumulation is not established all at once. When subsistence production evolves into commodity production by degree, its effects may be circumscribed with the deleterious social consequences of capital accumulation decelerated or modified by the continued functioning of the peasant mode (Wolpe 1980, 1–5). In short, articulation theory helped to identify and examine a two-part fundamental issue: (1) Capitalist expansion, as Cooper puts it, came into contact with "not merely cultivators, but social formations with their own coherence and forms of exploitation" (1993) and (2) in many instances these formations have not only maintained their coherence, they have acquired the means to maintain and reproduce themselves *via* their articulation with the capitalist economy.

Rey has been regarded as the most theoretically sophisticated of the articulation theorists, but his works are still mostly unavailable in English. Essentially, the strength of Rey's concept of articulation is that it is not a static state, but a process in time, a reworking of the problem of the "transition" to capitalism. Capitalism, according to Rey:

> can never immediately and totally eliminate the preceding modes of production, nor above all the relations of exploitation which characterize these modes of production. On the contrary, during an entire period it must reinforce these relations of exploitation, since it is only this development which permits its own provisioning with goods coming from these modes of production, or with men driven from these modes of production and therefore compelled to sell their labor power to capitalism in order to survive. (Foster-Carter 1978, 221–22)

As we will see in chapters 3 and 4, historically, copper mining and large-scale wheat production have left an enormous ecological and economic legacy in the comunidades. This legacy reveals itself as a key element in the processes of community formation, in the depletion of natural resources, and, in the case of mining, in the continued supply of labor to the mines that is produced and reproduced within the communities. As these communities have been integrated into the modern world system for such a long time, there is potential for further research that would examine how these communities have historically responded to the demands of mining in relation to changes in the world market. Specifically, there is room for a historical examination of the demand for labor in the mining sector during boom times for the commodity and analysis of the extent to which people were drawn away from the communities in search of work. Related to this is the need for research that examines the ways in which the communities functioned as places of retreat during downturns in the industry at particular points in time as a result of cycles of economic depression at the macrolevel.

Marxian historical materialism's rigorous insistence on specific and historically occurring relations provides an effective framework for understanding patterns of social change and dynamic power relations. Marxists propose that the economic elements of modes of production have a powerful influence (deemed a "determining" force in the stronger language of orthodox Marxism and a "shaping" influence when less strong language is used) over society's legal and cultural characteristics. Agriculture and mining have always been linked in the Norte Chico, and the mines, particularly processing plants, were highly reliant on the crucial variable of water. Labor migration is a key process in the relationship between communally organized farming in this ecologically tenuous environment and large-scale capitalist agriculture and industrial development. The "nonproductive" surface belies a long and complex history of a functional interrelation between rural cultivators/pastoralists and national and international industries, like mining. The use of long-range histories and the acknowledgment of people engaged in multiple subsistence strategies and social ties in a context where one form of commodity production is a conditioning dominant force but not intractably destructive is a notable advancement of more progressive approaches to peasant studies (Stern 1987; de la Peña 1989). As I will discuss, the rise of mining involved less the distortion or dissolution of preexisting forms of "use-value" (noncapitalist utility, rather than the "exchange value" of market commodities) economic orientations than the organic arrangement of commodity production and communal land.

Through this process, then, different modes of production possess different economic features and also distinct cultural traits, traditions, customs, and values. Importantly, since above all Marxian political economy seeks to explain how systems of inequality are reproduced, what is especially meaningful are the ways in which those ideological mechanisms that impart legitimacy to some economic orientations and "illegitimacy" to others are differentially experienced in various segments of the societal totality. As an illustrative example, in chapter 8 I describe a law designed to ensure the hygienic production of handcrafted goat cheese while stimulating economic development and the effects it is having on the family producers of this product in my study. While this law and the assistance programs and initiatives that are associated with it are well intentioned and seek to improve the market position of the small-scale producers of this commodity, the impact on the most economically vulnerable families has been largely negative.

This is because, as I argue, the plan is based upon a poor understanding of the importance of this petty commodity for families that must migrate in search of resources during periods of drought when the ability to manufacture the product on-site and sell it in nearby markets is crucial. In ideological terms, this failure of a standardized, market-oriented production model to reach those most in need of assistance is a blind spot in Chile's neoliberal economic worldview. In material terms, for those living in these economic and social margins who find themselves excluded from this development and targeted by this law, the stakes are much higher, as a critical piece of their livelihood is threatened. The policy that "makes sense" in formal economic terms can have detrimental effects on those who participate in the informal economy.

For Althusser and Balibar (1970) and Rey (1975), noncapitalist forms have not been replaced by capitalism in the modern world; rather, in the case of colonialism, the expansion of European capital through empire building seized and transformed other economies for its own uses while maintaining some of their original characteristics. These French Marxist anthropologists of the 1960s made an important distinction between "mode of production" and "social formation." In this view, the mode of production (or "the manner of producing" [Althusser and Balibar 1970, 209]) is an analytical concept indicating an aggregate whole that encompasses a specific alliance of connections between the elements of workers, owners, and the means of production. The main articulated connections entail (1) the processes by which "the appropriation of nature by man" (213) determines the system of productive forces and (2) the property arrangements that define the "relations of production" (not simply relations between owners and workers, but a specific structure of "the distribution of relations, places and functions, occupied and 'supported' by objects and agents of production" [180]). The mode itself is integrated (or articulated within) as the manner in which property is owned or possessed, the way in which surplus is appropriated and distributed, how labor is divided, and other aspects of production are arranged in a "totality of mutual interconnections" (Pollock 1989). A "social formation"—which exists in the day-to-day activities or "lived relations" of economic, political, and ideological practice—constitutes a multifaceted articulation of modes of production (Althusser and Balibar 1970, 170–81 and 207–24; Larrain 1989, 181). For Althusser, lived relations are ideological in that they are taken for granted, rarely questioned; residing in the seamless and unseen commonsense values of the status quo, they function to constitute individuals as subjects within the socioeconomic system (1971). If true, it stands to reason, then, that such lived relations will be different where production is organized in qualitatively and quantitatively different ways. Of relevance to my study is the manifestation that these relations take when, as others have put it, "community" itself is a relation of production because the continued reproduction of the individual household is dependent on collective defense and preservation of the community as a whole (Nugent 1993, 49; Roseberry 1991, 22).

In the conclusion to chapter 7, I detail the ways in which production is organized in Loma Seca as a distinct mode that has developed in response to the scarcity of resources in the region. In the dialectic between material and ideal elements, this mode is marked by cycles of resource scarcity, multiple integrated subsistence and income-generating strategies, and a community interface, in terms of property, between private possessions and corporate holdings and, in terms of labor, between household enterprises and group activities. In many ways, as I describe in chapter 4, the necessity of this unique human ecology is a result of the past environmental damage done by the appropriation and transformation of nature through mining and wheat production and the continued damage done by the low-input livelihood options of animal husbandry and rain-fed cultivation available to these largely "cash poor" households. The social formation generated by this dialectic generates surplus that serves both individual and community functions, reproducing both household livelihoods and the reproduction of the community mode itself. For example, in chapter 5 I identify two kinds of group economic relations in Loma Seca: "social forms of mutual assistance" and "work-focused forms of mutual assistance." In the first, money is raised through social activities (such as rodeos, dances, and horse races) for projects in the community that benefit the common good. In pooling funds for improvements from which all members of the community benefit, this form offsets to some extent concentrations of wealth and power in the hands of the limited number of right-holding comuneros. This, I contend, is an example of the circumscription of some of the negative effects of surplus accumulation described by Wolpe above. In the second form, production-driven efforts (such as wheat harvest and other group agropastoral activities) make use of collective resources and cooperative labor power in order to maximize the return and minimize the costs for individual families. Both of these, I demonstrate, are dependent upon the availability of both human and environmental resources and are key features of the individual/communal dialectic unique to this mode of production.

Articulation involves the connection and relations of many things: labor, goods, and, importantly, cultures. Althusser and Balibar purposefully conceived of the connections of "articulation" in a decidedly ahistorical and abstract language so as to understand modes of production as structures in their own right, operating under their own internal logic, resulting in what Wolf criticized as a mechanistic system that "moves people along as carriers of the system but leaves no room for human consciousness or history" (1982, 401). Despite such legitimate reservations, I contend that the concept is a useful tool for ethnography concerned with showing how distinct forms and relations of production can serve to consolidate rather than destroy peasant ownership of small pieces of land and, as Keyder observes, when articulated with state policies, the preservation of the peasant mode of production may spawn active "dynamic intervals" in agrarian relations (1983).

Looking at economic development as a mutually formative set of relations including both economic and cultural elements, it is possible to understand the power of the capitalist system and its material and ideological manifestations without impoverishing our understanding of alternative practices and motivations that are connected to it. At the material level, economic development policy influences and is influenced by local cultural practice. At the level of meaning, free market ideology is filtered through the experiences of local history, or, as Stern sharply observes, social relations of production are often more important than markets or the "profit principle" in the establishment of either capitalist or noncapitalist "laws" (1993). Similarly, Nugent argues in the introduction to *Spent Cartridges of Revolution* (1993)—his "anthropological history" of a peasant community in Chihuahua— "ideology" as a way of perceiving the world in which social meanings are organized and interpreted by people is not a free-floating force; it is both limited by and "expressed through" the material it organizes and the historical context in which the arrangement of meaning it provides are "*recognizable* to social actors" (36). Lest we forget this— that Althusserian "lived ideology" is premised on *living* people— Nugent cites Post's famous statement that: "The link between structures and history . . . is people, who are the bearers of structures, live through time, and perpetuate themselves and their labor-power through their children. In doing these things over a discernible period . . . they reproduce a particular pattern of association for the purposes of meeting material needs which implies cognition of material reality and the preservation of a certain distribution of power within and among structures" (Post 1978, 467).

Implicitly there is also an internal as well as an external dialectic at play. A community apprehends and functions in relation to an external imposition in ways that are shaped by its own specific historical processes of formation (Comaroff 1982). The anthropologist cannot casually position his or her community of study within the market's web and write another chapter on the history of expanding global capitalism. The specific cultural history with respect to the wider economic system must be thoroughly examined. The history of expanding capitalism into the periphery of the world economic system has been one of uneven development driven by the capital accumulation in core nations. Then, as political economy theorists such as Wolf and Roseberry contend, the integration into markets or the introduction of the relations of capitalism does not put peasant communities on any well-worn course toward any fixed or easily anticipated set of social transformations (Wolf 1982; Roseberry 1989b, 51–52).

An example of articulation as a dialectical relationship creating mutual costs and benefits can be seen in the work of Kearney. Looking at Mixtec peasants who migrate from Oaxaca to work the fields of northern Mexico and the United States, he shows how a distinct peasant mode of production reproduces itself, both economically and culturally, through the migration process and engagement with wage labor (Kearney 1986a, 341–45). Political and economic forces of poverty, environmental degradation, and failed land reform push these people from their farm plots to seek income. Both in northern Mexico and the United States, they are subjected to low wages and abysmal living conditions, rationalized by a prevalent racist ideology in the "receiving" cultures that sees them as "fit" for such work and an economic ideology that deems them a necessary low-cost component of competitive agribusiness. Today the "traditional" appearance of non-capitalist subsistence belies the villages integral articulation with national and international capitalism. The subsistence-based *minifundios* are the sources of cheap labor for agriculture in northern Mexico, across the border into California and as far away as the fields of Oregon and Florida just as a generation ago, they were similarly the source of labor power for the sugarcane plantations of the Gulf coast. Their economy is "an inextricable part of the encompassing political economies of Mexico and the United States" (Nagengast and Kearney 1990, 74–77). As migrants proceed along a network that was forged by previous movements, Mixtec communities in the north have become what Kearney calls an "encysted subclass" perpetuated by articulation through a network that is insulated, culturally dense, cohesive, and exclusive. Remittances are sent home to support both families and communities as a whole, and while there is a growing dependence upon this income, this link to external capitalism facilitates a revitalization of traditional Mixtec practices at home, a flourishing of institutions of ethnic identity in the north, and even a rise of worker consciousness that is seen in their active participation in labor organization (Kearney 1996, 174–95).

In the following, the reader will recognize some parallels and common factors between the process that Kearney describes among his transnational migrants and the experiences of the laborers and producers of the comunidades agrícolas of the Norte Chico. Although the communities appear situated on the socioeconomic and environmental margins, I argue that via the articulatory mechanisms of migration and commodity production both individual families and the community itself acquire means to bolster the rural mode of production. As the household survey and descriptions of one family's economic strategies will show, family members working for wages provide critical income during hard times, and as seen in chapter 5, migrants returning home to spend money at horse races, rodeos, and holiday festivals serves to some degree to redistribute wealth in ways that prevent the excessive accumulation of surplus and power in the hands of right-holding comuneros and their families. Also, as I describe in chapter 8 and have discussed elsewhere (2002, 27–28), associations of comuneros and their advocates have proliferated in the postdictatorship era, leading to higher visibility and a more prominent platform from which to voice their concerns. And while, as I also argue in that chapter, some development policy is based on a misguided understanding of the comunero livelihood in fancifully ethnic and historical terms (which I identify as "Policy-Positioned Ascriptions of Ethnicity and History" [see also Alexander 2006]) in order to push forward a modernization agenda, the community's own expression of its history and comunero identification with nationalistic themes and images associated with "frontier life" seem more vivid and vital than ever. These act not only as local counternarrative to a dominant discourse, as I detail in chapter 5, they are living expressions of everyday life and livelihood.

CONCLUSION: GETTING ON WITH THE WORK

In summary, this book makes use of an articulation of modes of production perspective in order to avoid the analytical breach between local culture forms and external pressures. In doing so, I put forth the following four postulates that should be useful for the study of the peasant culture in general:

(1) A mode of production analysis provides empirical details to fill in the gaps left by broad anthropological perspectives on "the Peasant question" in Latin America.

(2) There is no reason why macroanalysis of underdevelopment (such as world-system and dependency theory) cannot be more concerned with local cultures and histories. At the same time, there should be no reason why mode of production analysis cannot be more concerned with global structures and causalities.

(3) An identification of more than one mode of production participating in an overarching economic system suggests that a relationship of economic dependency of cultures in underdeveloped areas upon the developed world may not be a zero-sum game in which one "side" can gain only at the expense of another.

(4) Capitalism is a *process*, not a monolithic and coherent "thing" that affects all areas of the world in exactly the same way and in which all areas of the world participate in uniform ways.

A good deal of William Roseberry's sadly brief but highly influential career was dedicated to reviving interest in "modes of production" and "peasants" as relevant concepts and meaningful units of analysis. Another leading figure in the political economy of rural Latin America, Michael Kearney, has devoted much of his work (1996) to refuting the validity of "the peasant concept" in the present-day global economy. In this chapter I have made the case that the research presented in this book is deeply informed by articulation theory and that the tools of modes of production analysis are of great relevance to my study. At this juncture, I will heed the words of my personal mentor in the field of peasant studies, the late Daniel Nugent, who warned me of the torpor of unremitting scholarly sniping over the virtues of one analytical model over another, advising me that at some point one must take a position and "just get on with the *work*," lest we spend all of our time stuck in a quicksand of classificatory debate over *categories* and *meanings*. In an effort to pull myself up from that mire, I now get on with the work.

3

Comunidades Agrícolas in Chile's "Little North"

INTRODUCTION: INITIAL RESEARCH AND REFLECTIONS ON DIVERSITY

MY INITIAL INTEREST IN THE COMUNIDADES CAME ABOUT BECAUSE OF my involvement with a biodiversity and economic development project. Nations such as Chile that ratified the International Convention on Biodiversity (ICB) treaty in 1992 agreed to take meaningful courses of action for conserving biodiversity and developing sustainable uses of plant life. The goal was to integrate the objectives and principles of the convention into national environmental laws, policies, and strategies for managing natural resources and ecosystems. Countries in which "bioprospecting" for medicinal plants was under way or about to begin were encouraged in the treaty to take measures to preserve the traditional knowledge and uses of biodiversity by indigenous people and rural communities and to promote the active participation of local peoples who possess such knowledge. From August 1994 through May 1996 I was a research associate with the Biodiversity Conservation and Sustainable Economic Development subproject of the Bioactive Agents from Dryland Plants of Latin America project. As part of the International Convention on Biodiversity Groups (ICBG) program of the National Institute of Health (NIH), USAID, and the Fogerty Center, this project utilized principles established by the International Convention on Biodiversity treaty. The project involved botanists, pharmacologists, environmental specialists, conservation biologists, and anthropologists from universities in the United States, Chile, and Argentina. After a year and a half of project research at the University of Arizona, I spent January through May 1996 conducting preliminary fieldwork in Chile.

One of the goals of our subproject was to evaluate strategies for minimizing the negative effects on biological diversity and local culture that might arise from the discovery and exploitation of indigenous plants with medicinal uses. Another aimed to develop means for ensuring that potential economic and social benefits would accrue to local and national economies as a consequence of the sale of these drugs in an international market (Grifo and Downes 1996, 290; Weaver et al. 1996, 1999). Although the contributions of my colleagues and myself to the project ended shortly after my return to the United States, I was extremely grateful for the opportunity I was given through participation in that project. After these four months in Chile, I came back convinced that I should carry out extensive fieldwork in an agricultural community in Region IV and having the good fortune of making the acquaintance of those who would kindly introduce me to the people of Loma Seca upon my return the following year.

There are several reasons why I chose to work in Region IV. I went there first because there had been extensive plant collection carried out by the project in the area, particularly in the Limarí and Elqui valleys. Environmentally, the region suffers from seemingly interminable drought and is subject to extreme erosion and desertification. Economically, poverty rates are among the highest in Chile despite the fact that the region possesses great mineral wealth (Chile is the world's leading copper producer and a number of major mines are located in Region IV) and has experienced a boom in commercial agricultural production (primarily grapes and other fruit) as a result of the push for export-oriented development begun in the late 1980s. This dynamic between ecological degradation, poverty, exploitation of natural resources, and socioeconomic stratification has produced a range of subsistence strategies in Region IV as well as, it was argued, a diversity of traditional knowledge regarding plants and a likelihood for the sale of medicinal plants to become an income option (Castro and Romo 1996). Since the comunidades are situated in the most impoverished areas in the region and because they maintain a special relationship between economy and environmental resources mediated by a democratic framework for handling the management of land, I felt that it was vital that these communities be target areas of concern (Alexander 1995). When our project ended, I was convinced that for the rural poor in an area such as the Norte Chico, diversity in production was one of the keys to survival and that this diversity was bound up in a complex relationship not only with the land and the natural environment but with the socioeconomic environment as well.

In this chapter I present a general overview of the comunidades agrícolas of Chile's Norte Chico. I describe their system of land tenure, democratic decision making, resource use and management, and some production-oriented social relations. This is followed by a historical summary of their formation and some considerations of how some of what is known about their origins might be misinterpreted in both historical and cultural terms by outsiders whose worldview is informed by ideals of modernization development and free market capitalism.

GENERAL CHARACTERISTICS OF COMUNIDAD SECTORS

Three rivers running east to west divide Region IV into three provinces, each bearing the name of the river that runs through it. Of the 170-plus comunidades, 31 or 18 percent, are located in Choapa. The *provincia* of Elqui is home to 24 or 14 percent of the communities. Limarí has the heaviest concentration of communities, 118 or 65 percent, and this is where Loma Seca is located. The vast majority of comunidades agrícolas are in Region IV, but there are a few in Region III to the north, to the south in Region V, and a few in the marginal lands on the outskirts of the Region Metropolitana (CIPRES 1993). *Comunidades indígenas,* also called *reducciónes,* are what remains of the communal landholdings of the Araucanian (Mapuche) Indians, the only indigenous group in Chile of any significant size. (There are about a half a million Mapuche in southern Chile and about 15,000 people of Aymara descent in the far north.) The majority of these Mapuche comunidades indígenas are in the province of Cautín in Region IX, several hundred kilometers south of Santiago. They differ from comunidades agrícolas (which are, interestingly, occasionally referred to as *comunidades históricas* to distinguish them from their "indigenous" counterparts) in many respects. They are much smaller in area (reduced through usurpation by colonial and postcolonial governments, the average reducción totals less than three hundred hectares). People from a single kinship group typically populate each reducción. Also, the usufruct areas known as lluvias are absent there (Loveman 1988, 33–34: IREN-CORFO 1978, 17). Comunidades agrícolas, in contrast, are typically very large in area, maintain three forms of land tenancy, and are an organizational structure comprised of different families.

Only 7 percent of the land in the communities is arable (Castro and Romo 1996, 17). Of this, 98.4 percent is dryland (*secano*) and 1.6 percent is irrigated. The vast majority, 96 percent, of land that is used for production purposes, is dedicated to livestock, primarily goats; 2.2 percent is used for annual crops; 0.1 percent for fruits and vine culture; 0.1 percent for the growing of vegetables; and 1.1 percent for forest production (Ministerio de Bienes Nacionales 1998, 5–6).

The most comprehensive study of the communities was conducted between 1976 and 1977 by the Instituto de Investigación de Recursos Naturales para la Corporación de Fomento de la Producción (IREN-CORFO 1977). The work was published in two volumes, a veritable atlas of ecological, economic, and social characteristics. Subsequent studies continued to use the framework of grouping the communities into eight sectors based on location and natural resources that was set down by the IREN-CORFO project (figure 3.1). The data in the following description of each sector is taken from the second major comprehensive survey, a 1986 project that has since become the definitive reference work (Avendaño 1986).

(1) *extrema árido:* Only three communities make up this sector of "extreme aridity." Almost exclusively desert, only small aggregations of people can be sustained and only in the limited areas where water and resources are concentrated.

(2) *costero:* Stretching from the coastline to the interior, this "coastal" region benefits from morning and evening mist (*neblinas*) and accompanying humidity, which permits, in nondrought years, better and more frequent cultivation and a relatively good supply of natural forage in comparison with other interior areas. Loma Seca is among the fifteen comunidades in this sector.

(3) *interior árido:* In contrast, cultivation in the communities in this "arid interior" is possible only in the rare years when there is an exceptional amount of rainfall and a satisfactory distribution of this rain. There are thirty-two comunidades in this sector.

(4) Guatulame: A tributary of the Rio Limarí, the Guatulame River is home to eleven communities that more or less contiguously line its banks in a stretch of land between the Cogotti and Palmeras reservoirs. Because of a favorable microclimate and the absence of frost, there is a good deal of fruit production in slopes and valleys, and many growers have been successful here using specialized technologies such as growing tomatoes under clear plastic greenhouselike structures (*bajo plastico*).

(5) *cordillerano:* In this "mountainous" sector, the communities are scattered and isolated by the steep relief of the rough land. The presence of adequate forage is heavily conditional upon rainfall. What little subterranean water exists here is usually limited to drinking water and for irrigating some small gardens. There are seventy-three communities in this sector, more than in any other.

(6) *interior semiárido:* The "semiarid interior" is located in the southern part of Region IV in the province of Choapa. It receives an average of 200 mm of rain a year, distributed with the heaviest concentration in the months of May and August. This along with a geology that produces a good deal of subterranean water allows a relatively high amount of irrigated agriculture and can sustain a relatively high population base in the twenty comunidades located here.

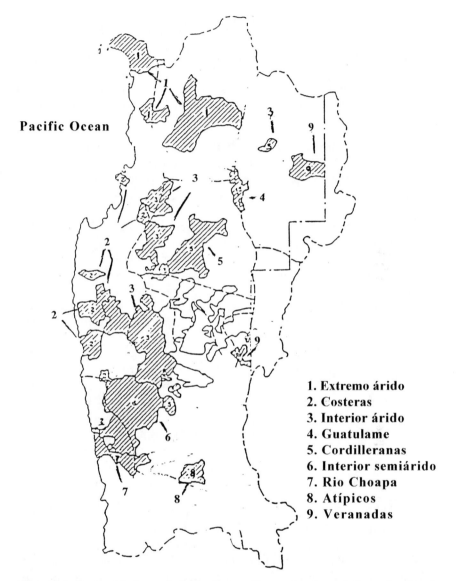

Pacific Ocean

1. Extremo árido
2. Costeras
3. Interior árido
4. Guatulame
5. Cordilleranas
6. Interior semiárido
7. Rio Choapa
8. Atípicos
9. Veranadas

Figure 3.1. Comunidades agrícolas by Sector. (*Source:* Instituto de Investigación de Recursos Naturales para la Corporación de Fomento de la Producción [IREN-CORFO]).

(7) Rio Choapa: In addition to being beneficially situated on the banks of the Choapa River near the provincial capital of Illapel, the six communities in this sector share some of the favorable climatic conditions of the "semi-arid interior" sector.
(8) *atípicos:* These are classified as unique, having "atypical" characteristics.
(9) *veranadas:* Five communities make up the high *cordillera* sector named for the "summer pastures" of the seasonal practice of moving goats and sheep into mountain areas. This rugged land is isolated and marked by difficult access.

The five columns in the table below (table 3.1) compare the eight sectors in terms of (1) number of communities, (2) land area, (3) population and population density, (4) number of people holding the title of comunero, and (5) number and percentage of comuneros living in their communities.

These figures represent information that was collected in 1986, the last time that a comprehensive census and study of all of the comunidades agrícolas was carried out (Avendaño 1986), but some basic themes still resonate today. The three sectors with the highest person-to-land ratio, the Guatulame, Rio Choapa, and interior semiárido communities (with ratios of 16.24, 13.29, and 11.68 people per square kilometer, respectively) are areas near or adjacent to prominent rivers and have relatively high rainfall. Since more irrigation and permanent agriculture is possible, the carrying capacity of these communities is higher. These sectors make up 22 percent, or 37, of the communities and 16.5 percent of the total land and account for 34 percent of the total population.

Conversely, in the veranadas and the extrema áridez sectors, the two sectors with the lowest person-to-land ratio (1.25 and 1.30 people per square kilometer, a fraction of the carrying capacity of the above communities) agriculture is not viable because of an utter lack of water and the precipitous terrain. Livelihood is almost exclusively drawn from herding. Although these sectors make up less than 5 percent of the total communities and only about 4 percent of the population, they account for 21.6 percent of the total land occupied by all of the communities, because the amount of land necessary to sustain even this small population in such an environment is extensive.

The remaining three sectors—the interior árido, costero, and cordillerano communities—fall in between these two extremes in terms of population density and livelihood. These "arid interior," "coastal," and "mountainous" communities have a population density of 10.88, 8.6, and 4.86, respectively. In these sectors agriculture is almost exclusively rain-fed, so there is a heavy dependence on goat and sheep herding when rainfall is exceptionally scarce. The population density

Table 1 Comunidades agrícolas of Region IV by sector

Sector	# of comunidades agrícolas and % of total	Hectares and % of total area	Population and Persons/km²	Comuneros	Comuneros in residence (%)
extremo árido (extreme aridity)	3 / 1.8	141,280 / 14.1	1,764 / 1.25	316	207 65.5
costero (coastal)	15 / 9.1	59,766 / 5.9	5,187 / 8.68	1,020	755 / 75.0
interio árido (arid interior)	32 / 19.4	17,060 / 17.5	19,155 / 10.88	3,375	2,305 / 68.3
Guatulame	11 / 6.7	31,548 / 3.1	5,125 / 16.24	892	629 / 70.5
cordillerano (mountainous)	73 /44.3	306,050 / 30.5	14,862 / 4.86	3,576	1,824 / 51.0
interior semiárido (semiarid interior)	20 / 12.1	106,948 / 10.6	12,498 / 11.68	2,072	1,676 / 80.1
Rio Choapa	6 / 3.6	27,648 / 2.8	3,675 / 13.29	904	626 / 69.3
veranadas	5 / 3.0	75,306 / 7.5	955 / 1.30	N/A	N/A

in the communities in these three sectors is more moderate relative to the above two groups. These are the "typical" comunidades agrícolas in that they employ a diversity of productive strategies closely linked to rainfall. This environmentally shaped diversity and flexibility has engendered what Avendaño called (in the subtitle to the 1986 study) *una particular relación hombre-tierra*, or "a particular man-land relationship." These sectors contain 72.8 percent of all communities, account for 54 percent of the total land area, and 62 percent of the total population.

As mentioned in the introductory chapter, migration is another key variable in this "particular relationship." Irrigated, permanent agriculture requires less land, can support more people, and is more labor-intensive than pastoralism. Because of the poor quality of the land in the Norte Chico, traditional pastoralism requires very large expanses of land and cannot support large numbers of people. Permanent out-migration is more extensive here. Rain-fed agriculture is possible when conditions are good—the chances for adequate precipitation are a little better in the misty coastal sector in which Loma Seca is located—but also requires a good deal of land for frequent rotation. Migration here tends to be much more cyclical. The last two columns of table 1 show that the percentage of comuneros residing in their comunidad varied between approximately 50 to 80 percent between sectors in 1986. Of the 12,155 comuneros accounted for above, 8,022 or 66 percent were still living in their communities of origin. A 1998 survey by Bienes Nacionales, the government registry providing legal assistance to the communities, found in a sample of 2,789 comuneros from 25 comunidades that only 56 percent were in residence (Ministerio de Bienes Nacionales 1998, 12). This reduced number of permanent resident comuneros illustrates the growing difficulty that people have in making a living in the communities because of the increasing environmental problems of the last decade.

The Traditional Land Tenure and Political System

Particular types of land tenure, resource management, and cooperative social relations of production both within and between communities distinguish the comunidades agrícolas from other rural villages in the Norte Chico. In these other communities all land is individually owned as private property that can be freely sold on the open market. They have neither rules of usufruct nor the political structure governing land that is held in common. Such enclosed smallholdings are called *parcelas* in Chile. What follows is a general description of the comunidad system.

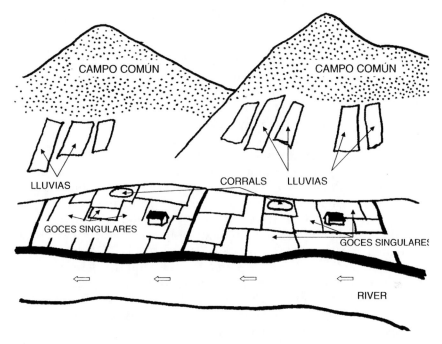

Figure 3.2. Composite View of Land Tenancy and Use

Land Tenure, Possession, and Use Rights

Just as families make use of a diversity of productive strategies, the communities themselves are composed of a combination of forms of land organization, each with distinct rules and practices of possession, transfer, and usage. The above illustration (figure 3.2) presents a composite view of three types of landholdings that are found in the comunidades agrícolas.

The areas referred to as *posesiones* or *individuales* have some characteristics of "private property" in that their boundaries are permanently fixed, they are possessed and used exclusively by an individual or family, and can be transferred or sold to other individuals within the community. However, the holder does not have the right to sell to people who are not community members without the consent of the other comuneros. These lands include both small pieces of land on which houses are built and goces singulares, tiny (generally less then 1.5 hectare) plots of irrigated land used primarily for growing food for family consumption. These are also sometimes referred to as *hijuelas*, from *hijo* (the Spanish word for "son"), denoting the practice of the original owner dividing the land according to the number of sons.

When there are irrigated goces singulares, houses are usually built fronting them.

Areas of land to which comuneros have individual usufruct rights are called lluvias and are located in the dryland above the water source. As the name ("rain" in Spanish) indicates, they are most commonly used for rain-fed cereal production. Limits on the size and number of lluvias that a single individual can possess vary between community, depending upon the availability and quality of land and the number of comuneros. There may be restrictions on both the size and number of the lluvias. This is usually the case in the few communities with prominent rivers and *esteros* (swamp or marshland). There may be a limited number of unlimited size. This principally occurs in the interior communities in which the carrying capacity of the land is low and the number of people with the rights to use the land is relatively high. Finally, least common are communities in which there may be an unlimited number of lluvias of unrestricted size. This only occurs in the largest and most sparsely populated communities. There are also some cases in which more than one family has the rights to use a single lluvia, and they share the labor of working it (IREN-CORFO 1978, 26–27; Iannuzzi and Salinas 1986, 50). After a period of continuous use, usually six to eight years, the land's productivity is depleted. The fences are pulled up and the land left to recover while the comunero petitions for more land.

The irrigated goce singular possessions are a scarce commodity in all communities, and many comuneros do not have access to them. However, being a comunero does give one the right (a *derecho*) to available lluvias and to use the campo común, the vast grazing area that comprises the majority of comunidad land. It is not uncommon for the campo común to account for up to 90 percent of the land within a community. These open tracts of hilly, rocky terrain, dotted with goats and sheep, are for many a kind of "summarizing symbol" (Ortner 1973, 1339) of the region's rugged interior as a place where people and animals scrape sustenance from the dry, infertile land.

Another type of land classification that exists in a few communities is the *lluvia común*, also located in drylands and foothills. Its boundaries are permanent and it is accessible to all comuneros. Each family contributes similar portions of work and all that contribute receive a share of the harvest. Occasionally, comuneros are mobilized for the recuperation of undeveloped land. This land from this *siembra colectiva* (collective harvest) is made indivisible and without any individual assignment. Those who are able to provide labor for the irrigation and development are entitled to use it (Batallán 1980, 109–11). Whenever children of comuneros who have no rights or possibility to

"Goats and sheep grazing on the community pasture (*campo común*)." Photo courtesy of the author.

inherit a *posesión* and who opt to stay in the community are verbally ceded land by the community authorities for building a house, this type of land is called a *piso*. These individuals, who are often artisans or laborers, pay a yearly fee to the community to use this land. This does not give them the right to use the campo común. If they wish to use the community pasturelands to graze their animals, they must pay an additional fee to do so.

Inheritance of Land and Use Rights

To be a comunero means to have rights to use the land and to have a vote in community matters. When a comunero dies, he or she leaves the title and its accompanying rights to the spouse. If there is no living spouse, the title goes to the oldest son. If the oldest son does not live at home, it passes to the oldest child living with the comunero at the time of his or her passing. When a comunero dies without leaving an heir, the right leaves the family and can be sold by the community to another comunero or "derecho-less" child of a comunero. The money goes into the community treasury. During my fieldwork the cost of a derecho was 360,000 pesos, or about $800. Since comuneros are very hesitant to allow this to happen, those who have no biological children will sometimes adopt a child in order to keep the right "in the family." This practice is fairly common in Loma Seca, and when I asked one of my informants who had done this very thing about it, he joked that it is because "comuneros are selfish." He then redirected my attention to the fact that derechos are very precious things because they are in limited supply, and they are in limited supply because of the poor quality of the land. If one has many children, he told me, he or she has the obligation to in some way pay—with money or possessions—the other children who do not receive the title. He phrased it this way: "We are a small group of people with a large area of land. Not a large group of people with a little bit of land. If the right went to all of the children, there would be more comuneros than land. . . ." He then added that because of the difficulties in making a living from the land and the enticement of improving one's life with wage employment in other areas, it isn't as common for the oldest son to be living at home as it was in the past. He summed up the limiting factors of restricted access structured by land of limited productivity: "This is one of the reasons that the community is small. If one person has one right to one hectare of land that doesn't produce much and there are ten kids, the others have to leave to find other sources of income. If the ownership was 'open' we would eventually lose the community." Such limits have been necessary since the communities' formation. To see out-migration today as evidence of the "failure" of communities to provide for their own people, I believe, would be to overlook this structural element of land preservation—a fundamental feature of the human ecology of the Norte Chico.

The traditional structure, however, is not without its critics within the communities themselves. It is definitely a kind of "limited" democracy, since only those holding the title of comunero have the right to vote in elections and meetings as well as the right to use the land. Although this form of "citizenship" has been described in the past as "limited to almost entirely aging men" (Rosenfeld 1993, 29), this is changing. As we will see, although there are, as to be expected, marked differences in wealth, productivity patterns, and resource use based on possession of derechos (chapter 7), there are internal mechanisms that work against extreme concentrations of wealth and power and that may curb potential extreme factionalism. For example, traditionally few women had derechos, most of them having been gained through inheritance on the death of the husband, and those young people who are in line for them often must wait a long time to receive them. Legal changes now allow derechos to circulate more freely within communities (chapter 4) and, in my example from Loma Seca, entrepreneurship via comunero access to resources is far from an exclusively male activity (chapter 5). As a result, women are increasingly assuming important roles in the community political body (chapter 5) and in regional organizations that lobby on behalf of the comunidades and act as intermediaries between community members and outside authorities (chapter 7). Finally, as I will elaborate in upcoming chapters, non-derecho-holding families, many of which are headed by single mothers or widows, receive assistance through the community projects (chapter 5) that benefit the common good as well as through state assistance as *vecinos* (non-comunero residents). Many of these "checks and balances" to the potentially socially detrimental results of the exclusivity of comunero status are, arguably, an outcome of the frequent necessity for community members to migrate as those who stay behind take the initiative and responsibility necessary to provide for themselves and their families.

Political Organization: La Directiva

A 1967 law, which I will discuss in the following section on legal aspects, established guidelines for the election of community officers and representatives and outlined their duties. Each community elects a *Directiva,* an administrative body that should consist of no less than five and no more than eleven members. The group's tenure is for three years, after which time another election is held. Within the community, their responsibilities include fixing the maximum quota of livestock per comunero, making decisions about community cultivation projects, establishing yearly dues that each comunero must pay, managing the community treasury, and resolving questions and problems concerning the distribution and succession of use rights. Among the functions the Directiva performs as an intermediary between the community and the wider society is the solicitation of assistance from public welfare agencies, the presentation of community projects to regional development offices, and the procurement of *abogados* (lawyers or legal experts) to represent the community in its relations with banks and credit companies. It is often noted that the people with the most power and resources make up the Directiva (Castro 1986, 225). The offices include *presidente, vice-presidente, secretario(a), tesorero(a),* and *director.*

Meetings are held throughout the year, depending upon how active the Directiva is in community affairs and in promoting projects. In Loma Seca meetings are held about eight times a year in the *local,* the town meeting place where dances, fiestas, and community business are conducted. At these meetings, the Directiva organizes and presents the issues to be discussed and every comunero has a chance to voice his or her opinion. Once all sides feel that they have had a chance to make their case, a vote is taken. Because simple majority rules, and once a decision has been reached the comunidad acts as a whole, strong efforts are normally made to arrive at a general consensus and to reduce conflicts.

As mentioned in chapter 1, rampant overgrazing is often attributed to a lack of centralized control in the community framework. Overgrazing is a serious problem. Owning a large number of animals is often a scattershot means of security: the more animals one has, the more animals will survive. However, communities have ways of constraining herd sizes, as each community limits the number of animals each household can put to pasture on the communal land. Families pay a fee to the community for any animals above this limit. This "tax" acts as a resource maintenance instrument as herders must weigh the price of this fee against the real or projected benefits of having excess animals. The collecting of firewood as a subsistence strategy is also regulated within communities. Though not as important as in the past, wood is still an important source of energy in the most impoverished areas. The selling of this wood may also provide a meager income supplement. However, people are only allowed by the comunidad to collect wood that is already on the ground, and there is a fixed quantity allowed per family for each collection. Additionally, communities in the interior charge a small fee and assign a specific trail to be used by pastoralists from the exterior coastal areas transporting their animals to the hills. It is their prerogative to deny access if the visitors allow their sheep and goats to graze in undesignated areas.

Intercommunity Relations

Since producing wheat with limited technological inputs demands sizable labor power, and since able-bodied workers are increasingly employed away from home, communities may still make cooperative exchanges between themselves. Castro and Bahamondes (1984) identify categories of traditional labor exchange agreements. These include *la minga,* in which laborers are paid with meals; *vuelta de mano,* in which reciprocal labor is traded at a point down the road; and *gallaíto,* in which payment is made in portions of the harvest.

In earlier times, *la trilla* (the threshing) was the use of a team of horses to separate the seeds by trampling the wheat. The driver, or *trillador,* a high-status person with the animals and machinery, would be paid for his services with a cut of the surplus. The image of a trillador and his horses working with a group of farmers to bring in a harvest is a familiar symbol of Chilean traditional rural life. Such representations of the trilla are almost as popular a subject matter for etchings, hammered copper bas-relief illustrations, and other souvenirs as that of Chilean cowboys (*huasos*) taking part in the *rodeo chileno* or that of a couple dancing the *cueca,* the nation's highly stylized folk dance, both of which I will discuss in chapter 5.

While combine harvesters replaced horses by the 1960s, as I will present in my description of the wheat harvest in Loma Seca, the *trilla* remains an important event in community life. Not surprisingly, with machinery in short supply, the trillador, who travels around the countryside to conduct his business, holds a powerful position, both respected and resented. Often still paid with a portion of the wheat, the size of his cut seems to increase yearly as the price of gasoline rises and the price of wheat falls. The switch to mechanized harvesting has led to a decrease in the number of people filling the position of trillador, and some regret that this change has led to a shift from cooperative relations to a more entrepreneurial form.

Another interesting traditional cooperative arrangement with a festive atmosphere is the *corridas de liebres y zorros,* the "running of jackrabbits and foxes." Here a large number of people are gathered together to hunt and eliminate these animals, which damage crops and livestock. The participants on horseback move in a line formation to cover large stretches of land at a time. The animals are shot with rifles as they are flushed out of the brush. The people are paid with food and drink for their participation and with the understanding that the hosts will likewise participate in corridas in their guests' communities when the need arises.

ORIGINS AND HISTORICAL DEVELOPMENT

As with the above assessments of the logic behind and function of community mechanisms of resource conservation, surplus redistribution, and power differentiation, there are varying interpretations of the history of these agricultural communities that are likewise positioned relative to various theoretical and ideological bearings. The exact origins of the comunidades agrícolas of Region IV are somewhat ambiguous, developing from a confluence of cultural and economic sources in the pre-Colombian, Spanish, and the early Chilean republic eras rather than following a linear history from a single and easily recognizable starting place.

Origins, Influences, and Explanations

The two most widely held accounts of the genesis of the mixed land tenure system involve as the essential historical moments and forces: (1) fragmentation of large agricultural estates in this colonial frontier; and (2) particular outcomes of the mining industry. Also sometimes cited are pre-Colombian and colonial "indigenous" origins, including the passing of the *encomienda* system and the forced relocation of Indian groups (Santander 1992b, 1–5; Castro and Bahamondes 1984, 144).

Four major indigenous cultural groups were living in northern Chile at the time of the Spanish arrival: (1) Aymara living in the mountain valleys of the far north, what is now Region I, Tarapaca; (2) Atacameño settlements around the natural salt deposits of the Atacama desert; (3) hunting, gathering, and fishing bands in the past colloquially referred to as *los Changos* (an unfortunate racist term, the word for "monkey" in Spanish) who lived in the coastal ecological niches; and the prominent Diaguita culture situated over much of Regions III and IV. Only Aymara culture and language have survived to the present day. The Diaguita, whose language belonged to the *kakan* linguistic group, was the first culture to disappear. It is believed that by the end of the seventeenth century the Diaguita had for the most part been absorbed into "mestizo" society mostly as a consequence of the influence of mining activities (Castro and Romo 1996, 8). After Chile's defeat of Peru and Bolivia in the War of the Pacific (1879–84), provoked in order to gain access to the valuable nitrate fields, the far northern reaches of the world's driest desert were annexed and became the "Norte Grande," changing Atacama and Coquimbo into Chile's "Little North."

Shortly after Pedro de Valdívia, founder of Santiago in 1541, laid plans for the building of La Serena (today an urban center of 150,000) in 1545, the Spaniards began to mine gold in the Norte Chico. This spot was strategically situated midway between Santiago and the Rio Copiapó, where there was a northern outlying Indian settlement. Originally destroyed, La Serena was reestablished for good in 1549 and given formal city standing in 1552. Francisco de Aguirre, a conqueror charged with the second founding of La Serena, was granted domain over the Indians and forced them to labor in the mines through the encomienda system. This was the earliest stage of the region's development as a center for copper production (Pederson 1966, 42–75).

By the time of the Spanish era, the Diaguita culture group had already been incorporated into the southern parts of the Incan empire. Before the coming of the Inca in the fifteenth century, the Diaguita farmed solely in the rain-fed valleys, practicing a small-scale cultivation that put little pressure on the land. As with the Spaniards who came later, the Inca were attracted by the area's mineral wealth and introduced new methods of animal husbandry and irrigation as well as mining (Alvarez 1987, 111).

It is thought that later when subordinate army officers were granted land as recompense for service, the Spanish and pre-Spanish systems remained side by side until the two systems converged into a single mode of production as a result of ecological pressures on land productivity and regional economic changes that formed a common class segment (Santander 1992b, 1–2). These *Mercedes de las tierras"* (land grants) helped to create an elite class that was both tied to the land and loyal to the Crown. Expansive tracts of land in the Norte Chico were ceded in this way to de Aguirre and other famous conquistadors in Chilean history such as Pedro Cortes Monroy, Geronimo Pizarro, Juan de Ahumada, Diego de Valencia, Augustín Jorquera, and Bartolome Rojo (IREN-CORFO 1978, 21–24; Solis de Ovando 1992, 18–19). Gallardo Fernández, while acknowledging the mercedes as a common denominator, insists that since only officers of the "highest colonial social strata" were granted land, this is an insufficient account of the formation of the communities (Gallardo Fernández 2002, 367).

The details of precolonial origins are largely a matter of inference and interpretation rooted in a belief in the persistence of cultural traditions and the politico-economic tools of empire building; the lines of descent drawn from the suspension of the encomienda system to the present-day community arrangement are drawn more clearly in the minds of adherents. While encomienda (the system in which conquerors were entitled to demand tax and labor from several generations of Indians within their domain with the requisite obligation of Christianizing them) was never as significant in the sparsely peopled north as in other areas of the colony, it existed longer here than in other regions, continuing on into the early eighteenth century (Loveman 1988, 47) It was during this time that Spanish mining went into full swing and the labor demands of mining, along with the associated development of the production of *semi-elaborados* (simple manufactured staples including dried fruit, wine, and the distilled spirit *pisco*), created a scarcity of manual labor. In conjunction with slavery, forced transplantation of indigenous people, and the luring of Spanish laborers with salaries and land, the encomienda functioned to meet this need (Castro and Bahamondes 1984, 143).

Santiago and other parts of central Chile reaped the benefits of the colony's satellite orbit in relation to the powerful Peruvian market, while the northern periphery was situated in a more insecure and economically vulnerable position. As a result of a commercial agriculture crisis in the early seventeenth century, many haciendas in the north were forced to sell their holdings or reorganize (Castro and Bahamondes 1986, 115). The hacienda in the Valle del Hurtado, for example, was fragmented into a self-contained entity of four interrelated *vecinidades:* small private properties, a reduced hacienda, small tenant areas, and lands for *medieros y talajeros* (woodsmen, or woodcutters). The requirement to contract commercially with Peru and the diminished state of viability in the Norte Chico are two reasons for such dissolutions cited by Alvarez (1987, 113). Gallardo Fernández concurs as well that these economic crises and the resulting falloff in wheat exports to Peru during the first decades of the eighteenth century no doubt played a formative part in the founding of the comunidades agrícolas (2002, 376).

Written records concerning origins are spotty. There is scarce recorded information spanning the colonial era's initial grants and the first divisions of land among later descendents and the first efforts toward legal recognition and codified land rights in the era of the early republic. For example, the comunidades of Yerba Loca and Carquidaño in the Valle Hermoso trace their founding to two events: a Spanish governor granting encomienda to a conquistador in 1605 and the breaking up and distribution of the land by his male descendents a hundred years later. The origins of the comunidad of El Espinal is described in a 1968 college thesis from the University of La Serena as in the early eighteenth-century division of property among the ten children of the daughter of Juan Julian de la Vega, recipient of the original grant (Acevedo et al. 1968, 29). Exploring the history of the comunidad of Jimenez y Tapia, Solis de Ovando cites an eighteenth-century document showing Ramon Jimenez Tapia leaving a large estate to his sons. Solis de Ovando asserts that because the holding was in bad condition, the sons and subsequent offspring preserved most of the land as common property. The next surviving document does not emerge until the end of the nineteenth century, by which time Jimenez y Tapia has long been designated a "comunidad" (Solis de Ovando 1992, 22–23).

The influences of mining and the relocation of indigenous populations are not really the initiators of the comunidad system but better fit the description of formative processes that shaped ongoing patterns and arrangements of land tenure, property rights, and productive activities. From the colonial period through the early years of Chile's independence, commercial mining operations were frequently endowed with ancillary land for owners and workers to use, and much of this land was held corporately (Alvarez 1987, 113). Santander (1992b,

5) cites Borde and Santana (1980) as the main advocates of the view that Indians driven from the productive encomienda land near the ocean brought their communal land tenure practices with them to the less fertile land in the interior.

Gallardo Fernández, in her innovative study of the comunidades agrícolas of the comuna of Canela, delineates a sequence of events that converged during the second half of the eighteenth century to bring forth this unique system of land use. Once property was divided into a number of large parcels, subsequent subdivision via inheritance took place as economic activities involved the concurrent practices of irrigated agriculture near water sources and cattle raising in the hills. She deems the fencing of flat, irrigated land and the persistence of the "earlier tradition of communal lands within the resultant properties" an organic result of the "economic rationale" of this ecologically specific mixed strategy of production. Recognizing that while this drawn out process is easier to conceptualize as a natural evolution, identifying "exactly how and in what order different elements contributed to that formation is more difficult," adding that along with the economic crises discussed above, the decrease in human population as a result of the spread of disease could also be offered as a factor (Gallardo Fernández 2002, 380–81).

Imagining the Past

Gallardo Fernández summarizes the key and somewhat idiosyncratic aspects of the mixed tenure comunidad system: Large semicommunal tracts of land in combination with small individually owned plots emerged during colonialism, evolving out of the big land grants in what she calls a "spontaneous process" that was not, as might be expected in a colonial empire, directly "imposed from above" (Gallardo Fernández 2002, 364–65). This understanding is no doubt the most plausible, yet, as we shall see, the lack of a clear lineage in this process-oriented model probably makes it less satisfying to both "folk" and "official" histories that draw heavily on popular assumptions regarding culture, ethnicity, and identity. Presumptions of a unilineal ancestry from a single source belie the complexity of factors involved. It should not be surprising, however, that particular land use traditions persisted among different groups across different historical eras considering the common challenges of drought, a short supply of arable land, and wider instabilities both economic and environmental that these groups faced. A flexible system of land management oscillating between "open" (pastoralism) and "closed" (agriculture) persists and is maintained via mixed land tenure, multiple income and subsistence strategies, and shared labor exchanges because then, as now, individual farmers on small private plots simply could not have survived by themselves in this capricious and unforgiving environment.

The members of the communities do not consider themselves to belong to any Indian group or see themselves as ethnically different from the majority of Chileans. Many comuneros are clearly proud of the association with the region's long history, colonial past of the comunidades, and their ancestors' important service as frontier settlers. As I will discuss in chapter 5, for many of the men, their self-identity is rooted in an identification with Chilean cowboy culture, and I will provide details from the horse races and rodeos, considering them in terms of the function that they play in reproducing the local economy and in promoting group cohesion, as well as individual expressions of identity.

Development specialists, seeking to change the "mentality" of comuneros, sometimes regard their practices as a lingering ill-informed cultural tradition. The mind-set associated with these customs was at various times described to me as an irresponsibly selfish "mining mentality" that extracts life from the land without remorse or as an antiquated "indigenous" tradition of rampant overgrazing and "non-capitalist" relations that the locals obstinately and irrationally refuse to change. Some, like Iannuzzi and Salinas, observe that pride in their Spanish heritage of comuneros projects a kind of arrogant superiority not found in other Chilean campesino communities (Iannuzzi and Salinas 1986, 46). Along these same lines, I was told more than once by outsiders that because they are isolated, people living in comunidades speak the "best" Spanish as they have somehow remained an isolated and "pure" linguistic group.

Others suggest that comunidad practices might possibly have been transplanted to Chile as an Arabic communitarian system as a consequence of the Spanish conquest of Arabs in Castilla, where wheat was the staple crop and the indivisible communal property was rotated between cultivation and sheepherding and regeneration achieved through a similar technique of "fencing" and "fallowing" (Santander 1992b, 7–8). This same attribution of transplanted culture was told to me by more than one development worker who were aggravated by what they perceived as the comuneros' stubborn insistence on growing wheat, despite warnings of its extremely detrimental effect on the dry soil and his assertion that "they don't *need*" to grow wheat.

Romanticized origins. Epic lineages. Folk linguistic ideas about language purity. The doggedness of ancient customs. Beliefs in dubious histories may tell us more about mainstream Chile's view of comuneros and their practices as foreign or antiquated relics than anything else. As I will discuss later, such assumptions are at various times legitimated by modernization and development discourse.

In chapter 8 I will revisit such images associated with this history, exploring other contradictions between state and local-level discourses over origins, identity, and ethnicity. However, it is meaningful to remark at this point another perhaps more ominous image that springs from the historical influence of mining, especially the leftist political affiliation related to labor organization and class consciousness. During my first trip to Chile I was visiting the village of Vicuña in the picturesque vineyard- and orchard-lined Elqui valley while searching for a community to study. A local business owner with whom I would become fast friends was somewhat incredulous: Why would anyone willingly choose to live in a comunidad agrícola in the rugged interior, especially when there are so many more beautiful, modern, and interesting places and things to see in the region? His home in the Elqui valley, for example, is a lovely locale renown for grape vineyards, pisco factories, and crystal-clear skies; the birthplace of Nobel laureate poet Gabriela Mistral, a world-class observatory, and a growing reputation as a tourist destination (spurred partly by a recent spate of UFO sightings and the valley's geographic location in a New Age energy vortex). I soon sensed that he was afraid that the North American visitor focused on such a poor and backward area would leave with a poor impression of his country. His comments were animated. He kicked the dirt to make his point: "There's no water. The land's no good." Shaking his head to illustrate confusion, he warned that it was a strange place where "nobody owns the land . . . *everybody* owns the land." Finally, he stuffed his hands in his pockets, lowered his shoulders, and shifted his weight to demonstrate idleness. "Comunistas," he said, practically spitting the word.

In the next chapter, I will show how from the beginning the communities were part of major historical moments of export production—primarily copper mining and wheat production. This history is important for more than descriptive purposes. In terms of operationalizing political economy toward goals of development and environmental policy, it is imperative to take into account the history of capitalist expansion into particular ecological niches in order to understand how this past has shaped the present-day relations between local communities and agents of development. The comunidades agrícolas are an interesting example of articulated mixed modes of production that were clearly not inward-oriented indigenous communities fitting the description of the semi-isolated, so-called "closed corporate institutions" presumed to have developed in response to the intrusion of capitalism; they bear many characteristics of Wolf's "open" peasant communities articulated with capitalism from their inception (1957). Noncapitalist relations of subsistence production and resource management have since colonial times been connected with the region's capitalist economic development. This historical connection has found expression in both material and ideological elements, or as Loveman puts it:

> Always . . . the interdependence of agriculture and mining persisted and has dominated the economy of the *norte chico* to the present . . . Like the *norte grande*, although to a lesser extent, the norte chico has played a disproportionate role in shaping the development of Chilean labor movement and working-class organizations while at the same time exporting its products to support the Chilean economy. Owing to the tendency of many rural laborers and peasants in this region to work alternately in agriculture and mining, depending upon weather conditions and access to cultivable land, the militancy of the mine workers spread to the rural regions. (1988, 23–24)

4

Resiliency in Hostile Natural, Social, and Political Environments

INTRODUCTION

IN THE MID- TO LATE-NINETEENTH CENTURY, THE FIRST FEW DECADES after Chilean independence from Spain, key events and processes shaped the communities in economic, ecological, and social dimensions. Mining was a powerful force in the formation of the comunidades agrícolas. Along with brief but intense periods of wheat exportation, mining transformed the land, the labor, and the livelihoods of people struggling to make a living in this intersection between commodity production and subsistence farming. As we have seen, the comunidades agrícolas of Chile's Region IV do not fit neatly into either evolutionist trajectories of the expansion of capitalism nor essentialist models of pure "persistence" or "resistance" covered in chapter 2: they are neither "precapitalist relics" that remained unchanged by modernization and development nor are they in danger of being replaced in the countryside by capitalist enterprises and proletarianization (transformation into wage workers). In fact, their origins are linked with early capitalist production of large-scale commodities (copper and wheat), and this complex mode of production developed in response to the need for diversity in production in the fragile and uncertain environment. In this chapter, I will discuss how commercial commodity production and economic booms also left a detrimental ecological legacy that further necessitates the particular subsistence, commodity, and petty commodity production and diverse economic strategies like those of the families in Loma Seca. In turn, copper mining left a social legacy in politicized migrants who returned from the mines with a leftist orientation, socialist ideals and practices that continue today. This brought great difficulties during the oppressive Pinochet regime and continues to conflict with many neoliberal rural economic policies of the post-Pinochet coalition governments.

73

I begin by looking at the impact of the large-scale production of the commodities of copper and wheat on the region's natural environment. Next I will consider how mining shaped the sociopolitical environment vis-à-vis the experience of comuneros and other campesinos as wage labor migrants. This is followed by a review of the significant laws and legal changes regarding the codification of land entitlement and community recognition that have affected the communities during Chile's political upheavals of the last few decades. Finally, some present-day problems of drought and water competition issues will be explored.

MINING'S IMPACT ON THE NATURAL ENVIRONMENT

Gold was the primary mining activity from the start of the eighteenth century through Chilean independence in 1818, but copper and silver ultimately became more important as a result of a boom that lasted until the early twentieth century. The boom brought in large-scale mines and processing operations and the accompanying growth in population. The system of *pirquen,* in which operators paid royalties and rents on mines that they worked independently, facilitated this development. As foreign capitalists financed the massive expansion and exploited the expertise and toil of *pirquineros,* Chile became the largest producer of copper in the world. A significant number of the miners and laborers came from the comunidades agrícolas, as animal husbandry and agriculture supplemented the often erratic income earned from mining (Pederson 1966, 157).

Mining quickly began to drastically degrade the natural environment. The depletion of woody species was initiated by their use as firewood, charcoal, and timber to support camps, mines, and copper smelters brought in between the late eighteenth and early nineteenth centuries. Their "reverbatory furnaces"—a process in which heat is radiated from the roof on to the material being treated—gobbled up the vegetative covering in a staggeringly short period and the industry by the mid-1800s was unsustainable in all but the far southern areas of Region IV (Schneider 1982, 114). Between 1601 and 1900 approximately 800 billion tons of copper were produced in the Norte Chico via a primarily wood-burning form of metallurgy, with nearly 85 percent of this total produced between 1835 and 1900. It is estimated that between anywhere from 4 to 7 million hectares of forest were cleared to make nearly thirty million tons of firewood extracted for mining (Santander 2003). By the time the boom was over, the "Little North" was left with, in the words of Leland Pederson, a historian of mining in the Norte Chico, "depleted resources, ghost towns, hulking ruins (and) railroads joining abandoned smelters to abandoned ports . . ." (1966, 289). During the peak years of this environmental destruction, when such primitive metallurgy generated 1.5 tons of copper annually while devouring woods at a rate of 7,000 hectares each year, some critics as early as the 1830s raised their voices, among them the respected Chilean naturalist and geographer Claudio Gay, who was seriously troubled by it (Alvarez 1987, 112). Santander emphasizes that although the scientific community reported the severity of the problem, the government did nothing until well after most of the damage had been done. The *intendiente* (or governor) of Coquimbo and the president of the National Society of Agriculture were on record in 1871 and 1872, respectively, lamenting the deforestation. The "timid and ineffective" "Law of the Forests" (1872) continued to permit cutting of what little vegetation had initially escaped clearing (Santander 2003). Today, many feel that attempts to deal with the Norte Chico's enormous environmental problems are still hindered by a familiar state patrimony and indifference and a lack of local collaboration for the common good. As mentioned, a good deal of environmental and economic development policy in Chile limits the blame for erosion and desertification to the local subsistence patterns of goat and sheep grazing and growing wheat on depleted soil. While these activities certainly exacerbate these processes, most environmental scholars with the long historical view are quick to emphasize they were put into motion by shortsighted commercial mining enterprises of the past. Although they no longer devour forests to satisfy their energy demands, the mines still compete with small growers and commercial agribusiness for the critical supply of water and have been the biggest source of resource depletion since their inception. Collier uses powerful words to describe their impact: "The smelter's insatiable demand for fuel made deep inroads into the exiguous timber resources of the Norte Chico and contributed to the southward advance of the desert—that usually unremarked but basic ecological theme of Chilean history since colonial times" (1993, 14).

REVERBERATIONS OF TWO WHEAT BOOMS

It is important to keep in mind that although the small-scale production of wheat and other cereals and overgrazing goats and sheep are usually blamed for the region's erosion and desertification, these uses of the land are for the most part a continuation of an ecological degradation that was wrought by mining. Commercial wheat production that occurred at key points in the nation's history when this region was articulated with other economies far beyond its boundaries should also bear some of the responsibility.

There were two periods when the production of wheat for export was important: (1) The above-mentioned period between 1620 and 1690, when the Norte Chico was a satellite dependency of the metropole of Peru and supplied wheat to the Peruvian market (Castro and Bahamondes 1986, 113), and (2) a brief boom during the second half of the nineteenth century, when sailing around Tierra del Fuego was the only passage between the Atlantic Ocean and the flourishing prosperity of California.

This second boom was abrupt and short-lived but its impact was great. Most of the wheat was grown in central and southern Chile but the environment of the Norte Chico was greatly altered by the expansion of wheat production into the region. To facilitate dry farming, wide expanses of wild vegetation, primarily along the coastline, were cleared and then abandoned once the rush to produce wheat had died away. The boom left scars on the land that remain today in the form of deteriorated shrub vegetation (Schneider 1982, 114). Thousands of hectares in the coastal range previously serving as natural pasture were broken up during this time. According to Bauer, the technique of dry farming (utilizing moisture-conserving tillage) was "virtually unknown." Driven by goals of immediate profit, the shortsighted agricultural practices, which included plowing hills vertically and giving little attention to the preparation of seedbeds, proved to be disastrous. The visible legacy of discounting the future for short-term returns can be seen in the eroded red soil that remains in much of this area where the land could not recuperate (Bauer 1975, 122).

Codifying Claims

As the 1830s was the high point for mining in the region and the most prosperous times in the history of the communities, it also saw the beginning of the process of legal recognition. Large mines not only provided employment, many small independent miners who struck out on their own were comuneros whose efforts were subsidized by these "communal modes of production" (Loveman 1988, 22–24).

The Codigo Civil in 1847 first inscribed those in possession of titles with their property. The Conservado de Bienes Raíces in 1857 outlined the prescribed means by which those who were not in possession of titles should acquire them (Iannuzzi and Salinas 1986, 46). It is significant that the confluence of the halcyon days of mining, the rise of the independent miner, and the concomitant necessity of the communities as a subsistence buffer resulted in both legal codification and bloodshed. Much violent activity took place outside of these prescribed means in armed struggles over land rights, and those with the most power and influence certainly fared better (Batallán 1980, 101). Today many of the descendants of those who came out on top in this "sorting out" period toil in poverty and uncertainty, clinging fiercely to what often seems from the outside to be a worthless privilege in a desert wasteland, but is their one source of security that has remained constant throughout times of state indifference, repression, and interference.

It would be nearly one hundred years before the comunidades were again affected by legislation. These laws primarily served to protect the interests of those who were involved in wage labor. As the large commercial estates grew, more and more people from the communities sought work away from home and for longer periods of time. Consequently, loyalties and community political structures changed as these new laborers were organized into *sindicatos* or *federaciones de inquilinos* (farm contract laborers). The reforms of the Asociación de Agricultura legislation in 1944 lumped small growers, comuneros, and others into a single category. Two years later, the Congreso de Trabajadores (workers' congress) in Salamanca established the eight-hour workday, improved working conditions, and set a minimum salary. All of this bettered the lot of the contract miners but did little to address the internal problems of the comunidades agrícolas (Batallán 1980, 102).

REFORM AND BACKLASH FROM THE UNIDAD POPULAR THROUGH THE MILITARY REGIME

Along with the history of regional economic development in general, the history of national and regional public policy as experienced at the local level should be considered as one of the factors in community formation. For example, using mode of production tools to enhance a World Systems understanding of the economic development of the U.S.-Mexico border in the years 1940–90, Weaver's analysis of the establishment of the Border Industrialization Program shows the importance of policy programs in facilitating the extraction of wealth from peripheral regions and its accumulation in centers in the core (2001).

There were two periods of great change in the Chilean agrarian structure during this century: (1) 1965–73, when the state broke up estates of more than 80 hectares, and (2) after the 1973 coup when the government reversed the reform process. Between 1965–70, during the reformist Christian Democrat government of Eduardo Frei, approximately 1,400 properties totaling 3.5 million hectares were appropriated. The socialist Unidad Popular government of Salvador Allende went even further, breaking up over 4,400 properties totaling around 6.8 million hectares. This period ended the domination of the great estates of the past and brought about a proliferation of medium-sized (20–80 hectares) and small-sized farms (5–20 hectares). Prior to reform in 1965, small and medium-sized farms only made up about one-third of Chilean agricultural land. By the end of land reform, two-thirds of the agricultural land in Chile consisted of small and medium-sized holdings (Gwynne and Meneses 1994, 7). In all, more than ten million hectares of *fundo* lands (the word *fundo* in Chile and Peru means haciendas or large rural estates) were expropriated and transferred to the previous tenants and wage laborers by means of cooperative frameworks (Korovkin 1990, 91).

Concurrent with land redistribution were government policies that increased agricultural production at a much higher rate than the increase in employment in the capitalist agricultural sector. Much of this was because of the replacement of full-time paid laborers with temporary migrant workers. While Chilean land reform, for a time, reversed the trend toward shrinking peasant holdings that occurred in most other Latin American nations, nonexpropriated lands were transformed into medium-sized capitalist farms with limits placed on ownership. During Allende's administration collective lands were often illegally privately appropriated in response to the extreme price controls of the socialist government (de Janvry et al. 1987, 397–98; 401). Jarvis persuasively argues that the lack of faith in (or embarrassment toward) the small farmer as an independent producer that led government policies to neglect the peasant sector even during the reform process was grounded more in antipeasant urban biases in Santiago than in empirical evidence of the "inefficiency" of peasant farming (1985, 3–5).

While there is no doubt that the subsequent Pinochet government's policies effectively concentrated land into the hands of large commercial enterprises and facilitated the transformation of many campesinos into wage laborers, some contend that the demobilizing of both the peasantry and the old landholding elite would not have been possible without the weakening of the landowning oligarchy that occurred with the progressive reforms that occurred prior to 1973. The military government could not have successfully challenged the landed aristocracy, and radically advanced capitalism in the Chilean countryside had not the governments of Frei and Allende successfully dismantled, in their words, the deep-rooted patterns of "precapitalist" development. According to this line of thought, the extreme and vast land reform of the progressive governments paved the way for the displacement of the peasantry and the rise of the business class during the military government (Martínez and Díaz 1996, 133–35; Portes 2000, 360–61). On the other hand, Boorstein claims that, forced to operate within the restrictions of the Frei government's reform laws, Allende and the Unidad Popular were never really able to either successfully control the landholding elite or bring about the scope of land distribution necessary to address the problems of temporary workers, *minifundistas* (the smallest growers), the Mapuche communities, and rural unemployment and underemployment. He shows that as of July 1972, more than half of all market production agriculture came from the twenty to eighty hectare farms, many of which had been large estates that were subdivided among family members during the Frei administration and, thus, whose owners were hostile to the Allende government (Boorstein 1977, 149–57).

After the Pinochet coup, most of the appropriated land was re-privatized, with 30 percent returned directly to the previous owners. The rest was auctioned off, with 28 percent going to individual campesinos or *cooperativa* associations (profit-sharing collective institutions), 10 percent to nonpeasant "haciendalike" commercial organizations, and 20 percent directly to private corporations (Castro and Bahamondes 1986, 114). The Pinochet government boasted that the "regularization" of landholdings, rather than bringing back the era of the large fundos, brought "real" titles to 45,000 land reform beneficiaries that had been (to use a still-in-fashion piece of "New Speak") "liberated" from government-run cooperatives in this new post-revolutionary setting. But, since the military regime offered little in the way of support, technical assistance, or input subsidies for small producers, by 1981 nearly half of the "liberated" had no choice but to sell their parcels of land, always at low prices and often to city-based professionals seeking to make money as farm entrepreneurs. This process of concentrating land into the hands of the economic elite and transforming smallholders into wage laborers was critical to the Chilean shift to export fruit production (Collins and Lear 1995, 190–92). Even when the lands of the smallholder were comparable in size to small capitalist farms, they were at a distinct disadvantage because they lacked the assets of machinery and technology, and received little to no financial or technical assistance from the state (Korovkin 1990, 91–92).

As the important agrarian unit became the labor-intensive, intensely capitalized farm geared for export production, job security dwindled.

Collier and Sater contend that "The new agribusiness had none of the paternalism of the old hacienda (fundo), and offered relatively few stable jobs. Thus the cost of Chile's dynamic new agriculture was an intensification of rural poverty—the poor now being the victims of capitalist modernization rather than of the inertia and hierarchy of the past" (1996, 367–69).

How did these drastic changes in land reform affect the comunidades agrícolas? For the most part, the communities, having possession of their low-quality land for generations, were touched very little by the land policies of Frei and Allende. In fact, the process of agrarian reform and counterreform in Chile during the 1970s and 1980s had only a marginal impact on access to land by small farm families in many regions of Chile. There is little exact regional information on the distribution of land in the Norte Chico, but it is assumed that the regional pattern was consistent with the national trend in which the impact was often regressive, with the wealthiest households in 1968 receiving the greatest increases in land (Scott 1990). Agrarian reform during the Allende government that succeeded Frei's was extreme and rapid. Most of the people I met in Loma Seca spoke of the Unidad Popular government (1970–73) as the high point of relations between the Chilean national government and the community and the best times for comuneros. They feel that it was during this brief period that the state was most attentive to their needs, providing a variety of rural social services, as well as a subsidized market for their products. Because of subsidization, there were good prices for wool, meat, wheat, and cheese. People had money in their pockets, I was told, and they could afford to buy more goods. Trucks would come to the community once a month selling food and household necessities at subsidized prices.

Chile's socialist governments were not a "peasant revolution." Democratic legitimization of land reform was, to a degree, obtained from the peasant sector of society (de Janvry et al. 1987, 400), but the real benefits that accrued to smallholders were offset by the impossibilities of wedding nationalist economic policies with concerns for rural poverty and by corruption within the progressive political framework of land reform. In discussing the potential for peasantry as a self-directed class, Hobsbawm's conception of modern peasants is not that of homogenous, harmonious, insulated, corporate entities but of dispersed, politically unmanageable isolates, having as little in common with one another as they do with other segments of political economy. Rife with internal conflict, these "prepolitical" subjects are subjected to the resistance-deflecting divide-and-conquer discipline exerted from above and therefore incapable of leading themselves in a successful struggle against the state (Hobsbawm 1973, 18–20). Corrigan counters this view by criticizing Hobsbawm for drawing upon a questionable extrapolation of the Eighteenth Brumaire and for suffering from the urbanization/industrialization-as-progress biased approach to rural society that afflicted both orthodox Marxists and anti-Marxist modernization proponents at that time. For Corrigan, it is misguided to deny peasants the integrity of their own actions. This is because (1) all production relations involve social relations and specific dynamic ways of interpreting these relations and acting upon them and (2) mutuality is a defining quality of peasant production. Corrigan uses the upheaval in Chile in the late 1960s, specifically early success of the Unidad Popular, as examples of a coherent popular conception of social change resulting in gains for the peasantry. He also sees the counterrevolution of 1973 as motivated by a "bourgeois democracy/necessary stages"-as-progressive logic that bears strong resemblance to the argument of Hobsbawm (Corrigan 1975, 344–46). This second statement is an exaggerated bit of theoretical infighting, but it does bring to light the problem of the perception of the peasantry as "backward" in "top-down" approaches with dissimilar political agendas.

While the modernization efforts of the progressive governments may have ignored communities and been met with indifference within them, the negative effects felt under Pinochet were painfully direct. During the dictatorship (1973–90), the comunidades agrícolas were dealt with in ways that varied from "benign neglect" (withdrawal of state support) to outright suppression of their democratic traditions. The military regime isolated and immobilized political opponents during this counter-reform era of systematic exclusion from assistance, subsidies, and credit to the small farm sector in general and to the recipients of earlier land reform in particular (Jarvis 1985, 3–5;188). The dictatorship's hostility was clearly a reaction to labor organization and political participation among the miners and comuneros of the north, a region where campesino participation had long been important in the Chilean history of labor relations and land reform (Silva 1991, 20–21). The Frei government (1964–70) initiated a sequence of steps to foment unionization in the rural areas. Also during this time, the communities were given status as a special category of landholding within Chile, and their tenure and decision-making customs were legally recognized. The law codified self-governance practices that comuneros had acquired from the unions through generations of mining and migration experience (Rosenfeld 1993, 31). The influence of leftist political leanings and tactics acquired via emigration to the north and subsequently expressed in the countryside in the form of organization and activism is cited by Gallardo Fernández in her compelling description of the struggle for land in the comunidad of Espíritu Santo in Canela. Land that was illegally sold in the mid-nineteenth century was successfully reappropriated a century later, Gallardo Fernández contends, largely as a result of the personal histories and fighting spirit of the former "protagonists in the nitrate fields and copper mines" who organized the struggle (2002, 326–27). As I have argued elsewhere, while mining had altered the natural environment and articulated the communities at a material level with external economies, involvement in wage labor had altered peasant consciousness and linked them ideologically to movements away from the countryside (2002).

Socialist ideals and practices placed people in great danger after the military takeover of September 11, 1973. There was widespread purging of leftists, labor leaders, and supporters of the Allende experiment that continued throughout the brutal early years. Thousands "disappeared"—kidnapped, tortured, and murdered by the military and secret police—and tens of thousands of others were forced into exile during Pinochet's seventeen years in power. The military government greatly restricted comunero democracy. Meetings had to be approved by the local police force and could only take place under the watchful eye of police presence. So-called "political" topics could not be discussed and those who defied this were jailed. The government installed handpicked leaders to replace left-leaning representatives who were fortunate if they escaped at all.

Comunero democracy was silenced during this bleak period but it did not perish as informal, and secret meetings were held whenever possible. The spirit survived persecution by the state and a series of legal changes designed to convert land into private property. The radical changes to the law before, during, and after the dictatorship—blown forward and backward by the turbulent winds of political change—produced a politically hybrid legal framework that the very active NGO Juventudes para el Desarrollo y el Producción (JUNDEP; Youth for Development and Production) judiciously deemed in 1996 "a synthesis of four different laws passed during different historical moments" (JUNDEP 1996, 1). Decree Law Number Five of 1967 established standards for the setting of boundaries for each community based on right-holding, possession, and usufruct. It clarified how communities could "regularize" (a process referred to locally as *saneamiento* or "cleaning up") the composition and ownership of property as long as all comuneros were in agreement. However, fearing that such standardization under the watchful eye of the state might lead to the breakup of their communities (the usually wise recognition that such "visibility" and "definition" are often the first steps toward having something taken away from you), most comunidades opted not to regularize property ownership at the time of the progressive governments (Gwynne and Meneses 1994, 13–14). Tellingly, 120 of the 173 communities that had regularized by 1998 had done so during a ten-year span (1974–84) during the dictatorship. This is almost three times as many as had done so during the nearly nine years of the reformist governments under Frei and Allende (1965–73). This is not surprising considering that the dictatorship had pushed for communities to standardize themselves so as to ease conversions from communal property to private property and sometimes installed community leaders who supported such changes. Through manipulation and coercion the dictatorship succeeded in ways that the progressive governments could not. Standardization by itself was not "privatization" of the communities, but it was the beginning of the process of breaking up of some communities following subsequent legal changes during the military regime. In chapter 8 I will describe another type of standardization in the form of a controversial law regulating goat cheese production that is met with strong resistance in the communities during the post-Pinochet era.

Decree Law 108 passed in 1978 permitted comuneros to sell their rights to parties outside of the comunidad, as long as ownership had been regularized (Gwynne and Meneses 1994, 7). Although some of the comunidades disaggregated land for private use that was sold to a handful of wealthy families in the region who invested in the grape production, the majority resisted the lure of privatization. In a Chilean publication written toward the end of the Pinochet times, Castro and Bahamondes (1986, 114) observe that as the drive for regional export-orientation marginalized many campesinos and comuneros, it led them to rely more heavily on their own production of food for family consumption. This capacity for subsistence production, in combination with wage labor migration, insulated communities during the period of inactivity when they could not produce commodities for market or hold regular community meetings. The "peripheral" nature of the communities in some ways worked to their advantage since because of the poor quality of the land where most of them are situated they were for the most part ignored.

As comunero-style rights and consensus building and the immutability of common land came to be viewed as obstacles to economic progress, further changes were enacted. Legislation in 1984 enabled free transference of rights, opening the door to dissolution of the communities (Solis de Ovando 1989, 58). The government executed a house-by-house program between 1986 and 1990 to promote—

sometimes using strong-arm tactics—the idea of conversion of communal land to private property. The prevailing thought of the free market ideology was that converting collective land into private property would spur economic growth and that the creation of titles would help people gain easier access to credit and rural housing subsidies. There was, however, a duplicitous underside to these capitalist ideals. Community members were generally not informed that the conversion of their land to individual property would result in taxation, which many in these poverty-ridden areas could not afford to pay. Neither were they told that selling their land meant the loss of their derechos, the suspension of their positions as comuneros, and their entitlement to any new land. Due to their strong ties to their property and suspicious of the government's motives, most families were reluctant to change. Still, although only 22 percent of the total number of those holding rights converted and sold their holdings, this small percentage for the most part comprised large tracts of the best irrigated and potentially irrigable land that was purchased and developed by transnational fruit-exporting companies. Such privatization also benefited some individuals who enjoyed favorable treatment from the government, many of them coming from local elites and powerful families. Also, many of the dictatorship's chosen community officers were able to obtain the most valuable pieces of property (Rosenfeld 1993, 33).

PRIVATIZATION AND EXPANSION OF COMMERCIAL AGRICULTURE

The expansion of the production of table grapes is an export-oriented development venture that has led to accelerated economic differentiation, social disruption, and nonsustainable exhaustion of natural resources within what is classified as a "poor" region. Between 1974 and 1986, agriculture's share of export production increased from 2 percent to 13 percent. During this time, Chile became the most important temperate climate fruit exporter south of the equator, topping the market in nectarines, peaches, and table grapes (Hojman 1990, 2). Throwing open the national economy to transnational capital and trade engendered regionalized economies built upon specialized production. Those areas capable of specializing in the production of higher-priced commodities for external markets have fared better than those limited to production for a shrinking domestic market. Yet, it is a facile gloss to divide the "haves" and "have-nots" of Chile simply along regional lines. Even in seemingly dynamic regions where export-oriented development policies have taken hold, there arose clustered cores of economic power and a gross inequitable distribution of access to sources of income (Diaz 1990, 132–34).

Fruit-producing regions in general and the Norte Chico in particular exemplify such inter- and intraregional uneven development. Although the commercial production of table grapes is based on a large number of producers, there are differences in the "pace" of resource accumulation and hence differences in profitability. Rapid commercialization and export-orientation resulted in rapid differentiation through waves of sales in which more successful commercial farmers have tended to purchase the land of the less successful. By 1980, 48 percent of the *parceleros* in Aconcagua, the province abutting the Norte Chico to the south had sold their land. Only a few were able to make a go of it alongside large capitalist producers (Korovkin 1990, 91–92). In the Norte Chico, some long-established landholding families were in the vanguard of table grape planting, borrowing large amounts of money and developing highly profitable businesses. To expand production, they purchased a good deal of nonirrigated communal land, which is of little direct value to comuneros but is used by them to graze their herds. Such pasture land is cheaply priced, but to convert it to grape production requires considerable investment in the forms of leveling the rough terrain and installing pump irrigation systems to draw water and distribute fertilized water to individual vines. The decision to take up grape growing was influenced by the availability of irrigated or irrigable land and the ability to purchase land and invest in irrigation. For cash poor comuneros living from season to season, the decision to sell was undoubtedly influenced by whether or not it had been a year of drought and those who did not sell came into strong competition with grape growers for water. There soon arose serious doubt as to how much further development can be sustained, and it has been suggested that the government exert control over the concentration of land, provide start-up subsidies for farmers endowed with insufficient capital and who are at greater risk to the capricious nature of the environment, and regulate the strain on and inequitable distribution of water (Gwynne 1993, 288–89). In short, export-oriented economic development during the "boom" years of the late 1980s and early 1990s, when the country's economy experienced an unprecedented ten consecutive years of growth, meant prosperity for some but has also led to (1) an amalgamation of land for commercial enterprises; (2) a reduction in land for alternative strategies such as pastoralism; (3) greater competition over resources; (4) intensified susceptibility for some to the prospect of disastrous drought; and (5) increased stress on land and water in an already fragile environment.

The comunidades in the Guatulame valley (see "Guatulame sector" in the previous chapter), because of their favorable microclimate, were the most altered by these policies. Those who privatized property participated in a brisk land market connected to the rapid growth of the production of table grapes, but the expansion was not without cost. There is what Gwynne and Meneses have described as a rising tension between water use and economic development. Warning that an environmental crisis looms, they call for policies to control land and water use that consider the long-term impact of climate change and reduced precipitation in the enclosed valley systems. These researchers doubt that the rapid growth of table grape production can be sustained, and they describe a bleak and ironic cycle in which better irrigation methods mean less water waste but also less surplus to leach out the accumulation of salt in the soil. This rising salinity will in turn require increased water use for flushing the soil and a decrease in the amount of soil that is conserved. All of this sets the table for another cluster of dry winters to bring about major ecological crisis (Gwynne and Meneses 1994, 34–35).

Although herding is not a major activity in the Guatulame, pastoral livelihoods have suffered in other areas where grape production has been expanded. As described, herders use a wide-ranging system of foraging and moving herds to different areas depending upon the time of year and the environmental conditions at hand. In the past, an important part of this system was a strip of pastureland in the hills that was preserved for herds to graze on before being moved to the mountains. The installation of vineyards has in many instances cut off access to these areas and disrupted the seasonal movement of animals.

"RURAL DEVELOPMENT" BEFORE AND AFTER THE DICTATORSHIP

In 1964, startled by the narrow margin by which socialist Allende had lost the 1958 election, both the Chilean right-wing and the United States backed Eduardo Frei, a Christian Democrat, who pledged a "revolution in freedom." Between 1964 and 1970 Frei brought 51 percent of the copper industry under state ownership and minimum wage and unionization rights for agricultural workers. It was during the Frei reform years that the "Plan Punitaqui," the most extensive attempt at rural development aimed specifically at the comunidades agrícolas, was undertaken and when government seemed to first take notice of these people in a concerted way. Loma Seca was one of twenty comunidades lumped together collectively as part of what was deemed the "Punitaqui System." These geographically contiguous communities are grouped together because of their common characteristics of production, resource exploitation, and types of intracommunity reciprocal relations like those that I have previously described. The other communities in this system included: Punitaqui, Las Damas, Cerro Blanco, Los Trigos, Cuarto Cajon, Los Pozos, Fernando Avarez, Lorenza Araya, Espinal, Loma Seca, Salala, Barraza Alto, Socos, Alcones, Calera, El Durazno, Rinconada, Potrerillo Alto, Divisadero, and El Altar (Batallán 1980, 137). Punitaqui, with approximately two thousand residents, is the largest of these communities.

There was an early attempt to transfer technology through pilot demonstration programs. The overall goal was to attain the best proportion of people to land. "Regularization" of legal titles to land was encouraged. Small salaried jobs were subsidized. Construction efforts were carried out in which people were paid with food. Post offices, schools, and other facilities were built. Most agree that the plan was not successfully carried out by the government, and any attempt at bringing significant changes to the comunidad system were for the most part rejected by the comuneros (Batallán 1980, 91).

It is still claimed by some that the Plan Punitaqui failed in Loma Seca because the people felt no motivation to change, and because of fear that to do so would mean that they would become subject to more taxation. For example, I met a man who is now an upper-level administrator at one of the government assistance offices in La Serena who upon finding out that I was working in Loma Seca began relating to me his personal experience with comuneros when he worked on the famous "Plan Punitaqui." It more or less failed because, from his perspective, the people ultimately refused to be helped (*La gente no se aceptaba la asistencia!*). Some schools and roads were built, some seeds and materials were given, but when the program ended after five years the people did not continue to work as a group or to legalize their boundaries and rights at that time. He summed it up by saying that *comuneros son muy individualistas* (comuneros are very individualistic)—that they are "isolated" and "old" and that as "miners of the land" they refuse to give up their claims to their "own space." In short, he said that they do not really participate *as* communities. The land tenancy system is the biggest reason for this, he elaborated, which of course is perpetuated by the migration of young people. In the next chapter I will describe activities that suggest that this is certainly not the case in Loma Seca.

Most previous studies from the era of the transition from the later years of Pinochet through the earliest parts of the return to democracy, agree that poverty, drought, and desertification are serious problems for the people of the comunidades agrícolas of Region IV. They also agree that action must be taken to stimulate the local economy, and that, for the most part, the communities are not nor have they ever been entirely independent, self-supporting entities. Where they differ dramatically is their assessment of the abilities of the communities to produce for themselves and the degree to which they believe that the communal land structure and traditional means of livelihood should be altered. The studies fall into three categories: (1) those that see indivisible, communal land as the biggest obstacle to economic improvement and that place the blame for erosion and poverty on traditional subsistence practices (Azócar and Lailhacar 1989; Contreras and Gastó 1986; and Iannuzzi and Salinas 1986); (2) more moderate assessments that stress the link between poor practices and environmental damage but that also acknowledge the degree of control over scarce resources and unstable conditions that is afforded by the communal institution and multiple subsistence strategies (Bravo 1989; Gastó et al. 1990; Paez 1991; Gwynne and Meneses 1994; and Ramirez 1991); and (3) those that believe that community production could thrive if given the proper attention and that advocate for preservation of community democracy and traditional life ways, seeing them as appropriate adaptations to the environmental damage and economic marginalization initiated and aggravated by large-scale mining operations (Bahamondes, et al. 1992, 1994; Batallán 1980; Castro and Bahamondes 1984, 1986; Castro 1986; Santander 1992, 1993, 1994).

At the extreme end of the first "pro-transformation" group is a study by Iannuzzi and Salinas. They assert that hereditary tenancy and the "lack of decision-making organization" are the primary reasons for underutilized resources, low levels of investment in productive inputs, and lack of access to markets (Iannuzzi and Salinas 1986, 6). The main underutilized resource is labor, too much of which they say goes unused between the months of April and September. According to them, by doing away with hereditary tenancy and transferring technology and training to change the "inflexible campesino mentality," the state can assist the communities in rising up from atomized "subsistence only" exploitation to diversified cultivation, access to credit, and full market integrated commercial production (1986, 107–14).

The second group of studies sees some value in traditional practices and arrangements and thus advocates less radical measures of change. After briefly considering "decolonization" (simply evacuating the most ecologically degraded areas!), the Gastó group dismisses it as a "low internal cost" strategy with high "external cost" demands (full employment for the transplanted population would be needed). Maintaining the current subsistence system would require increasingly expensive state support because of the growing deterioration of the ecology. Increasing employment, credit for seeds, credit for cheese production, and production bonuses is deemed only temporary help and not "real" development. This is because since there is no structural change of the communities involved, there is no hope for sustainability. Their final recommendation is the implementation of "communitarian farm businesses" with a new stronger centralized management that is educated in terms of administration and commercial production methods (Gastó et al. 1990, 209–16).

The third group is exemplified by the work of Castro and Santander. Castro stresses that (1) maximization of available resources through traditional knowledge, (2) the ecological integration of moving herds throughout the year, (3) intracommunity cooperation, and (4) the income integration of internal multiple subsistence strategies and external wage labor work in conjunction with strategic cultural adaptations in the forbidding environment of Region IV (1986, 242). Santander's work moves along similar lines. In addition, he makes recommendations to greatly diversify the economic base of the communities by providing a productive structure that is less vulnerable to drought. He proposes, among other things, plans to foster "ecotourism," install industry, construct and improve affordable irrigation in communities closer to river valleys, and encourage new cultivation activities (such as hydroponic cultivation). He also emphasizes the concomitant need to improve public works and infrastructure, create permanent employment opportunities, and protect and conserve the environment (1992; 1994, 80–98). Studies and recommendations such as those of Santander seek to increase the income opportunities by adding to (not reducing) the diverse strategies used in the comunidades agrícolas and by making use of the traditional management and communitarian structure (the emphasis is on community, rather than solely on individual entrepreneurial development). These studies also emphasize the capacity of the community structure to continue to produce, and to produce more effectively once the socioeconomic factors that serve to marginalize the communities are mitigated.

Post-Pinochet "Privatization within Limits"

Pinochet begrudgingly stepped down in 1990 after the public responded with an emphatic "No" vote in a general plebiscite in which he had expected to be granted eight more years of one-party rule. This began the gradual transition to democracy and the undoing of some of the more severe policies of the dictatorship. In 1993, JUNDEP began working with the communities to make key changes to the land law. By this time the reform process was far enough along to permit substantive modifications that would correct some of the injustices of the state's exploitation of the communities. Separate rights were established for the *derecho de comunero* and individual property, permitting comuneros to sell individual parcels without losing their community rights and privileges. Significantly, it was no longer possible for an individual comunero to unilaterally usurp his or her goce singular from the community by selling it on the open market. As part of a plan to foster community economic planning and development, the decision now must be approved by the Directiva. And while parcels of land may also be developed or sold collectively as a community, the survival of the communities is guaranteed in this "privatization within limits" plan as no more than 10 percent of all land can ever be sold (Rosenfeld 1993, 34).

At this point, it seems propitious to return briefly to matters of "origin." Situated on the "outside" of one of the poorest regions in Chile, the communities are economically and socially "marginal" and "peripheral." Some contend that if we look at contemporary legal origins, a kind of structural marginalization becomes very apparent. Both Paez and Solis de Ovando argue that, as set down in the 1967 law that established them as they exist today, these communities are *marginal by definition*. This legal definition identifies them as rural lands belonging in common to various proprietors "in which the number of comuneros will be manifestly larger than the productive capacity of the property to provide subsistence necessities" (Solis de Ovando 1989, 21; Paez 1991, 20). In practice, however, while the limited number of comuneros with rights (or "shares") assigned to a community acts to maximize individual utility by limiting users, the productive capacity of the land during years of rain is augmented by collective work projects involving family members who often do not reside in the community. Solis de Ovando rightly points out that such a legal definition of subsistence is inexact and focuses on poverty, stressing the inability of community resources to provide for its members. This definition does not take into consideration the important *social nature* of community *productivity* as identified by the comuneros themselves, nor does it acknowledge the noncapitalist relations within and between the communities (Solis de Ovando 1989, 22). It is the hope of organizations such as JUNDEP that restricted privatization will serve communities best by freeing up limited amounts of land for entrepreneurial development while still maintaining the community structure and these traditional benefits of the system.

DROUGHT

The erratic and sparse rainfall is generally clustered during the winter season. There may be entire winter months with no rain at all and entire winters with minimal rainfall. Nearly a quarter of the years recorded since 1540 have been drought years. During the "Great Drought of 1831" over half a million animals perished. For the past century or so, the pattern has been one year of adequate rainfall followed by three or four years of insufficient rain. The five worst periods during the twentieth century were 1909–13, 1916–18, 1935–37, 1968–70, and 1993–96. Until 1998, the single worst years of this century had been 1968 and 1970, during which time 45 percent of livestock were lost, almost a quarter of a million people were unemployed, and damage was estimated at one billion dollars. The period 1989–91, though not as bad as 1968–70, brought destruction estimated at 200 million dollars. The winter of 1987 was a season of high rainfall that was followed by three consecutive years of winter drought before the rains returned in 1991 (Santander 1994, 4–9).

Many contend that although the region has always been affected by drought, the phenomenon seems to be getting worse. Since the region pattern seems to be a concentration of dry years followed by a year of rainfall, a 1993 article by Gwynne maintained that it is necessary to take decade-by-decade averages in order to get an accurate picture of this trend in precipitation. Between 1950 and 1980 data from reporting stations throughout the region showed a 54 to 66 percentage of years with rainfall below the mean average. There was a profound decline in average rainfall, from a decrease of 45.3 mms between the 1920s and 1970s at La Serena and Vicuña in the Elqui valley in the north to a decrease of 28.6 mm at Combarbalá in the south (Gwynne 1993, 282–83). A report filed by a special drought commission in 1996 stated that 40 percent of years over the last four decades have been dry enough to significantly "affect human activity" (Intendencia Región IV 1996, 1).

I arrived in the Norte Chico in February 1996 at the beginning of the last year of a four-year drought. The pattern had been typical. In 1992 reporting stations from all three provinces showed that they had averaged twice as much rain as normal for the year. For the years 1993 to 1995 these same stations reported a reduction of 56.5 percent, 44.5 percent, and 85 percent for the Elqui province, 52 percent, 64 percent, and 73 percent for the Limarí province, and 11 percent, 58 percent, and 47 percent for the province of Choapa (Intendencia Región IV 1996, 5). When I returned in October 1997 the drought had been broken by fierce winter rains. Exceptionally intense periods of rainfall in June and August caused by the El Niño phenomenon had brought the

Elqui stations up to four times the average amount of precipitation by August 31. The Limarí and Choapa stations showed between a 200 to 300 percent increase by the same date (Ministerio de Obras Públicas 1997, 2). When I returned for my final extended stay in September 1998, drought was again at crisis proportions.

Geologists call the soils found in agricultural and grazing areas "relic soils" from a "humid phase" that occurred around 30,000 BP and a climatic optimum during the late glacial period around 19,000 BP. In subsequent eras the climate became increasingly arid and hotter with sparser vegetation cover and the land left more susceptible to erosion caused during periods when there was heavy rain. The present-day semiarid conditions developed some 3,000 years ago rendering a fitful environment (Veit 1993, 139–44) that has engendered the comunidades' unique human ecology. After bringing about massive deforestation, mining and wheat drained scarce supplies of water and accelerated soil depletion, and today more than 80 percent of the land in Region IV is undergoing processes of erosion (Ministerio de Agricultura-Chile 1995, 31).

WATER ISSUES

If market integration of the comunidades agrícolas is the ultimate goal of those promoting sustainable and environmentally responsible development, then the difficulties of small commercial growers are plainly relevant. Another example from the Elqui valley is illustrative. There, poor irrigation practices, the lack of capital necessary to improve irrigation, and the loss of land and water rights are the primary problems, where there are fewer comunidades and a greater number of small growers fully integrated into the market economy. The main source of this integration is the production of a special variety of muscatel grape used in the making of pisco. In the Elqui, pisco, Chile's unique "jam brandy" is king. The road between La Serena on the coast and Vicuña in the interior that winds through the valley alongside the river is lined with vineyards. Poverty is not as great in the Elqui as in the drier areas of the Norte Chico, but it is a mistake to characterize the valley as "prosperous" simply because of the presence of these vineyards.

Government agencies promote the use of "drip" or "sprinkler" irrigation over the use of "ditch irrigation," an antiquated system of river canals. The efficiency of the canal method is low because plant life growing in the path of the canals saps the flowing water and because the flow contributes to and is drained by the already eroded

"Abandoned houses and corral during year of drought." Photo courtesy of the author.

soil. Not only is water lost, but this diversity of plant life, with a variety of local uses, is lost in the erosion process. There is even greater water loss in this way under more difficult conditions in the interior of the valley among the population centered around the town of Pisco Elqui. Here the terrain is sloping and much water is wasted in supplying the vineyards. At present, about half of the growers in the Elqui make use of the efficient drip and sprinkler systems. Most of these are in the larger vineyards, which can afford the cost of the maintenance and installation of the pumps and necessary structures.

Most of the pisco factories are supported by cooperativas, associations of growers both large and small who contract to produce the special varieties of grapes. The price for pisco grapes fluctuates depending upon the regional yearly yield. In the absence of extreme shortages, prices are generally the same from plant to plant. When yields are low and the price is high some growers may clandestinely bypass their obligation to their cooperativa and sell to whichever factory will pay the higher price. Drought and the erosion of soil bring about such "erosion" of cooperative values of self-regulation and solidarity (values necessary for the common good in this hostile environment). The environment presents what we might call a "stratified paradox" for pisco producers. Drought years mean higher prices, but only for those who can afford to efficiently use water. Years with adequate rainfall bring lower prices with access to profit spread more equally. Differential access to resources and profit interact with processes of drought and erosion within the total biocultural milieu.

The Elqui River is practically the sole source of water for growers in the valley. Every grower is allowed access to the river and is allotted a certain amount of water, called *acciones* (in English "share capital"). In exceptionally dry years, such as the five years of drought between 1992 and 1996, there is a tendency for small growers, having weighed their chances of having a successful harvest, to sell their water rights to large growers and companies. This short-term infusion of cash, though far from preferable to a good harvest and not enough to support families without other income, may be the best option during a drought. It may be the only option for growers surviving on the margin, where the prospect of a low water supply is combined with the lack of capital to invest in efficient irrigation methods. A water code adopted a few years ago facilitates this selling of irrigation. It has been noted that through lack of knowledge and the spread of disinformation, many small producers have sold their water at prices well below what it would bring on the market. Many communities possessing water rights have not taken advantage of their possession of traditional waters. By not registering them through common law means, they are susceptible to losing their water without receiving any recompense at all (Bahamondes et al. 1994, 12). This exchange of water rights for money by rural people represents a loss of control: control over their means of making a living as well as over their social status and identity as producers.

Another development reveals a permanent loss of such control. Some foreign companies have loaned small growers money for production purposes contingent upon their harvests bringing a certain price at market time. After some consecutive years of a negative return on the loans, land is seized as payment or is purchased by the company at a reduced price. It is a common strategy for men to sell their land and use the money to purchase a taxicab to drive in the regional cities of Vicuña or La Serena as an alternative to wage labor or the piecework income of picking someone else's grapes. These developments in the selling of land and water are classic processes in the separation of rural people from their land and livelihood. Limited access to capital for irrigation investment further concentrates land, wealth, and control over production into the hands of an economic elite. While poor canal irrigation threatens sustainability and the selling of a year's water rights suspends livelihood, the final expulsion of small growers from their land is the end of any chance for either sustainability or livelihood.

These problems demonstrate what the comuneros (through their decisive rejection of privatization) seem to have known all along: There is not an adequate safety net in the market economy for the marginal producers. How, in the name of "biodiversity and sustainability" (the issues that brought me in 1996 to the Norte Chico in the first place) can comuneros be asked to risk the security of land for the considerable uncertainty of a private enterprise that carries with it the ecological and economic hazards of fruit production in the desert? Of course, agriculture itself—especially large-scale—always represents a fundamental reduction in biodiversity. On the other hand, because land and livelihood are one in the same in subsistence production, such practices seem less likely to engender practices that threaten its existence. Drought and poverty are inextricably linked and give the appearance of chronic conditions as extreme fluctuation of rain has been the normal state of affairs in the Norte Chico since drought was first recorded in the sixteenth century. The government that took office in 1990 continued but modified the agroexport model, saying that it will provide technical support to small farmers, and there is a supposed revitalized interest in the livelihoods of campesinos. The government has vowed to reduce rural poverty, introduce price supports for domestic crops, and in general strengthen the state apparatus to address inequities in isolated and "marginal" environments in socially and ecologically sustainable ways (Kay 1993, 27–31).

POVERTY

Chile's economy for most of the late 1980s through mid-1990s was praised as a success attributed to both neoliberalism and democratic reforms. Until the downturn precipitated by the "Asian Crisis" as the twentieth century drew to a close, the economy was averaging a 6 percent growth rate every year for the previous ten years. During these times of growth, however, the state's attempts in the post-Pinochet era to increase social spending and combat poverty in rural areas were not enough to redress the income disparity between economic classes. In an upcoming book on neoliberalism in Chile during the period of "transition to democracy" politics and neoliberal economics (Alexander, forthcoming), my colleagues and I explore the impact of these policies on the poor and disenfranchised in areas including the public health system, homelessness, affordable housing, urban markets, workers' benefits, privatization of water rights, gender, national parks, and salmon fishing.

Today the country is dealing with the results of prior inattention to small farm development and rural poverty. In the 1980s while the "Chilean Miracle" brought prosperity to the upper and middle classes, shantytowns began to spring up in the countryside, populated by many of the peasants who had sold the parcelas that they had received in the postreform privatization (Collier and Sater 1996, 366–67). By the end of the first Concertación (moderate coalition) government, the labor force in the Chilean countryside amounted to about 700,000, of which 600,000 are seasonal wage laborers, with the majority of these people working in the export agribusiness sector (in the Norte Chico, of course, many labor in the copper mines). Before the 1973 coup, there was one seasonal worker for every four permanent workers. By the mid-1990s there were fifty *temporeros* for each person who is permanently employed in the countryside. Less than 10 percent, or approximately 60,000, of these temporary laborers are organized today, while before the Pinochet regime the number of organized rural workers was more than 200,000 (Petras and Leiva 1994, 154).

About three-quarters of Region IV are deemed areas of "extreme poverty or indigence" and all of the comunidades agrícolas are located within this sector (Castro and Romo 1996, 18). Coquimbo is among the regions in the nation with the highest poverty rates, having (1) more than 30 percent of the population living in households in which the amount of income is insufficient to satisfy basic needs and (2) up to 10 percent of the population living in conditions in which basic nutritional needs are not being met (INE 1996, 38). Coquimbo has the second-highest infant mortality rate in Chile at 16.8 deaths per 1,000 births, just below Region IX with 17.2, and well above the national average of 14.5 (INE 1996, 17). In 1992 the per capita gross income for the region was eleventh out of Chile's thirteen regions, averaging $2,240 U.S. dollars per person, less than 60 percent of the national average of $3,786 per person (INE 1996, 17, 33, 38).

This was in spite of the fact that between 1985 and 1992 Region IV's economy had grown at a rate of 6.5 percent per year (INE 1996, 29). This mirrors the economic growth rate for the nation as a whole during that period. It also demonstrates at a regional level the same tendency for growth statistics to mask disparities in wealth and inattention to poverty in the poorest segments of society as a whole. In Region IV 38.4 percent of the workforce are classified as *obreros*, primarily unskilled agricultural workers whose jobs are low-paying and temporary in nature. The percentage of the population who work in agriculture in the region is second in the nation at more than one-third (INE 1996, 49). For the decade leading up to the onset of the "Asian Crisis" in 1998, Chile's economy was held up as the shining star in Latin America, a success usually attributed to democratic reforms, privatization of industry, and unrestricted foreign investment. The national economy had averaged a 6 percent growth rate every year for ten years. Before this ten-year boom period had ended, the government was officially admitting that a quarter of the population was living in "poverty" and a quarter of these people (over a million people out of the national population of fifteen million) struggling in conditions of "extreme poverty."

Unemployment in Chile doubled following the "Asian crisis," and in 1999 the country elected its first socialist president since Salvador Allende. From 2000–2006, the coalition government was led by Ricardo Lagos, a socialist of the so-called "Third Way" variety fiercely pursuing "free trade" while advocating "socially responsible economic growth." Sometimes called "neoliberalism with a human face," profit motives are still considered the best means of organizing the economy under this philosophy, however, there is an increased role for state regulation in remedying "market failures" (monopolies, manipulation, impeded access to markets, etc.) and providing basic social services, such as health care and education. Even in those areas, it is held that there should still be some imitation of the market through competition and the operation of profit-minded enterprises. Opponents of "the Third Way" say that it is no more than a centrist political ideology simply substituting for the familiar right-wing market principles of deregulation, decentralization, and bare-bones taxation; that in replacing "real" socialism for capitalism with a modicum of progressive policies it continues to privilege the corporate and multinational financial interests over those of the working class and poor and mainly serves to help its adherents reclaim political power. Still, Lagos can be credited with some impressive reforms. A progressive domestic subsidy program, Chile Solidario, attempts to provide a sufficient safety net for the more than 20 percent of the population living in poverty. While the poverty rate is lower than in the past, it has leveled off and is now characterized by many as a kind of "entrenched poverty" that is dangerously permanent in nature. In Chile the top 10 percent consume more than 40 percent of the national income while the bottom 20 percent scrape by on less than 4 percent (Saveedra 1999; Reyes 2002; InternationalReports.net 2002). Lagos also worked toward health care reform with a program to provide medical services for two-thirds of the population unable to pay for a private system. With regard to the plight of vulnerable temporary workers in the fields, Lagos vowed in the 1999 election to revive labor reforms, particularly in the rural sector. After Pinochet lifted a ban on unions in the 1980s, the greatest indictment of unions continued to be the deplorable conditions of temporary agricultural workers, which make up the majority of the country's rural labor force (Saveedra 1999). Conditions for temporary workers greatly worsened as Chile's job market struggled to recover from the 1997–98 recession. Sixteen-hour days and lack of basic facilities were not uncommon, and the majority of the more than 400,000 rural workers were women with families. Initially, Lagos limited his promises to help temporary workers to modest goals such as education in the wearing of protective clothing during spraying and temporary child care during harvest seasons (*Economist* 2001). However, in January 2002, Chile finally updated its labor laws to provide seasonal workers in fruit harvesting with employment protection under sweeping labor law reform that was hailed by workers' advocates and scorned by agribusiness. At long last, temporary workers were given official employment status and subcontractors are now required to register the workers they recruit and provide them with contracts. The new provisions make them eligible for social security and extend their right to collective bargaining, from which they had long been excluded even after Pinochet restored the right to permanent workers. The official workweek was reduced to 45 hours beginning in 2005, and there are restrictions on overtime and new protections against antiunion persecution (Jay 2002). Many in the private sector interests oppose such labor reform and see it, along with other welfare programs, as obstacles to growth even as they welcome the accelerated free trade agenda (InternationalReports.net 2002).

Since I left Chile in mid-1999, a backlash against neoliberalism has spread across the continent in the form of leftist or left-leaning elected governments (including Brazil, Venezuela, Bolivia, Argentina, and Uruguay), which are listening to antiglobalization popular movements and taking measures to reverse the negative influence of free trade and unrestricted privatization. Their reversals of previous policies include programs supporting agrarian reform, nationalization of resources and industries, and rejection of "Washington Consensus"-style economic development international lending institutions. March 2006 saw the historic inauguration of Lagos's successor Michelle Batchelet as president of Chile. This was a significant event for a country long-considered to be among Latin America's most socially conservative. As a result, there is optimism among progressives as Batchelet is affiliated with the left-wing of the Socialist Party; her father died after being arrested following the 1973 coup, and she herself was detained and spent years in exile during the Pinochet era. Echoing Lagos she promises to improve efforts to address inequality, wants to guarantee greater access to education, create progressive child care initiatives, reduce the unemployment rate, and provide subsidies for firms who hire the poor. Also like Lagos, she says that she will govern as a moderate socialist and will maintain economic discipline and respect for markets that neoliberals believe have sustained rapid growth. Skeptics feel that she is just repeating the promise that somehow both "continuity and change" is still a possibility.

CONCLUSION

So far I have provided a general backdrop of historical, environmental, legal, social, and economic information in which I will next place specific details from my research in subsequent chapters. Recognition of this wider context is important because if policy makers conceive of local culture as autonomous and isolated and do not consider aspects of national economy that impact local communities, they are apt to make decisions that are simply imposed from above. It is especially easy to overlook how the relationships between people and their environment have been articulated across time and space with regional, national, and international economic systems when the target areas of study are in objectively "marginal environments," such as arid regions where natural resources are insufficient and degraded and where subsistence is precarious. Development policies typically neglect "nonproductive" sectors of society. But underneath this veneer often lies a long and complex history of a functional interrelation between rural peoples and national and international industries and markets. Perhaps the image of marginality is overdrawn because these people, living in fragile environments, make use of an array of subsistence strategies that may lack coherence to outside eyes. The level of poverty, especially in terms of per capita income as compared with other sectors is distorted. A broader historical, social, and economic context prevents us from confusing "marginal environments" with "marginal people."

Although the communities are usually thought of as uniformly poor and desolate, across the eight "types" of comunidades there is a range of ecological niches, each engendering particular subsistence practices linked to environmental conditions at hand. In the following chapters, I will examine the diversity of specific resources and productive activities available to the "costero" community of Loma Seca (chapter 5) and to a specific household living in the community (chapter 6). I was in a good position to observe the full range of this diversity and flexibility because my fieldwork spanned periods from times of an overabundance of rain to the driest of droughts.

5

Forms of Mutual Assistance in Loma Seca

INTRODUCTION

LOMA SECA IS LOCATED ABOUT SIXTY KILOMETERS SOUTHEAST OF THE comuna capital of Ovalle and lies about fifteen kilometers east of the Pacific coast. The community established itself legally as a comunidad agrícola in 1978 during the period when the majority of comunidades normalized boundaries and rights in the process of *saneamiento de títulos de propiedad* (or "cleaning up the titles"). According to land registry information at Ministerio de Bienes Nacionales, the total area of Loma Seca was set at 6,587 hectares. These boundaries had been informally in place since the mid-nineteenth century after the community, like others in the region, evolved into a *comunidad sucesorial indivisa* in which land is indivisible and use rights are passed down within families. It is believed that the land was originally a seventeenth-century royal land grant (mercedes reales) to a captain in the Spanish army named Don Gabriel de Santander, who bequeathed the land to seven sons whose descendants continued to maintain it as common property without legalization because of the impracticality of dividing the poor-quality land into private shares (Acevedo et al. 1968, 85).

There are forty or so permanent households in the community and less than two hundred residents. The number of residents at any given time varies depending upon the year's productive activities, the need for labor at home, and the opportunities available for outside employment. The most important of the productive activities are the rain-fed cultivation of wheat and the raising of goats and sheep. In good years, in which there is more than 80 mm of rain spread throughout the growing season, the community harvests up to 1,200 hectares of wheat. When rain is insufficient, livestock accounts for almost all production. Corn, onions, beans, peppers, and potatoes are grown in small quantities on the tiny amount of available permanently irrigated land. As with most villages, a good deal of family income is earned

101

away from home through temporary wage labor and from pensions typically earned from years of work in the mines.

In my preliminary fieldwork, in Region IV from January through May 1996 while I was working for the biodiversity project, I interviewed many environmental and economic development officials and experts in order to grasp the scope of assistance offered to the communities and the types of projects being promoted. Often when I expressed my specific interest in the comunidades agrícolas, I was told that I should meet a man in Illapel recognized as perhaps the singular authority on the subject living in this region. I finally caught up with Lazaro S. toward the end of my first trip to Chile. Fleeing Chile shortly after the military coup in 1973, he and his family lived in exile—first in France, where he earned a master's degree in agronomy, and then in Mozambique—for the seventeen years of dictatorship. Since returning he has worked with the local government in Illapel on efforts to expand irrigation for small growers. He recommended Loma Seca as a community to study when I returned to Chile in 1997. A "typical" community in terms of production, it is also where his family is from and he offered the use of a rustic house that he still maintains there and occasionally visits. Living adjacent to this house at the time were Lazaro's niece Amelia, her husband Pablo, and their two sons Tomás and Felipe, then thirteen and six. They became the closest friends of my wife and myself and were my invaluable guides to life in the community.

To a great extent, my fieldwork movements mirrored the travels of this particular family and their activities in response to the availability of resources and changing climatic conditions. The first half of my first field season in Loma Seca (November 1997 through January 1998) was spent at Lazaro's adjacent house while the family was engaged in goat and sheepherding and making and selling cheese and lamb. Julie and I lived with Amelia and Pablo in an isolated interior sector of the community, surrounded by the rough, steep hills of the campo común. Every morning after the animals were milked in the corral, they were put out to graze on this common land. Then the day's cheese was made, followed by various other household duties and routines until the animals were brought back at dusk. Descending the steep hills as light was fading, the return of the animals to their corrals brought every day to a colorful and noisy conclusion.

In the second half of my first field season (January through March 1998), we moved to Loma Seca "proper" into the house of other members of this family, Pablo's mother Elena and his brother Eduardo. Another brother Gustavo worked away from home during the week but returned home almost every weekend. They were anxiously awaiting the arrival of the rented combine harvester so that they could bring in the wheat from their lluvias and from their share of a section of common land that was being worked as a group project. Living there allowed me to observe both harvests from start to finish and it provided easier access to other daily activities and special events in Loma Seca. I also had fortunate access to community meetings and records, as Elena is secretary of the comunidad.

I returned to Chile for the final time in September 1998 for a nine-month stay as a Fulbright Fellow. This time I came alone as Julie and I had gone our separate ways during the interim. Since the drought had returned and many community members had dispersed in search of pasture and jobs, I made a permanent base for myself in Ovalle. From there I made the best of "town and country," continuing to get information from development agents on their most recent projects, making frequent visits to Loma Seca, and visiting Amelia and Pablo at various areas in the comuna where they moved from site to site renting pasture to maintain the animals through the hard times. Because of the winter rains of 1997, most of the comuneros planted wheat in August and the February 1998 harvest was abundant. Pasture was adequate for forage, so milk, cheese, and lamb production was relatively high. No wheat was planted when the drought returned in the winter of 1998. The population of the community was reduced by 30 percent by emigration. Those herders who could afford it rented pasture away from the community. Since the government no longer subsidizes loans for dryland cultivation, families carried out a group project in which they pooled labor and resources to harvest wheat on a section of sloping, nonirrigated common land. The profits were then used to finance the harvesting of their individual plots. After paying off their production costs, of which renting of harvesting machinery is the highest, individual profit from all of this work appears from the outside to be very small. Development agents often ask why the comuneros continue to engage in this labor-intensive, low-profit activity. One reason, of course, is that because they lack capital, they have no other alternative. Another answer that I will put forward is that while the harvest is not greatly "profitable" from an outside perspective, it serves to reproduce the community system and the benefits of security and assistance that are not easily recognizable to a development model.

Along with the wheat harvest (*la cosecha*) and threshing (*la trilla*), there were other community efforts that I observed. Comuneros shared the cost and labor of chemically treating all of their sheep against parasitic arthropods in a three-day group project (*baño de ovejas*). Community members also participate in small groups called *comités* to raise money for specific projects to improve the quality

"Fields of wheat in the *lluvias* during year of rain." Photo courtesy of the author.

of life in Loma Seca. These groups raise money by staging events throughout the year. These events include horse races (*carreras*), dances, song festivals, soccer games, and fiestas, the most important of which is the Day of the Dead (called El Día de los Difuntos [Deceased] in Chile and El Día de los Muertos in most other parts of Latin America). Once these groups have raised a certain amount, the government provides matching funds. There is one comité to assist in the construction of houses (Comité Pro-Casa), another to install electricity (Comité Pro-Luz) and running water (Comité Agua Potable) in sectors lacking these services, another to help pay for the new school that replaced the one destroyed in the earthquake, and one to bring a television relay transmitter (Comité Pro-Antena) to improve television reception in the community. There are also charitable efforts for the benefit of specific individuals in need of expensive medical attention. These activities are greatly looked forward to by the people in the community as they break the tedium of day-to-day life with a festive atmosphere in which friends and families get together. During non-drought years, when wheat is harvested and when more people remain at home, these events are staged more frequently. The community makes the most of the availability of people to contribute toward these projects during these good years.

In this chapter I will describe these various forms of mutual assistance that I observed in Loma Seca. In my presentation of community livelihood data in chapter 6, I will analyze these forms of assistance in terms of how particular households make use of them. For clarity's sake, I divide them into "Social Forms of Mutual Assistance" and "Work-Focused Forms of Mutual Assistance." However, it will also be clear that this distinction between social life and livelihood in this community, as it is in many parts of the world where labor is based on reciprocity rather than the wage relation, is to some extent an analytical artifice.

Social Forms of Mutual Assistance: Comités

I had been meeting with Lazaro in Illapel the day before the October 14 earthquake struck. He suggested that I accompany him and his family to Loma Seca on November 1 to meet the family members with whom I would be living and to get my first look at the community. They, like so many people with ties to the community but living afar, were going home for the Day of the Dead celebration.

El Día de los Difuntos: When the Town Seems Most Alive

The holiday provided the perfect opportunity for my entrance into Loma Seca. Not only would I observe one of the more important events of the year, I would be able to meet a maximum number of people in a minimal amount of time. This would be a first step toward them becoming accustomed to the idea of having this stranger in their midst. Even more important was the fact that I was being introduced as a friend of Lazaro, a well-respected man from a well-respected family. He had done much advocacy on behalf of Loma Seca and for comunidades in general. Although his work requires him to live in the city of Illapel (about two hundred kilometers to the south and in the interior valley of the Choapa River), he returns often and maintains strong ties to the community. He is known as someone who has made a name for himself but who has not forgotten his roots, someone who works to improve the lives of people in the communities and who understands the importance of preserving the comunidad system. His endorsement of my work eased any potential suspicions or concerns about my motives.

As we wandered through the crowd, Lazaro told me that this day is one of the four days in the year—the other three being Christmas, New Year's, and Independence Day—when Loma Seca is crowded by the return of so many of its sons and daughters who return for the holiday. These people live and work in local cities and towns such as Ovalle and La Serena, and as far north as the mines near Calama and Copiapó and in the capital of Santiago four hundred kilometers to the south. "Tomorrow, the town will be empty," he said, kiddingly preparing me for what he thought would likely be boredom during the course of my stay.

All of the grave markers in the cemetery were decorated with flowers and wreaths that families had made for their deceased relatives. Before we left Illapel, Lazaro's wife had spent the better part of the previous day making elaborately arranged wreaths of fresh flowers. The day's activities, because of their reverential nature, were relatively subdued. Those gathered in the cemetery were intently focused on their work while others milled about the gates and the *local* (meeting hall) to reunite with the emigrants and to enjoy the food and drinks being sold. The Pro-Casa comité was well represented as its members—men, women, and some children—were busy serving the hungry throng.

The meals were the typical Chilean fare of *cazuela* (a hearty stew made with chicken or beef in the cities and usually with goat in the countryside), *porrotos* (green beans), salad, and fruit. We ate these huge lunches under a large canopy made from sewn-together fishmeal sacks. This was one of my first indications of the prevailing method of making the most of whatever materials are available and an admirable lack of waste of discarded objects and fabric. The other specialty food that is usually available at events such as this is the meat-filled pastry *empanada de pino*. Distinctly Chilean and delicious, because their preparation is a labor-intensive activity, they are not (to the chagrin of many tourists misguided by the guidebooks) readily available at most restaurants. It is relatively easy, however, for the committee volunteers working together to produce a large supply of them, and their preparation and availability contributes to the festive atmosphere of such events.

Dancing began in the afternoon and the party was certain to increase in vigor as night fell. Lazaro had to return to Illapel, and I had to get back to Vicuña to begin preparations for our relocation. (The first order of business would be to tell Julie that we would begin our stay living deep in the interior with neither electricity nor running water, next door to a delightful family and a hundred goats. I myself could not have been happier with the ease with which this arrangement was made.) In later days spent in the community I reflected upon how my first impressions of Loma Seca were colored by El Día de los Difuntos: the obvious irony that "The Day of the Dead" is one of the times when the town is most "alive"; my recollection of a description of a typical comunidad by someone from the city the year before as a place where the old miners "go home to die"; how the crowd and activities were an absolute contrast to days spent on Elena's front porch watching seamless expanses of wheat undulate under a cloudless crystalline blue sky; waiting for the man who owned the harvester to finally arrive, the town so quiet that the rare occurrence of a motorized *vehículo* approaching was heard from over the hills long before it was seen, giving practically the entire town enough time to utter a collective "Who's that?" These contrasts and ironies, however, were mostly seasonal in nature. If my first impressions were colored by my arrival following a winter of plentiful rain, that color was most certainly green.

Seasonal and Permanent Changes

On returning to the Norte Chico the sight of the desert blooming with cactus flowers was far different from the barren land that I had described to Julie after my first trip to Chile the year before. In Loma Seca on the brisk spring morning of November 1, most of the steep rolling hills in which the main part of the community is nestled were verdant with a vibrant blanket of green wheat fields. Practically all of the available lluvia land had been planted with wheat. When we moved into Pablo's mother's house here in January in anticipation of the harvest, the color had turned to brown. After the harvest, the land would be stripped back to the dry, bare fabric of its lifeless state during my previous visit and would remain that way throughout the rest of my time in Chile as the country endured yet another drought.

The cemetery is the community's most prominent feature. The brightly painted stone markers burst into view when one makes the big curve on the high dusty road that leads into town. On closer inspection many of the tombstones have faded in the cramped, walled burying ground, but a few of the sky-blue ones still stand out brilliantly. The road winds its way to the bottom of the steep grade where it splits to form Loma Seca's main street. About twenty houses are located in this vicinity. The remaining are scattered in isolated pockets of the community's 6,500 hectares. Fronting this road, across from the locked entrance to the cemetery, sits a little store (*el almacén*) with a small selection of canned goods, drinks, and other kinds of food. Across from the store is the local, the long concrete three-room building that serves as a town hall for meetings and dances. Next to the local is a flat pebbly general purpose open area that during my stay functioned in turn as a makeshift soccer field, a temporary storage place for sacks of wheat, and an open-air plaza where food was sold during celebrations. Just down the road from this are Loma Seca's schoolhouses and the tiny church made of concrete blocks and corrugated tin.

During my first extended visit, the little schoolyard next to the church was crowded with evidence of the recent earthquake. All that remained of one of the school's original structures was a foundation and a scattering of adobe blocks. Adjacent to this was a badly damaged small wooden building with broken windows and a caved-in ceiling. Across from the foundation stood three temporary unpainted wooden one-room buildings with paneless windows cut into the wood. These were some of the temporary *casas de emergencía* that were quickly built for people whose houses were damaged beyond repair. All of the houses in Loma Seca were damaged to some degree, but the oldest ones made of adobe fared the worst. Twenty houses were rendered uninhabitable by the earthquake. There was not enough state relief money to go around, and by the end of my first visit only fourteen of these emergency shelters had been erected. The occupants of the other six houses were left to live with relatives in order to make do. The government made emergency loans available for people to make repairs to their damaged houses, but because the interest rate was not much more favorable than normal bank loans few, if any, residents here could take on the extra financial burden.

A new school, however, was built in very short order. When I returned the following year it was the pride of the community, the three peach-colored brick buildings with blue trim smartly shining on the little dusty road. I got my first look at it when I visited to attend a horse race. The head of the school committee drove me over, telling me that the structure itself was paid for by emergency government funds and that the race was being held to raise money for supplies to furnish the school. Everyone was proud of the fact that the school was built in only five months. The *jefes* of the construction team were experts from Ovalle but most of the labor was provided by men from Loma Seca. A few were paid a small wage for manual labor, well-digging, and masonry work while others contributed their expertise in installing plumbing and electricity.

Another quality of life improvement that had arrived in the community during my absence was the installation of a telephone in the general store. Previously, the closest telephone was located twelve kilometers away at a restaurant on the Pan-American Highway where the owner charged what most agreed were extortionist rates to use his cell phone. Now residents only have to go to the little store to communicate with the outside world. The dueña stands diligently by with watch in hand, but the cost is only 100 pesos (around 25 cents U.S.) for a three-minute local call, the same price as any public pay phone. Transportation and communication are also limited because of the poor conditions of the roads in the rough interior, and we soon came to appreciate the quality of patience necessary in making plans that involved life outside of the community. We were frequently impressed by the adaptability of most people in response to expected visits that never transpire and unexpected visitors who arrive unannounced. Since there are very few motorized vehicles in the community, horse or burro is the usual means of transportation, and when most people go to Ovalle they take the "Parral bus."

The Parral Bus and the Feria

The bus to Ovalle leaves the nearby community of Parral well before the break of dawn, picking up its Loma Seca passengers at about six in the morning. Its destination is the Feria, a bustling market on the east side of the city that is transformed three times a week (Monday, Wednesday, and Friday) by people brought in from the countryside by rural buses. The hectic pace of shopping and socializing is due to the fact that the Parral bus departs the Feria at three in the afternoon and does not return until the next market day. I was warned that "the bus sleeps in Parral." If we went to Ovalle on a Friday morning we either had to be ready to leave at 3:00 PM or wait until the following Monday.

A converted school bus, the machine is several decades old. It is often very crowded and seats are at a premium. Whenever I boarded in the morning almost all of the passengers from other villages down the line were already sleeping and continued to do so even though at times the engine ground loudly as if it were running without oil. It wheezed and heaved itself at a slow pace down the narrow dirt road that winds the eleven kilometers to the Pan-American. I was thankful for the early-morning darkness, which spared me from seeing exactly how close we came to the edge of a sheer precipice while taking a particularly impressive curve. Once on the highway, this plodding beast would have seemed like an abomination among the other vehicles that more acceptably fit a reasonable standard of highway traffic had it not been only one of a succession of such "buses rurales" making the Monday-Wednesday-Friday run to Ovalle.

The Feria is a remarkable sprawling marketplace. In the open main area shaded by a high roof, scores of vendors sell all types of fruits and vegetables at very low prices. Around the perimeter of this main section and in a connected covered area, there are tightly packed stalls where merchants sell cooked meals, candy, clothes, and every imaginable general household item. Because of the time limitations, the majority of the people who take these buses limit their experience of Ovalle to the Feria and its all-inclusive environment. The shouts of vendors hawking their wares and offering the occasional free sample clash with the sounds of musicians playing for tips in the eating area. To a certain degree, many aspects of rural culture outside of Ovalle are reproduced three days a week within these chain-link-fenced confines on the outskirts of the city. A view of the parking lot filled with old buses shows the extent to which Ovalle serves as hub for people throughout the Limarí comuna who come here out of necessity and choose to pass a pleasant day with others from the countryside.

Finding a seat for the return trip is even more difficult than in the morning because of the bulging sacks of goods from the Feria that the riders bring back with them. Loaded down with this extra cargo, including an assortment of packages, bales of hay, sacks of seed, and building materials hoisted to the top and tied securely to the roof, the bus moves even more slowly than it does in the morning, and at frequent long stops the young man working with the driver climbs to the roof to untie and retrieve the goods.

What is a forty-five-minute drive to Ovalle down the Pan-American Highway by automobile takes up to three times that amount of time from Loma Seca on the rural bus. In the campo común the Parral bus is not an option. There one must make a long hike over the hills in order to catch a national bus on the highway. My friends Humberto and Marta in Vicuña, who I had met during my previous visit, offered to move us to Loma Seca in their new truck shortly after I returned from the Day of the Dead celebration. Although I stressed to him that we were going to be living in a rugged area away from the "town" and that the road was in poor condition, Humberto insisted that his truck could handle it. When I came with Lazaro the week before, we arrived at night, but in the light of day, the road felt bumpier and the distance into the hills seemed much longer than I had remembered. I was embarrassed and felt bad for Humberto. We bottomed out a few times and even lost a taillight. Although he took it in stride, he did pointedly remark that this was more of a "burro trail" than an actual road. Mostly he and Marta were concerned that Julie and I did not know what we were getting ourselves into. Their looks chastised me as if to say that as a man I should know better than to bring my wife into such a miserable living situation.

A couple of days after this, after Pablo and Amelia made it clear that our living here would be far easier than we could have imagined, I wrote about the paradox of our physical isolation in my journal: "On the one side of us we feel isolated from the world. The dreadful 'burro trail' is a pitiful umbilical cord. On the other side of the hills, the Pan-American, paved all the way to Alaska, they say. Situation of tension? Peasant dualism? Metaphors abound . . ."

I was grasping to find a metaphor to express a theoretical position in the back of my mind. The people in Loma Seca are not far from Ovalle in physical proximity but are isolated in many respects. The connection to the city is necessary, but there are structural obstacles. Lack of vehicles, poor roads, and restricted means of communication make the connection a tenuous one. Their market integration is partial and they seem to occupy the "intermediate place" in classic definitions of peasantry (chapter 2).

"Chamagote" and Radio Norte Verde

Because of these limited means of transportation and communication, one of the important ways that information is transmitted to Loma Seca, and other places like it, is via a colorful radio personality known by the nickname of "Chamagote" (*chilenismo* slang for "the Mexican") whose daily afternoon radio program has long been a favorite in the rural communities surrounding Ovalle. The station, "Radio Norte Verde," plays a mixture of Latin American "country music" and traditional Chilean *cuecas* (waltzes). The sound of this station is a ubiquitous background presence throughout the daily activities of most every household. Chamagote's specialty is Mexican *ranchera* music, the songs of peasant life and the Mexican Revolution, themes that resonate with many of the rural people of Chile. A former schoolteacher, his gregarious personal demeanor is augmented over the airwaves by liberal use of sound effects and a scratchy tape loop of canned laughter that clumsily punctuates every punch line of the corny jokes he tells in a comic campesino accent.

Chamagote's program is popular not only for the entertainment it provides but also because it serves to inform the people of the scattered, isolated interior communities about comunidad and comité meetings, festivals, and other upcoming events. A special segment is devoted just to horse races (carreras) with the recording of the crescendo of pounding hooves of two racing horses accompanying his announcement of soon-to-be-held events. The great number of these events reflects the enthusiasm for horse racing and the passion for all things having to do with horses among this segment of Chile's rural population. Government and development agencies in Ovalle also use his program as an effective means of reaching the communities with announcements of times when they will be visiting to meet with comuneros to discuss current programs and other matters pertaining to rural welfare and development.

The radio is also an important means for sending personal messages. Once when we were living with the family tending the animals deep in the campo común, Pablo met us on horseback at a place where a bus had let us off after one of our weekly trips to Ovalle to buy food and supplies. After hearing a description on the radio of a lost child at the Feria fitting the description of one of our neighbor's children, he had come to meet an earlier bus to inform the surprised mother that she had absentmindedly left one of her kids at the market. Our lifeline to Ovalle was this hour-long hike over the hills to the highway where we could with relative ease normally flag down a passenger bus heading north. The walk offered magnificent views: a glimpse of the ocean through the distant valleys, the Pan-American snaking through the rocky terrain, and wide vistas of the dry, heavily eroded land cracked as if it were being pulled apart from underneath by some unseen force. Return trips were less pleasant when making the climb while carrying bags full of groceries and fighting the sometimes fierce winds at the tops of the hills. Until the various drivers became familiar with us, we sometimes had a little trouble convincing them that we really knew where we were going and that we really wanted to be dropped off at a place where there was no access road and that lived up to the designation "middle of nowhere." The other passengers were likewise at times incredulous at the sight of what appeared to be two lost tourists weighted down with groceries and forging their own path over the steep hills.

Just a few days after we had settled into the campo común, on the morning after one such particularly arduous trek, we were awakened at 7:00 AM by Pablo knocking on our door. In our absence a vehicle had been secured and arrangements had been made to take the entire family to the rodeo being held in Parral. I was delighted to be invited along and given the opportunity to observe such an important event so early in my stay. At the time I did not realize that this was another benefit of my fortuitous timing to be living in the community during a year of rain because, as with so many such events, there would be no rodeo next year.

Rodeo Chileno

Pablo's brother-in-law, who works for a car dealer in La Serena, had come with a pickup truck to take a dozen of us to Parral. After we arrived at his mother's house in Loma Seca and began rousing the others, Pablo slaughtered an especially meaty goat for our barbecue that afternoon. The twelve of us piled into the truck along with our food, a bale of hay for Gustavo's horse, and a case of bottled beer in a plastic rack. With the truck weighted so heavily, the driver, to my relief, was forced to take it easy on the curvy dirt road that wound, climbed, and dipped past twelve kilometers of mountainous scenery and vibrant green fields of wheat. The rodeo ring is the major structure in the small community of Parral. They were charging 1,000 pesos at the gate, which, along with the money earned from food and drinks, would benefit the Parral comités.

Rodeo competition is an important event in most parts of rural Chile, with the national championship held in the central valley city of Rancagua occupying the national spotlight every March. Rodeo is a time of festival that promotes certain key images in Chilean folklore and history as key elements of national identity. Two of the most prominent and romanticized of these images are that of the *huaso*, the Chilean cowboy, and the cueca, the "courting dance" between a man and a woman, which is the official national dance.

The *rodeo chileno* was initiated in the colonial era as a yearly event for rounding up, counting, and marking cattle that grazed the unfenced range. Founded on the antiquated idea that heifers must be "broken in," the present-day sport is a test of the ability of two riders on horseback to work together as a team, called a *collera*. Since the early rings were crescent-shaped, the circular padded stockade is still today called the *media luna*. The team maneuvers the cow around the edge of the ring, stopping at the end by pinning the hindquarters against the fence and then turning the animal back in the opposite direction.

After doing this three times, the heifer is freed from the ring. Three judges sitting in a box high atop the grandstand assign points on a scale of one to seven for skills of horsemanship. The highest scores go to those teams whose efforts are graceful and smooth, a performance of teamwork, ability, and elegance. For the animal, it's a one time show, as rodeo convention says that the ordeal is only effective when it comes as a "surprise" to the heifer. In areas where cattle are numerous, many farms have their own rings where the breaking in takes place not as a public event but as part of the everyday routine of stock raising.

Huasos

Pageantry is in full color, however, during the public performance of rodeos, especially in the dramatic outfits of the contestants: wide-brimmed hats with short square crowns, vividly colored ponchos, and polished boots with hefty iron spurs firmly set in the ornately carved

"Rodeo: Two-man *collera* team performing in the *media luna*." Photo courtesy of the author.

nineteenth-century-style wooden stirrups. Proudly astride their finest horses, the men who participate in the rodeo compete dressed in full huaso regalia. The simple poncho is long and plain in color and design, serving simply to protect the rider from the wind and the rain. Mantas are shorter and are divided into four sections of bright colors. More extravagant are the *chamantos,* double-sided mantas made of fine material and adorned with intricate thread patterns in a variety of motifs. Sometimes sashes, called *fajas,* of single color or the familiar Chilean red, white, and blue tricolor are draped across mantas and chamantos. Whatever the degree of lavishness, most of the teams wear matching outfits.

Less familiar to the world at large than the gaucho of Argentina, the image of the huaso as a working man with an ardent individualism and a dignified demeanor emerged as a representation of the new republic's independence from Spain. Located "at the end of the world" (as many Chileans still say), and possessing a limited supply of gold, the thin slice of latitude wedged between the Andes and the Pacific was of little interest to the Spanish empire except as a frontier buffer. In an ethnological essay, Lago contends that the word huaso quickly became shorthand for the self-sufficient *campesino montado* (peasant on horseback) in both folklore and popular usage (Lago 1953, 10). Horses were a valued symbol of status and independence in the countryside for tenant farmers, and as the image was popularized by writers and musicians, the landowners—from whose power and demands the horses were a means of freedom for peasants—began to appropriate the huaso style and fashion (Collier and Sater 1996, 11).

While the huaso is represented as thoroughly adapted to the frontier to survive on little, and as doing so with quiet decorum, analogous qualities are often attributed to the horses they ride. Lago describes the typical *caballo chileno* as an animal of minimal stature yet strong, muscular and elegant (1953, 11). In short, they are *grueso*—compact, solid, and of good quality—a prized attribute for work animals. The people in this part of Chile pride themselves on having horses that are both tough and beautiful. According to Lago, the race of horse adapted to the dry and stony terrain of the Norte Chico is marked by tough hooves, sure-footedness, and leaner in build than those in other areas (1953, 79).

From ten until one, the men lined the front of media luna in pairs, waiting their turn underneath the judges' booth and the Chilean flag. For a while Pablo took the microphone and announced the judges' scores. His brother Gustavo and a friend participated as a collera, and although they did not perform up to their own expectations, they were good-natured about it. Pablo later dug a pit by the truck and made a fire with sticks and branches. After lunch we went back to our seats to watch more of the competition. Around four in the afternoon, the first round was over and most of the people went into an area covered by a large tent where a four-piece band from Ovalle was playing traditional Chilean cuecas.

La Cueca

A female singer danced the cueca with little Felipe, the six-year-old, who was dressed in his huaso outfit. The "queen of the rodeo" in her traditional checkered print dress with a yoke of white lace around her neck, a small, flat, black hat on the back of her head, and her hair fixed into long black braids struck an impressive figure on the dance floor. She circulated among the crowd, dancing with many partners, including Felipe, whose mother Amelia was quite proud.

The cueca has been danced in Chile since the early nineteenth century. In music houses in the cities the traditional accompanying instruments were harp and guitar, while in the countryside the guitar was usually supported only by the rhythm of a washboard. Always, however, clapping hands and shouts of encouragement to the dancers from the audience accompany the music. As was humorously explained to me on many occasions, the name of the dance seems to be derived from the Spanish word *clueca* for a "broody hen," or one suitable for producing offspring. This is because the dancers imitate the movements of the persistent amorous rooster in pursuit of the halfheartedly defensive hen. These roles are apparent in the coy advance-and-retreat movement and the lively waving of handkerchiefs held aloft in each dancer's right hand.

The composition of the dance adheres to a rigid structure. Cuecas are short, played in three-quarter waltz time and consist of three movements or *vueltas*. In the first vuelta, the couple approaches one another. As a four-line quatrain is sung, the couple moves in a circle or in a figure eight of semicircular advances toward and away from one another. The second vuelta consists of six lines. The dancers continue the same movements but turn and approach one another from opposite sides. The final vuelta is an abbreviated two-line couplet. Between these three episodes are two brief pauses for the dancers to rest during which time it is customary to serve them drinks, and depending upon the atmosphere of the dance it is not unlikely that the refreshments will be shots of pisco. While the structure of the dance is set, the dance is energetic, and there is much free play in the steps and in the movement of the handkerchiefs. The man's knees are slightly bent and his body arches back. The most common steps are wide, sweeping moves called "the broom." The dance arrived in Chile from Peru in the 1820s where it was called the *zamacueca*. It is descended from the Spanish fandango. Chileans soon made it their own. Though ubiquitous at national holiday celebrations such as Chilean Independence Day on September 18, at less formal gatherings, such as the dances during the frequently held horse races, the music is almost exclusively divided between the wildly popular dance music from Colombia known as the *cumbia* and the more traditional Mexican ranchera music. Since rodeo is an expression of patrimony, the cueca is preferred over these more popular but more recent imports. Some describe it in almost sacramental terms, lauding both the rigid structure of the dance as a kind of timeless link to the past and the fact that young and old in all regions of the country participate in this expression of national unity.

Expressions of Nationalism and Peasant Identity

Given that the guidebooks promote the cueca as a cultural experience that is not to be missed, and because images of the dancing couple and the two-man collera rodeo teams predominate in the souvenir kiosks in Santiago and La Serena, until I had attended this rodeo I was unsure of the extent to which the huaso, the rodeo, and the cueca were still important expressions of campesino identity or simply embellishments of tourism. Yet at the Parral rodeo I was without a doubt the only gringo within many kilometers.

After enjoying the music and dancing, the people in the crowd returned to their seats. The finale began at 5:00. Before the two-man team competitions continued, four huasos competed with one another performing various skilled maneuvers on horseback. Afterward the Chilean national anthem was played on the crackly loudspeaker. Some in the crowd began to tire at this point, especially during a long break after a cow burst through one of the wooden doors and new planks had to be securely nailed in. The competition was still going on when we had to leave so that the people in our party from La Serena could get back to their home at a reasonable hour.

The rodeo serves many functions apart from that of a recreational and sporting activity. At one level, it is an expression of national pride and patriotism that is reflected not only in the preponderance of Chilean flags, the display of national colors, and the multiple playing of the national anthem, but also in the serious tone of the event itself. Many of my impressions from this day that made it into my field notes reflect this. The crowd was relatively quiet during the competition, and soft music serenely played on the loudspeaker during the long periods of quiet between the performances of each team. There was no real rowdiness among the spectators, and there seemed to be genuine good sportsmanship among the participants. The winners were awarded their prizes of trophy saddles and spurs in a dignified, almost solemn fashion.

The rodeo is also a public display of important images of peasant identity. The image of the huaso, the importance of horsemanship, and the dancing of the cueca all demonstrate campesino participation in national history, a valued image that is rural in character, despite the country's modernization in recent decades and the urban shift in population (almost 80 percent of Chileans today reside in cities, with nearly 40 percent of the total population in metropolitan Santiago [INE 1996, 12]). But while in other areas and contexts these images may appear to be a quaint affectation (one evening while watching television at Elena's house, I was delighted by my host family's laughter at the absurdity of an ersatz campesino character in a Chilean soap opera who always walked the modern streets of Santiago in a full huaso costume of manta, sombrero, boots, and spurs) here they largely remain important features of everyday life.

Gustavo, like the other participants, prepared for the rodeo well in advance of the event. Even when there is no upcoming rodeo, the men

"Rodeo: Expression of cowboy (*huaso*) identity." Photo courtesy of the author.

seemed to spend almost all of whatever free time they had in their work-filled days doing something related to the horses. They constantly groomed, shoed, trained, and generally tended to the horses or mended saddles and stirrups. Julie keenly noted that it reminded her of the fastidious attention that many men in the United States pay to their automobiles. Once while relaxing after dinner we were discussing with Pablo the differences and similarities between Spanish and English expressions. We learned, for example, that "burro" in Chile can have the same meaning as a "coyote" in the U.S.-Mexico region, someone who is transporting contraband. What spurred this discussion was my question as to the severity of six-year-old Felipe's insult of "burro negro" that he directed toward me earlier in the day when I had to cut short our soccer game. We all got a good laugh out of this and began to think of other comparable terms. When I offered the expression "to work like a horse" as a way of describing someone who thanklessly works very hard, Pablo did not agree. He corrected me by pointing out that a burro would better fit this image since they do menial, hard labor because they are too stupid to be bothered by the monotony. Horses, on the other hand, are very much appreciated for their elegance and their necessity in the countryside. As he went on to give me a fairly long dissertation on the many functions and practical value of horses in an area where the land is rough and vehicles are scarce and often useless, I smiled and thought back to a conversation I had with an agriculture specialist the year before who complained that the old-fashioned status associated with horses in comunidades was an impediment to progress. His complaint was that resources used to support horses, particularly the growing of varieties of wheat, which produce a lot of straw, could be used more effectively and profitably.

For the people in Parral, the rodeo serves the important function of raising money for their various comités. It is a special event that requires a great deal of organization and resources that are normally only available during "good years." In Loma Seca and most other communities, an effective and frequent way of raising money is to stage a carrera.

Carreras

I attended five of these horse races, three in Loma Seca and one each in the nearby communities of Maitencillo and Los Cienagos. On those days with a strong turnout, when the weather was good and when there was no major competing event in the area, there would be two to three hundred spectators in attendance. The race occurs in a flat field over a straight course that is about the length of an American football field.

Two side-by-side lanes are cordoned off from the crowd by lengths of string. Prior to the contest, the two contestants slowly pace the horses back and forth, allowing everyone in attendance to size them up and assess their chances. Then, those anxious to wager wave bills in the air and solicit takers by announcing which horse they are backing. After this, the crowd disperses along both sides of the course and awaits the fun. Despite the spirited anticipation the spectators must wait what may seem like an interminable delay before the race finally takes place. Since there is no gate to make sure that neither rider gets an unfair head start, a man holding a handkerchief stands at the starting line, and if the horses take off together cleanly, he drops the handkerchief. In the carrera at nearby Los Cienagos that I attended, it took a full hour and a half for the first race to finally come off. That race, which was held on a Sunday afternoon in early March after all of the wheat harvesting had been done and the rented harvester had gone back to La Serena, was an "end of the harvest" celebration for all of the neighboring communities. It drew the largest crowd and the Parral bus even made a special Sunday run to bring people to this carrera. Even though a number of cars and trucks brought in people from nearby towns, the "parking lot" still held far more horses than vehicles.

Regardless of the frequently long periods of false starts, the brief time during which the race actually takes place is pure excitement. I never warned any outsiders who accompanied me to these races about these possibly long lulls in action, and every one of them commented that the brief moment of the two riders streaking past at lightning speed and followed by the rising dust trail made it worth the wait. The crowd roars and the young winner waves his whip in victory circles above his head, and even those who may have been on the losing end of a bet are in thrall with this electric atmosphere. After the president of the host comunidad formally declares the champion, another hour or two may pass between races, which is put to good use eating, drinking, dancing, and catching up with the friends and family who had traveled to see the event.

Along with earning money for their specific project by selling food and drinks, the community takes the occasion to generate extra funds through wagering on the race outcomes. The host community sponsors a rider to race against a contestant from another town. People ante up cash to back their respective riders until a certain agreed-upon amount, usually 100,000 pesos (about $220 U.S.), is raised by both communities. The winning side receives what remains once the cost of putting on the races and dance are covered. This recoups expenses in food and drinks, assuring that a maximum amount of funds are earned for the comités. Such social forms of mutual assistance serve to effectively transfer surplus funds from pockets of individual accumulation into areas that improve the lives of all of the rural residents.

Fútbol

In mid-December of my first year there were two soccer games held in Loma Seca against a team from the town of El Teniente. The money from the food and drinks sold at the dance after the games were for the benefit of a man in Loma Seca who needed to travel to Santiago for cancer treatment. The local team won both of these and a rematch occurred in late February in which El Teniente would attempt to avenge these defeats. About twenty men participate as players, some of whom come from Ovalle and other places in order to play. Gustavo, Pablo's middle brother, who had been working for the construction company on a highway project, made a special trip home in the company van that they allow him to use for his personal transportation. Loma Seca was well represented as we packed the van and another vehicle with players and supporters and made the hour drive south.

El Teniente is the name of both the pueblo and the famous bridge on the Pan-American Highway that was destroyed in the earthquake. The remains of the dead trucker's cab were now gone, but the bridge, still reaching only two-thirds of the way across the dry riverbed 150 meters below remained closed. The local and the soccer field of El Teniente lie just to the ocean side of the bridge in a low area under a scattered patch of tiny houses built precariously on the rugged hills that line the highway. Our team won the first game and the second one ended in a tie. Although the host community was denied its revenge, the competition was friendly, the food and party afterward a success, and money was raised for a comité in El Teniente.

Chancho

Another way in which money is raised for the comités is the selling of pork, or *chancho*. Hogs are not kept in large numbers, so this is done only on special occasions. The spicy flavorful meat was for sale only twice while I was in the community, once in February for the benefit of the Pro-Luz committee and once the following November for the benefit of the Agua Potable committee. A large boar was brought to the local and slaughtered, and all of the next day was spent cooking the meat in a large copper pot over a big wood fire, a woman committee member tending the pot with its contents bobbing vigorously in the rolling, boiling water under great gray clouds of smoke and ladling out the blood that floated to the top of the cauldron into a small pan.

Inside the local a small group of women prepared the cooked meat with a combination of chilies and spices. There was a long list of people, many from neighboring communities, who had ordered meat, and we were lucky to get an order of *arrollado* ("rolled" pork fat)— the prized delicacy of the operation—before it sold out. These long strips of fat and meat chunks tied together with string and spicily flavored sold for 3,500 pesos, or roughly $8. A comité can raise several hundred dollars in this way.

WORK-FOCUSED FORMS OF MUTUAL ASSISTANCE

Comuneros also share the cost and labor for specific work projects important to the reproduction of peasant livelihood. Two that I observed during my time in Loma Seca were the baño de ovejas and the trilla.

Baño de Ovejas

Once a year all of the comuneros who have sheep get together to share the considerable cost and labor of treating the animals with a chemical wash to eradicate parasites. Each person pays 150 pesos (about 30 cents U.S.) for each sheep that is bathed. The extensive manpower makes the work of treating two thousand sheep pass by relatively quickly. One day in late December, we went to the Los Fuegos sector of the community, where there is a nearby source of water, early one morning when the atmosphere was lively and the work was well under way.

There were fifteen workers running the sheep through the pesticide bath. At one end was a large corral filled with comuneros working fifty or so untreated bleating sheep. About half of the men worked in this corral, herding, pushing, prodding, and generally bullying the sheep one at a time through the open door. When the push began, the action quickly swelled into great excitement. Both men and sheep were yelling, and the animals kicked up great clouds of dust that at times obscured the activity. What met the sheep at the other side of the door was a drop-off into a long narrow trench filled with the sheep dip mixture. The trench was just deep enough for the animals to keep their heads above the liquid. Pablo was one of the men who grabbed each sheep at the door and plunged it into the trough. Once in the water, the animals were met by a gauntlet of men standing side by side along the length of the fifteen-foot trench, moving them along with long forked sticks and pushing the animals by the neck under the water for a second or two. Every now and then a particularly strong and *rencoroso* (spiteful) animal would protest enough to make big splashes, soaking the men working nearby. A couple of the uncooperative creatures even made it over the trench wall before being wrestled back into the water. All of this made the affair an animated and laughter-filled work project

At the other end of the trough a ramp led the sheep to another holding pen where the wet animals were tightly packed. The family's elderly bachelor, Uncle Osvaldo, who earns a little money shearing sheep, stood near the entrance, keeping track of those animals that had been bathed and those that were still waiting. After one group was treated, a new group was brought in from a nearby pasture. About 650 of the approximately 2,000 sheep in Loma Seca were treated that day. A couple of weeks before about 1,100 were run through the trough. The remaining were scheduled for the following day. It cost Pablo the sizable sum of 30,000 pesos (or $60 U.S.) to treat his 200 sheep, but because the sheep dip is so expensive and because it takes so large an amount of mixture to run the animals through it, without the group effort it would have cost him as much to treat his animals separately as it costs to do all of that day's 650 sheep at one time.

"Group work project: Chemical treatment of sheep (*baño de ovejas*)." Photo courtesy of the author.

La Trilla

As described in the previous chapter, the trilla was traditionally accomplished using a team of horses to thresh the harvested wheat. For the most part, mechanization of this job replaced the use of horses in Loma Seca in the 1960s. At various places in the community, including one near the house that Lazaro keeps there, the remains of stone circles now overgrown with grass sit as relics of this practice. Harvesttime is still a festive time, and reciprocal forms of labor are widely used.

In mid-June of 1997, before I arrived, when it was apparent that there would be enough rain to grow wheat that year, a community meeting was held. One hundred hectares of lluvia not in use in the Nogales and La Mesa sectors of the community were designated and forty-four members of the community were inscribed as *socios*, or "partners." In a later meeting, it was announced that a man in La Serena who owned combine harvesters and rented them to communities in the area had been located. He would charge 18,500 pesos (about $40 U.S.) per hour for the use of the harvester, always referred to in the community as simply *la máquina*. This would include the cost of fuel and the labor of two of his workers, who were fed and housed by the socios.

The women among the socios provided this food, cooking large lunches and *onces*—the traditional Chilean midafternoon simple meal usually consisting of sandwiches and tea or wine. They provided food every day throughout the harvest for all of the workers, who usually rode back in from the fields in the La Mesa and Nogales sectors to take these meals at the local. The men worked from early morning until dusk. At any one time, there were usually twelve to fourteen men working with a few teenagers often helping. After threshing, the wheat that was not cleaned adequately for storage by the combine was cleaned by hand to separate the chaff, immature grains, sand, stones, and other foreign material from the grain. They worked in shifts with five men at a time working on a tall pile of freshly reaped wheat spread out in the center of the group. Dozens of seed sacks were sewn together to make a tarp on which the work took place. Two of the five men held wooden shovels that had been carved out of a single piece of wood while the other three held long "brooms" with bundled twigs tied together to form the whisk part. The men with the shovels turned up the grains and those with the brooms whisked away at the pile. They moved slowly in unison in a circle around the pile, separating the good kernel part of the grain from the rough chaff that was being swept to the side on the outside area of the tarp. When those working in the center finished, the others stepped in to scoop the wheat into old seed and flour sacks. After a sack was filled, it was sewn tightly shut and hoisted by three or four men onto the shoulder of another who scampered hurriedly to get it to the place where scores of other sacks like it were stacked high.

The work went on in this way for two weeks. We had moved from the campo común in anticipation of the wheat harvest in early January. It was more than two weeks before the máquina finally arrived. Day after day people tensely waited for news of the progress in the nearby community of Alcones where the machinery was being used, knowing that the longer the wait the higher the risk for disaster. Timing is the most critical decision in harvesting. If a harvest begins too late, the grain becomes too dry. This increases the amount of wasted grain that shatters and falls to the ground. Also, the longer that a ripe crop stands in the field, the greater the chances of loss from birds, rodents, and weather. With so many communities harvesting wheat that year, and with the scarcity of farm equipment in the area, it was a seller's market for the man who owned the harvesters. The high production also meant that the price for wheat was especially low. The best price that the socios could find was 75 pesos per kilo from an intermediary buyer, or *comprador*, who then sells it to a manufacturer. The comprador came from Santiago and would be making his way through this area with his truck by the end of February.

CONCLUSION

After paying for the use of the máquina, each socio's share of the collective harvest was approximately 6,300 kilos, or about fifty-odd 120-kilo sacks. About 20 percent of this was set aside to put in the family bodegas to save for seeds and family consumption in anticipation of two to three hard years ahead. Selling the rest to the comprador middleman at seventy-five pesos per kilo, each partner in the project could expect to earn about a thousand dollars. This would then be used to offset the cost of harvesting their individual *particular* family harvests. Paid usually with a share of the wheat, the modern-day trillador owning machinery rather than horses can expect to receive almost a 40 percent cut of an individual family's harvest. Pooling group resources of land and labor in combination with utilizing individual land and labor is necessary in light of the high cost of mechanized production and the low price of wheat. The reciprocal relations expressed in the social and work-focused forms of mutual assistance go far in accounting for the resiliency of the comunidad of Loma Seca.

In the following chapter I will present a detailed description of the

"Group work project: Threshing wheat (*la trilla*)." Photo courtesy of the author.

day-to-day life, division of labor and income acquisition, and resource maintenance strategies of the family with whom I lived. One general characteristic that will stand out in what follows is the great effort that these people make to maintain their productive resources during tough times when productivity was very low. The amount of cash that is available through the sale of their products is cyclical, with great variability both within and between years, but the goal is to keep resources at a constant level. The incarnation of wealth as money, in other words, is seasonal. An interesting way that this is expressed, I believe, is in the use of the word "plata."

"Plata," or silver, in Chile as in other parts of Latin America, is common slang for "money," whether in coin or bill form. In the Chilean countryside it is used almost exclusively, while the more formal "dinero" is hardly used at all. There seemed to be another level of meaning in the use of the word, a situational one related to the physical presence of money in one's pocket and the time during which one does or does not have it. People will say things such as "when I have plata I will buy this" or "we couldn't buy that because we didn't have any plata." There is little of the self-consciousness or embarrassment in these statements that one might normally expect to be associated with the words "I have no money." Also, something particularly dear is said to cost "plata dura," or "hard money." With two hundred sheep, one hundred goats, and access to a large expanse of land for agriculture and pasture, Pablo's family is far from poor by community standards, but there are times when they are in dire need of cash. Plata is one form of wealth, but as I learned, resources are to be conserved, maintained, and increased wisely so that money can be earned without losing the means and tools for meeting future and potential needs.

At the community level, a similar situational logic operates. The people who live in Loma Seca show a distinct ability to marshal human resources for specific projects at crucial times. Wheat growing in and of itself may not be very monetarily profitable at the individual house-hold level but it is an important part of an overall "package" of bene-fits that one has access to as a member of the community. If there is rain, they grow wheat and keep their animals within the community. If there is wheat and pasture, there are people. If there are people, there are successful group work projects and forms of mutual assistance related to both individual needs and the common goals. The com-munity makes the most of the good times, taking advantage of the availability of labor and the wealth redistribution aspects of the com-ités, because of the probability that bad times, at least in terms of rain, are ahead. The "value" that is gained from this availability of human resources is reinvested into the community in the form of houses, electricity, running water, a new school, medical assistance, and other provisions of welfare and security, which the larger society fails to provide for them.

Loma Seca has a reputation among some development workers and government agents as a comunidad that is forward-looking and ame-nable to change. They have a slightly higher standard of living and level of education. As one such person in Ovalle told me, because of the land and the microclimate, they can continue to produce wheat, though at a diminishing rate and at an environmental cost, because they "have families." What he meant was that the community was alive with people living and working there, as opposed to others where there is little incentive to stay. The spirit of community and the spirit of capitalism are not incommensurable here. They manifest them-selves in the various forms of mutual assistance, both social and work-focused, that I have described in this chapter.

The value of social relations is something that is quite clear to people in the "face-to-face" world of peasant communities. Once upon re-turning from the city, we told Amelia that we had seen our friends Humberto and Marta and that they had kindly offered to let us stay at their house in Ovalle whenever we made our trips in from the country. Amelia was happy for us and deemed this situation as "puro oro," or "pure gold"—something that is more valuable than silver.

6

Productive Diversity in One Household

INTRODUCTION

IN THIS CHAPTER, I WILL DESCRIBE THE REMARKABLE EFFORTS OF ONE family from Loma Seca with whom I lived and worked closely from November 1997 through May 1999 who maintained their livelihood through flexible and mobile production strategies during times of plenty and times of scarcity. Making use of multiple sources of income and subsistence, combining individual and communal means and relations of production, and enduring their "itinerant seasons of sacrifice" in extended periods away from home, their economic activities are articulated with both capitalist and peasant modes of production and thus challenge both dualistic views of peasant/capitalist culture and "bounded" conceptions of community.

One of the first things that struck me (in retrospect, an utterly obvious observation) was how hard these people work. The animals particularly require constant attention and the performance of a variety of tasks necessary to maintain them because of the relative lack of natural forage even during years of rain. In debunking the "myth of the idle peasant," Brush challenged rural "unemployment" figures that were distorted by the cultural biases of development workers who had different ideas about, in his words, "what peasants should and should not be doing with their time" (Brush 1977, 77). I recalled this study whenever personnel from outside agencies would describe the traditional method of grazing in comunidades as one of low-input, low-maintenance but high environmental cost, a system that they inherited from their "indigenous" past and one that gives them plenty of free time to do nothing when they should be working to plant, harvest, and store food for the animals to get them through the year. This criticism, of course, ignores the fact that most of these families lack the capital necessary to install irrigation which this improved system would require. When one development agency staff member demonstrated the comunero attitude by telling me, "You send the animals out in the morning, then . . . [placing his hands behind his head and leaning back in his chair], you take a siesta." I, having spent the field seasons described in this chapter, bit my lip and nodded politely.

El Arroyo: Life in the Campo Común

For three months, beginning in November 1997, Julie and I lived in the campo común in a sector of the community called "El Arroyo." Here Pablo and Amelia were staying in a house that had been in her uncle Lazaro's family for many years. It is a simple structure made of adobe with a tin ceiling and a dirt floor. It consists of two enclosed rooms; one that serves as a bedroom and another that is used as a workroom and storage area. There is neither electricity nor running water in this sector. The rooms are quite dark except for the natural light emitting through a plastic-covered skylight cut into the bedroom ceiling. Because of this, most social activities during the day took place in a semiopen area where the small dinner table was located and in which Amelia did the cooking over a small propane burner. Behind the house are three corrals made of stone and wood. Every day we fetched buckets of drinking and cooking water from an old well at the bottom of the hill on which the house sits.

On the other side of this hill is a quebrada that runs during the rainy season but was dry the entire time that we were in El Arroyo. Scattered about the property are various markers of family history that belie the lifelessness of the desolate landscape. In front of the house, a single narrow cross is hammered low into the dry ground, marking the place where an uncle fell from his horse when he was fatally stricken by a heart attack many years ago. Lazaro's grandfather's derelict stone trilla remains on the outskirts as a reminder that parts of this land had been used previously for purposes other than goat and sheep pasture. Pablo told me that in the past, before desertification and erosion had taken their toll, wheat was planted even in this isolated area. Julie and I lived in a more recently built wooden frame house adjacent to the one in which Pablo and Amelia were staying. Lazaro used this place as a cabin when he wanted to get away from his work in Illapel. His mother-in-law, Daniela, well into her eighties and who lived with them in Illapel, also stayed for extended periods of time in the cabin when her health permitted. Like many elderly people who had left the community, she wanted to spend as much time as possible in her later years in the place of her birth.

Six-year-old Felipe attended school in Loma Seca and stayed with Pablo's mother Elena during the week. An energetic and sweet-

natured little fellow, he immediately became fascinated with his foreign guests and attached himself to us right away. Every Friday afternoon he made the hour-long trek to El Arroyo unaccompanied, returning early Monday morning. Thirteen-year-old Tomás likewise
came to El Arroyo most weekends as he was attending an *internado* in
the nearby town of Socos. An internado is a public boarding school
subsidized by the state that is designed to help adolescents from the
countryside adjust to urban life. Although more shy and introspective
than his younger brother, Tomás also became a close companion, and
we became "Tío Willy" and "Tía Juli" to the both of them (as well as to
most of the neighboring children) almost as soon as we arrived.

While Pablo and Amelia and their children worked with the goats
and sheep in this sector, the other members of the family lived in Loma
Seca. As the oldest son, it was Pablo's responsibility to oversee the
livestock. During the week, his middle brother Gustavo operated a
road grader for a construction company that was expanding the La
Serena to Los Vilos section of the Pan-American Highway from two
to four lanes. Returning home on the weekends, his labor was especially needed in late January when the wheat harvest was brought in.
Eduardo, the thirty-year-old youngest brother, is the only one of the
three brothers who lives in Loma Seca full-time. Because a childhood
riding accident seriously impaired his vision, he lives at home with
Elena and makes extra money by assisting other people in the community with the care of their animals. He is the family member who is
almost always available to participate in community projects, such as
the alfalfa project that I will describe in a later chapter.

For clarity's sake, I include an abbreviated kinship diagram (figure
6.1) below that names the individual family members referred to in
this chapter, giving their age and where they live. Those holding the
title comunero are designated as having a "right" (derecho) in the
community.

In the campo común Pablo kept about one hundred goats and two
hundred sheep. We arrived as the cheese production season was at its
peak. *Crianceros,* or those who keep goats and earn money from their
products, can only make cheese for about five or six months of the
year because the animals are not productive and have little to eat
during the winter. The workday began every morning just after sun-
rise with Amelia and Pablo milking the goats together.

Goats and Cheese

A small portion of the milk is taken for the family's consumption. The
rest is used to make cheese. At the height of the production season this

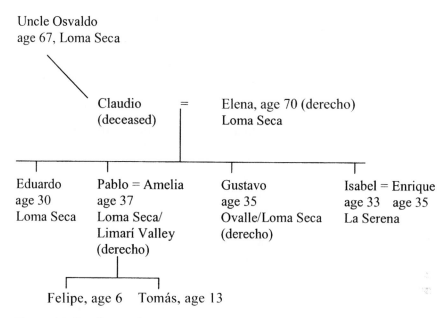

Figure 6.1. Family members

amounts to about 80 kilos of milk per day. As cheese making requires a good deal of milk, this could be made into about five or six kilos of cheese. During November and early December the price of such *queso artesanal* was 1,000 pesos per kilo (or about $2.50 U.S. The exchange rate fluctuated between around 420 to 480 Chilean pesos per U.S. dollar during my nineteen months in Chile. Here and elsewhere in this study, when giving dollar figures I use a base rate of 450 Chilean pesos per U.S. dollar). At the end of the season, the price was up to 1,500 pesos or more because the production was so low at that time, and by the end of January there was only enough milk to make one or two kilos per day.

A spoonful of a coagulation agent is poured into a large bucket holding the milk. The agent, sold commercially under the name "Cuajo," costs about 1,000 pesos for a jar and lasts about one week during the peak season. Traditionally crianceros acquired this enzyme necessary for the conversion of milk into curds and whey from a preparation made from the stomach lining of a baby goat. Cuajo is manufactured through genetic engineering in which cells from a goat's stomach are inserted into the genomes of bacteria and yeast. The microbes then make an exact copy of the enzyme. Promoted over the past decade by health workers seeking to improve the sanitary conditions under which goat cheese is made, crianceros like it because it works fast and is relatively inexpensive. After a wait of about a half hour, the milk has solidified to the right consistency. The cheese maker (*quesero*) reaches into the bucket and slowly churns up the solid chunks of curd by hand. Once there is enough curd to work with, the pressing can then begin.

Amelia and Pablo either pressed the cheese in the breezy room where they usually took their meals or, as the summer days grew hotter, in the cooler dark back room where the finished product was left to age on a high shelf just below the roof beams. The move to the back room was also made in an attempt to evade the swarms of flies that became a bother throughout the summer. Two wooden hoop molds about eight inches in diameter and two inches deep are placed on a small wooden trough balanced on a folding chair. The trough is built on an incline and has an open end so that the milk that is pressed out drains into a bucket. Two big handfuls of the coagulated milk are placed in each mold, making a tall pyramid of wet white curd. One wraps one's hands around this pyramid and squeezes slowly and firmly. As milk streams out and through the trough, the curd is gradually reduced to just above the level of the mold. The hard pressing then begins as slow, steady, firm pressure is applied to the cheese. The key to achieving maximum pressure is to barely touch the mold, just gently holding it in place with the sides of the hands. If the mold is not held firmly in this way, cheese will squeeze out from under the mold and will be wasted. Amelia began calling this *queso de Felipe* because if the little boy was around, he would quickly grab the wasted cheese and pop it into his mouth.

Once the cheese has begun to hold its shape and while it is still pliable, the mold is flipped over with the flattened solid underside now on top. Next, one pokes deep holes in the flat top with one's fingers, perforating the entire area and digging out the side that has been made flat and hard. Another big handful or two of the curd from the bucket is scooped into these holes, making another pyramid as before, and this side is slowly pressed and drained of milk.

The next phase is a monotonous process of constant, hard pressing. As the cheese continues to solidify and come into shape, it is squeezed and kneaded with fists and palms. The milk drains out ever more slowly. At first glance, pressing cheese does not look very physically challenging, but it soon became so to inexperienced queseros-in-training from the United States. Even Amelia, whose arms are well muscled from the work, complains of the soreness in her wrists from this routine. It is difficult to stand bent over for long periods of time, the lower back, upper thighs, shoulders, and wrists aching after a while from the constant pressure that is needed to complete the job.

Adroit pressing at this point would result in an occasional fountain of milk unexpectedly spouting out from a pocket of space inside the cheese that had not yet quite been reached. The trick is to balance by putting all of one's weight on the hands. Amelia and Pablo could do this quite expertly, but Julie and I could rarely achieve this. When I decided that the cheese that I was working on was finally finished, Amelia or Pablo would apply the final squeezes to it. If it was my second cheese of the day, there was usually more milk to be squeezed out than if it was my first, proof of my lack of stamina for this kind of work. It became an internal source of pride for me to have them do as little of the finishing as possible. Nevertheless, they usually complimented us on how *duro* or "firm" our cheeses were. They got a kick out of telling us that our cheeses were selling in La Serena, that their customers were not aware that they were buying *queso Norte Americano.* Once a week Pablo's sister would come by to take that week's cheeses to La Serena where she would sell them to a market there and to friends and acquaintances at the bank in which she worked.

After the cheeses are pressed, the top of each one is covered with an ample layer of salt. This type of salt is comprised of large crystals (similar to the kosher salt—finely ground table salt would dissolve quickly into the moist cheese), which are slowly absorbed down into the cheese. After a week or so of drying and aging, they are ready to be sold. They usually had two people working simultaneously. Our assistance freed one of them to do other things. Most of the time, the midmorning chore of pressing cheese was Amelia's responsibility as Pablo was usually away tending to the animals. Julie and I would take turns assisting Amelia. They appreciated the help. Amelia especially welcomed the company and the lightening of her work. For my work, it was encouraging to know that there would be a specific amount of time set aside every day during which I could easily gather information about their lives in a comfortable and informal setting. Visitors to the house were delighted or reacted in mock reproach to learn that Amelia and Pablo had "put us to work." When I made my next visit to Loma Seca word of this had preceded me. I think that this did much to show that we were not just curious guests but were willing to pitch in with chores whenever possible. It was during this shared work experience that began as soon as we arrived in El Arroyo that we became close to both of them, as well as the rest of their family, in a very short period.

Every day Pablo would go off on horseback to check on the sheep, which roamed freely day and night on the open pastureland. He returned later in the day to do various tasks such as mending the corral or attending to the horses. He would ride off again in the late afternoon to herd the goats back to the house. Often Pablo would come back with a sick animal or a newly born kid whose mother was rejecting it. On our first day in El Arroyo we arrived in the late afternoon. As the sun began to set, the herd of goats being driven by Pablo began to slowly emerge over the horizon and make its way down the steep hills. I had not seen Pablo since our meeting during the "Day of the Dead" celebration a week earlier. The image of him on this first day emerging from the hills on horseback with a newborn lamb cradled inside his jacket is one that I will never forget. The baby lamb's skin hung from its bones like an oversized dirty wool coat. Occasionally sickly lambs will be brought in from the pasture to nurse from goats in the corral. Because lambs are more valuable than goats, greater efforts are made to save them. A lactating goat was tied to a post in the corral and the sickly lamb got its milk with little problem.

It was always a constant fight after the goats had been rounded up into separate corrals for the adults and offspring to feed the babies from the recalcitrant mothers by force. It is usually the smell of other goats in the corral that makes the mother reject them. They are fine in the hills, Amelia told me, but when the baby acquires the smell of others, often the mother will not feed the kid. The mother must then be roped and held securely while the kid is allowed to feed. Pablo's dexterous use of the lasso was impressive. Young Tomás was also adept, but his shots were not yet as effortless as those of his father. Very sick baby goats are fed with a bottle rather than roping the obstinate mother goat. In the last months of cheese production, when the price of cheese is at its highest, crianceros will use a powdered milk substitute to feed the babies because the goat milk is too valuable.

The family kept about ten dogs of eccentrically mixed breeds. Fed just the excess whey from the cheese production and the occasional bones of a chicken or goat, these animals were lean, fierce, and hungry. All families with livestock in the countryside keep a large number of dogs to act as an "alarm system" against thieves and foxes. They also proved to be great help in maintaining order in the corral. Packed fairly tightly, occasionally a few rambunctious goats would push open one of the corral doors and some would spill out into the yard. Although they probably had little intention of straying very far, the dogs made sure that they did not. The dogs would jump to attention in an instant—barking, bullying, and circling the escapees into terrified acquiescence and leaving Pablo and Amelia free to continue with what they were doing. With the dogs chasing them, the madly scampering goats were more than happy to return to the corral. They hastily jumped and climbed back over the prickly fences, with one of the dogs hopping up on to the top of one of the stone walls to oversee things like a prison camp watchtower guard.

The hot summer days quickly turn cool once the sun goes down. Frequently a heavy fog will blow into the valley and the goats and sheep in the hills behind the house become very noisy when they are wrapped in the mist. The animals rarely get lost, but it upsets them and they slowly find their way home by keeping their heads close to the ground. Holding one's palm in the air, one can feel the incredibly fine mist in the air. For most of the year, the moisture of this *neblina* is all of the "rain" that the land gets. In the morning, everything outside will be damp and moist from a full night of this barely perceptible moisture. It can be an eerily beautiful site with everything beyond the immediate parameters of the property obscured by the gray vapor. Pablo joked that when it is very foggy he occasionally has to "divine" where the animals have gone when he is out on his evening horseback ride to round them up. To demonstrate he covered his eyes with one hand and groped for divine revelation with the other.

There are other natural elements that affect the animals' production. When there is a lot of wind, the goats find a place to shelter themselves. Staying in one place they eat less and produce less milk. In the wintertime, because it is colder in the hills, they are also less active and produce little. While the goats must be brought in every day, the sheep remain out to pasture. Most of the time the sheep are out of sight, grazing far from the house. When the temperature is very hot, the sheep will move to the top of a hill because the wind keeps them cool. Thus, it is occasionally possible to keep an eye on them from the front porch. A well-aimed loud whistle from Pablo or Amelia will direct them back into the hills if they begin to wander too closely to the house.

Sheep and Cordero

Pablo normally keeps about two hundred sheep. Around 15 percent of these are lost over the course of the year as they are killed by condors or foxes. Of the remaining, he saves about a quarter to breed for the next year. Selling lamb stops after the September prime market seasons because they need until March to reproduce themselves. He makes his decisions to conserve or sell depending upon the year's climate and the availability of pasture. Very little is sold throughout the year and only in rare instances, such as once when Tomás's teacher in Socos bought some lamb for a special occasion. In the early summer the price of lamb (*cordero*) is only about $2 U.S. a kilo, but this goes up to as much as $5 a kilo in the month of September when so much cordero is consumed all over the nation during the Independence Day celebration. In Chile, lamb is traditionally eaten during this holiday in the same way that turkey is consumed in the United States for Thanksgiving.

Early on, Pablo showed me some raw wool, handling it with disdain. They can only get about fifty cents per kilo for it, so it is rarely sold. In the past it was much more, he said, but the availability of synthetic fabrics are to blame for the low price. One sheep produces about two kilos of wool a year, so it is not worth the trouble. Every now and then, Pablo would work on a lambskin to sell or to use to make a saddle. He would clean it with detergent and hang it up to dry. If the lamb has been getting enough nourishment, the skin is soft and of fine quality and very strong on the underside. After washing it and drying it, Pablo scrapes the underside of the wool with a shovel. Proud of the strong but flexible soft underside, he said that one could treat it with chemicals to remove the fat but that this way is better because it is handmade, or *artesanal,* a term that he and the others used with pride especially when describing their cheese. He sells the lambskin for a couple of thousand pesos to a leather bodega in Ovalle where the craftspeople would fashion it into a finished product and sell it for up to 25,000 pesos. In a small way, the added value of the artisan handiwork tries to compensate for the market that was lost to the industrialized production of cheap imports.

During the first year that I was in the community, rabbits were not a big problem. In a year of drought after a good year of rain, however, they can become a major pestilence and threaten crops. The situation will be, as the people there termed it, a *plaga,* and an organized hunting effort (*carreras de conejos*) will be carried out to rid the community of them. Foxes are also a threat to the goats and sheep. When the sheep are far away in the pre-cordillera foothills and do not have the dogs to watch over them, Pablo loses about two animals a day to the foxes and to condors. The condor is one of the national symbols of Chile and the government has made efforts to protect them. Despite this, Pablo would sometimes fire his rifle without success at the condors circling overhead. Amelia confided that this was more of a show of frustration than anything else.

Occasionally there would be rabbit for dinner. Quail was an even more uncommon treat. Both were delicious, but Pablo had little time for hunting. They kept about twenty chickens, ten geese, and two pigs. It was the children's responsibility to feed these animals when they were at home. The chickens produced more eggs than the family needed, but it was impractical to sell the surplus considering their isolation from any market. The geese were kept for aesthetic purposes, more or less, as Amelia enjoyed having them around. The pigs were being fattened to be slaughtered and sold as *chancho.* This mobile resource was particularly useful the following year. They took the pigs with them in their search for pasture away from the community and made a little money from the sale of the meat.

Lamb was eaten only on special occasions because of its high market value. Male goats were much more expendable, since only about six or so were spared for breeding purposes. Crianceros in the community exchange breeding males periodically in order to reduce genetic risk within each family's livestock population. Goat was the primary source of meat protein and was eaten about once weekly, usually boiled in stews and sometimes barbecued. Pablo and Amelia slaughtered and roasted a lamb on our second day in El Arroyo, which happened to be my birthday. Although I was appreciative and delighted by the gesture, at the time I did not realize the extent of the cost that it meant for them.

Cardon (Puya chilensis)

The newly born kids are kept in a separate corral adjacent to the one in which the mothers are held when they are not grazing. After about a month one morning the little ones, with little fanfare, will go off to pasture with the other animals. In the weaning transition from mother's milk to pasture, the kids are gradually fed a little grass and often given a freshly uprooted *cardon (Puya chilensis)* plant, which is in abundant supply all around the campo común. After the animals have eaten the leaves and meaty plant material, the sticks are dried and used for building and repairing fences for the corrals and as general purpose building material.

Cardon is ideal for use in the corrals because they are covered with pineapplelike sticky points; they serve as a kind of natural barbed wire. The gnarled thick and heavy roots are also used for firewood. The plant, which can grow up to fifteen feet in height, is a tall, thin perennial with an enormous flowering spike with spine-edged leaves at the top. Extending from Chile's Region VIII in the south (where it acquired the name "puya" from the Mapuche language) to the Region IV, the plant thrives in the desert environment and sprouts yellow flowers that are especially vivid in spring seasons following winter rains. Along with its use as fence-building material, (it is also called *coto de pastor,* which loosely translates as "shepherd's fence"), its leaves furnish a fiber that is used to make mats and cords and to make fishing nets in coastal areas (Muñoz 1985, 25).

Christmas

As December came to a close, the goats began to produce less milk each day. By the end of March cheese production would stop altogether as the fall air began to turn crisp and edible pasture became scarce. As one phase of family production began to wane, anticipation of the wheat harvest began to rise. We made an arrangement with the family to move from El Arroyo to Loma Seca in accordance with the shift. Pablo's mother agreed to let us rent one of the rooms in her house in January. Amelia and the boys, who were now on summer vacation, would remain out here with the animals while Pablo would ride in every day to participate in the harvest.

It was a delightful and most memorable Christmas. Marco's excitement about the coming of *el Viejito Pascuero* (Santa Claus in Chile) was infectious. The old man arrives in the countryside on Christmas Eve night on a burro, and it is good policy to leave a little alfalfa for the animal to eat. For us it was a great gift to be able to spend the holiday with people whose limited means was far surpassed by their spirit and resourcefulness.

A few days before Christmas, in the late afternoon, Pablo, Amelia, and Felipe came to our door to take us with them to cut a branch to use as the family Christmas tree. We hiked down the hill to the quebrada that runs between theirs and another house where an oasis of tall green pines breaks the austere monotone of the brown desert. In that one little spot it is like a condensed lush forest, and from the inside one could scarcely guess that one was in the middle of the desert. It was remarkable to watch Pablo get the branch. He tied one end of his lasso to a big bowie knife and snagged high branches in the same manner in which he lassoed goats in the corral. The first one that he caught, he cut by simply tossing the knife into a high branch and yanking it to the ground in one fell swoop. This branch was short and full, but he decided on another that was taller, thinner, and more "treelike." The sun was going down and the cool fresh air in the woods was a welcome respite from the heat and the dust of that summer day.

We took the branch into the *comedor* and brought in the gas lamp that Julie and I used at night in our room. Amelia wrapped an old tin can in Christmas paper to use as the tree stand. We brought out wine and chocolates that we had bought in Ovalle. Julie and Amelia decorated the tree with some garland and decorations. Pablo bent some old wire into a star shape and wrapped it in garland. Amelia apologized for the tree, and she said that they had more decorations that were lost during the two years when they had migrated to the south. She did not need to apologize. We meant it when we said that the tree was beautiful. Wedged into one corner of the room, spread out against the wall, nearly reaching the ceiling, Pablo said that it "looks like a tree." I said that it *is* a Christmas tree. Understanding what I had meant, he repeated that, yes, it is a Christmas tree. That night I wrote in my journal before going to sleep:

> It seems so cliché, but it is true nonetheless. The spirit and joy and excitement of occasions like Christmas seem to be stronger with people who have little means to spend celebrating. Felipe and Tomás are anything but jaded consumers, and they appreciate and value whatever extras they receive. The branch is filled with so much more meaning than the fifty-dollar Christmas trees that are being dutifully (happily? grudgingly?) purchased in the United States today. Christmas itself means little to me, but it is hard not to be moved by Felipe's excitement and the family's genuinely celebratory spirit of being together rather than of just getting stuff. Of course, this is not to say that Felipe isn't like every other little kid this time of year—anxious and a little bit greedy. But when he talks about the coming of el Viejito Pascuero it seems to be more of anticipation of the time rather than of the arrival of piles of toys. In fact, he hardly talks at all about presents specifically.

After we decorated the tree, it was time for bed. Felipe was finally sleepy. I've never seen him tired before. As usual, the clear night sky was filled with stars. We saw a satellite pass by and two falling stars. Pablo pointed out the Southern Cross.

Harvesting Wheat in Loma Seca

In mid-January, we moved to Pablo's mother's house in Loma Seca. Modest by urban standards, the three-bedroom house with gypsum board walls and tile floors is one of the nicest in town. There is electricity and drinking water, but the water system is not pressurized "running water." Rather, water from a community reservoir is pumped via a hose to various houses that have holding barrels. Every day or so it was Eduardo's job to climb the ladder to the *mangera*, a kind of miniature water tower located behind the house, and to fill it by lowering a wooden bucket into the barrel. Gravity then moved the water through a hose to the pipes inside the house.

The community was abuzz with the expectation of the arrival of the máquina and the upcoming wheat harvest. Numerous visitors stopped by throughout the day. Elena is not only the secretary of the comunidad, but also serves an important function in the town's religious life. Because the priest comes to Loma Seca to say Mass only about once a month, Elena and three other ladies act as a kind of secular liaison in organizing religious activities. These include conducting catechism classes in her home and preparing families for baptism (*bautiza*) and other religious ceremonies. Neighbors and relatives also come in and out to socialize and exchange bits of news. Many times a crowd gathered to watch the popular nighttime soap operas (*telenovelas*) that make up the bulk of the few nationally produced entertainment programs. Although the reception is poor in Loma Seca, Elena's large color television seems to make the prevalence of "snow" on the screen more tolerable.

Pablo, Elena, and his brother Gustavo all have derechos, or rights, as comuneros. Together they have access to thirty to forty hectares of lluvia, which is always planted with wheat. When Pablo's father passed away several years ago the three rights that had accumulated in his family were passed on to his wife Elena and to Pablo and Gustavo, the two oldest sons. Eduardo, the youngest, will inherit Elena's right when she dies. Because of the changes in the law, people within the community may buy the derechos of others. At present the purchase price is 360,000 pesos, or about $800, and Elena is considering saving enough money to purchase a right for Isabel, the daughter who lives and works in La Serena.

For two weeks after we moved to Loma Seca the town waited anxiously for the men with the máquina to arrive. A few times news came for the farmers to expect them the next day, but there were always more delays. When they finally arrived, the general tension was broken by relief that the work could finally begin. Still there was a feeling of urgency to bring in as much of the crop as possible before too much was wasted as it stood in the fields. Don Hernan, the owner of the harvesters from La Serena, brought two shiny Massey-Ferguson combine harvesters and four workmen to operate them. First, the two group projects in Nogales and La Mesa were completed and then, finally, one of the harvesters and a team of two of the workers pulled up to cut Pablo's family's wheat.

As the harvester brought the grain in from the surrounding fields and from their lluvias located on the other side of the community, a trilla (threshing) like the group project that I described in the previous chapter, only of smaller proportions, commenced on the high, flat hill just behind Elena's house. Elena spent many hours sewing wheat sacks together by hand. Pablo, Gustavo, Eduardo, and a couple of other comuneros (with whom they were exchanging labor) worked together, using the broom and shovel method of separating the grain and loading and stacking the heavy sacks. Eight days passed from the time that they began to harvest until the time that the comprador came to buy their wheat. By then the area in the back of the house was stacked with more than 250 sacks.

Elena had to house and provide big meals for the workers, even on days when there was no work because of the weather or if the machinery broke down, which it frequently did. There were some days when work was halted by the fog or a mechanical problem. As a result of the wait, much of the wheat turned bad and was not worth harvesting. The increasingly damp weather was also a problem. As summer faded it was often too cool and damp to cut the wheat until the afternoon, as the wheat has to be dry for the machine to harvest enough to make it worth the price of operating it. While we waited, the workmen oiled and made little repairs to the machine. Usually after lunch, the sun would appear and burn off the fog and dry out the fields. One day the weather took a drastic turn after lunch. Around 1:00 PM I walked outside and was stunned to see great clouds of fog rolling in from the west, a little reminder that the Pacific Ocean was really just over the western hills. Fog rapidly poured in through the valleys, imbuing the land with an otherworldly appearance, and in a matter of minutes, the fields of summer wheat disappeared under the opaque shroud.

After about an hour and a half, a group of us went to the back of the house to perform a test run to see if the wheat was still too *húmedo* (damp). Pablo, his head down and hands clasped behind his back, walked with a couple of the others along behind the harvester as it cut a wide row. He occasionally kicked a clump of cut wheat. While they were doing this, Eduardo brought a beautiful mare and pony to graze in the swath that the machine had cut. The pony was two months old and its color was changing from brown to black. Eduardo said that they were feeding the mare right away because the pony needed milk. The animals were a little skittish when the harvester made its passes. After two such passes, Pablo decided that the field was too damp to cut. It would not have produced enough sacks to pay for the machine and the helpers. In the late afternoon, the harvester moved to another sector that had been dried out by the sun. The unharvested wheat, much of it located in the hills high above the house, was to be used to pasture the animals to sustain them through the winter. As soon as the harvest was over, some of the horses were led up there to feed upon the wheat. The sight of the blackened fields of the unharvested wheat was a sore spot for Pablo, but Elena was more philosophical about it. The farmers say that the community's proximity to the ocean is a double-edged sword (*de doble filo*). The location sees enough rain in good years to produce wheat, but the damp ocean air necessitates timely harvesting. Even if the cost of buying a combine harvester were not prohibitive, the erratic rainfall would make such a purchase impractical.

At around five in the afternoon on the day that the comprador from Santiago came, an empty tractor-trailer pulled up to where the wheat was stacked behind the house. A young driver in a loud print shirt watched the activity, occasionally moving the truck slightly in order to position it properly. Later a pickup arrived and the wheat buyer named Esmeraldo, who owned the truck and was in charge of the men, used a hanging-weight scale to weigh the sacks before they were put on the truck. Pablo and the other men loaded the sacks three at a time onto the scales. Esmeraldo shouted out the weight and Elena and Eduardo each wrote down the figures on separate notebooks to compare later. Three workers carried the sacks on their shoulders up two long, narrow planks, providing some comic relief as they diligently plodded up and down the plank. They were rowdy little muscular guys, one of them quite advanced in years. They wore ripped white wheat sacks that covered their heads and draped down over their backs. This was to keep the wheat off of them and to protect them from the rubbing of the heavy sacks. Pablo and one of his helpers lifted and rolled the sacks onto the carrier's shoulders and they trod slowly single-file up the planks. This went on for nearly two hours. In the end, Esmeraldo purchased 23,841 kilos of wheat. About thirty other sacks were left behind for the family bodega. The farmers keep enough grain in storage to last their families through two bad years. Normally, Pablo told me, he sells 60 percent of what he produces and keeps 40 percent in his bodega. This year because the production was relatively high, he sold much more.

After the counting and re-counting to get the two sets of numbers to jibe was finally completed, everyone relaxed and the atmosphere of anxiety and hard labor was soon eased away by the recognition that the cosecha was finally over. Sitting around the kitchen table, Elena informed us that because they had operated the harvester for over forty hours, "Don Hernan [the trillador machinery owner from La Serena] gets 10,000 kilos," and all of this effort had hardly been worth the trouble. Don Hernan came and went a few times during the weighing of the sacks, uneasily negotiating his payment with Pablo, Eduardo, and Elena. After he left, the high costs of the machinery and gasoline were freely discussed between the buyers and the sellers of the wheat. Pablo and Elena complained and Esmeraldo, the comprador, agreed that the person with the machine and the gasoline is the person who makes the "real money." Although there was no serious animosity directed toward Don Hernan, it was interesting to note that most people were more critical of the expense of renting the machinery rather than of the low price that the comprador was willing to pay for the wheat this year. Esmeraldo also owns a large parcela in Ovalle, producing fruits and vegetables, and Pablo seemed proud to be associated with such a successful agricultural entrepreneur.

The workers and the truck went off down the road to Nogales to pick up another family's wheat. That evening they returned to enjoy a small celebration that Pablo and Elena put on in the front yard. The party was both something that was expected as a way to thank those who had helped them with their work and was also a way for the family to celebrate a successful harvest. There was delicious roasted lamb (*cordero asado*) eaten directly from the grill (*parilla*-style), drinking, music, and dancing until the early morning hours.

According to Pablo, the 1997/1998 harvest that I witnessed was a fairly good year in that they harvested about 40 percent of what could have been produced. As mentioned, 30 percent of the seeds that had been planted were lost due to the previous winter flooding and the eroded soil. Another 30 percent was lost in the field because of the long wait for the harvester and the damp weather conditions. Before that year, 1993 was the last year that they grew wheat because of the four consecutive years of drought. In 1993 they harvested a little less than 1997/1998. Pablo said that the last really good years were in 1980 and 1984 in which almost everything that was planted was harvested. Thinking back, he told me that there were four good years in the 1970s, six good years in the 1980s, while only 1993 and 1997 were good years in the 1990s. His personal experience reflects the overall diminishing return for wheat production in the region's unforgiving environment. Always defusing pessimism with wry humor and ever-skeptical of the news reporting of the impending Y2K disaster, when I spoke with him about this shortly before I left Chile in May 1999, he joked that things will certainly be better in the "new millennium"—if the world does not come to an end.

ITINERANT SEASONS OF SACRIFICE

As mentioned in chapter 3, the veranadas are one of the eight sectors of comunidades agrícolas located in the cordillera high in the mountains near the Argentine border. The word is also used to describe pastures in Argentina. An agreement exists between the two nations that allows herders from both sides to pasture their animals in the mountains for a nominal fee. A combination of the words *verano* and *paradas,* the word means "summer lands" and is often used to refer to the "time" for taking the herds into either the cordillera or to fundos in the green south rather than the specific "place" where they are taken. The time is usually November or December through February. In the past, the trip from Loma Seca to the cordillera would take twenty days by foot. Now it is about a two- to three-day trip transporting the animals by truck. Families usually go to the same place each time where they have made an arrangement, taking many of their belongings and materials to make cheese on the site. It is necessary for them to produce cheese there in order to use this mobile capital and to defray the cost of renting and moving.

Pablo's family has been well served by their mobility in the past. As the eldest son Pablo manages all of the family's farm and livestock activities. At times it is a big sacrifice for him and Amelia because the animals are especially demanding and require constant attention. Having to move them south for two years was a particularly big sacrifice. Pablo and the family took the animals and moved their entire operation to a fundo near Viña del Mar, an upscale resort city four hundred kilometers to the south of Loma Seca that is adjacent to the important port of Valparaiso. Viña, kind of the "Rio of Chile," is famous for luxurious beaches and a summer musical festival, and attracts thousands of South American tourists every summer. They took 200 sheep and 150 goats with them, a number of the animals dying en route. They spent two of the previous four years of drought there, returning to Loma Seca in 1997. They rented land near the ocean for the animals, produced and sold cheese on the site, sold some baby goats to the tourists, and even rented their horses to tourists for rides on the beach.

At six thousand pesos per animal, the costs to move to Viña were very high, but they could make and sell cheese to the tourists. Without cheese, the only other option is to sell the goats. In exceptionally dry times, people will sell their animals if they have no other choice. Because of the extended drought, the number of goats had rapidly decreased—dying from starvation or illness or by crianceros giving up and selling their animals—in the decade before I arrived in 1997. Ten years before there were about four thousand goats in the community. This was down to about nine hundred when I arrived in 1997. So much depends upon the weather and availability of pasture. If there is nothing for the goats to eat, Pablo says that he has no choice but to leave. So far he has resisted selling his animals. He often talked about the adaptability of goats and sheep and about how cows could not survive on so little to eat. Speaking in Marxist terminology that echoes the comuneros' leftist political genealogy, in which participation in union activity in the northern mines gave rise to socialist ideals in the agricultural communities, Pablo emphasized to me that all of the crianceros make cheese because the animal is the "means of production" and that as "capital" it must be protected. The best that they can hope for during times of drought is to maintain the animals and to wait for better times.

While I passed the summer of 1998 in Arizona with a typical monsoon season bringing afternoon storms like clockwork, a winter without rain was passing in Chile. Pablo, like most of the other crianceros in the community, moved his family and animals in search of pasture. When I returned, my fieldwork mirrored their itinerancy. I kept a room at a *pensión* in Ovalle but spent much of my time moving, following them from place to place in the Limarí valley and making frequent trips to Loma Seca. In addition, I found myself moving between the "worlds" of peasant life in the country and the economic development offices in Ovalle and La Serena. In the last field season, I was also experiencing an uncertain season of transition on a personal level—a retrograde passage through the liminal phase between married and single status and doing so outside of the familiarity of my own culture. By the time that I returned to the United States near the end of my fieldwork for a two-week trip home to present my work at the 1999 Society for Applied Anthropology annual meetings, my journey seemed nearly complete. When questioned by friends if it felt strange to be back, I said that although, yes, it is remarkable that one could be making goat cheese in the northern Chilean desert one morning and making plans to give a talk at a luxury hotel in the United States the next, with every trip between the two Chile is becoming less strange and Tucson is becoming less familiar.

Independence Day at San Julián

In September 1998 I returned to Chile and arrived in Ovalle two days before the Independence Day holiday on the eighteenth. The brothers have an aunt who owns a small hotel there, where I often stayed when I was in town. Knowing that it had been a dry winter, I doubted that they would be living in Loma Seca, and I assumed that she would be able to tell me where I could find the family. I found that, in fact, Gustavo had taken a job at the hotel.

Gustavo arrived at Hotel Venecia that night, and the next afternoon he took me to a fundo in an area called San Julián that is only about a twenty-minute drive from Ovalle. Pablo was renting land there to pasture the animals because of the drought. The man who owns the land is a friend of theirs and was renting to them at the fair price of 120,000 pesos per month. The sheep were being kept in another area high in the hills for the cost of about 100,000 pesos per month. Pablo was living in San Julián full-time. Gustavo slept at Hotel Venecia after putting in a shift as the night man but was spending all day on the fundo tending to the animals. His labor was also greatly needed to help Pablo with the animals, and the proximity of the job at the hotel was ideal.

By mid-July they knew that there was not going to be any rain in Loma Seca, and they had been living in San Julián for almost two months. On the day that I arrived the whole family was there, butchering and selling lamb and *cabrito* (goat meat) for three days leading up to the next day's Independence Day celebration. Throughout the day people arrived in cars and taxis to buy the meat. The customer would pick the one that they wanted, and Pablo would slaughter, skin, gut, and butcher it on the spot. I always marveled at the precision with which he used his knife as cleanly as a kosher butcher, never nicking an internal organ. In keeping with the holiday spirit, the buyer was usually given a glass of wine to share with Pablo and the people helping him. One man bought a live goat to take home with him. They tied its feet and put it in the trunk of a taxi. I could not resist making the joke that it was the first time that I had ever seen a goat take a taxi. They laughed, but the sight certainly seemed more absurd to me than it did to them. They sold more than one hundred animals over the course of the three days, weighing the meat on a scale made from a rusty weight attached to an old rope looped through the roof beam of the slaughtering area. They made about two thousand dollars over the course of the three days. This may seem like a lot but, as mentioned, this represents almost their entire cash income from the sheep for the entire year. "Nada," said Gustavo, in a resigned but not bitter way.

On Independence Day, Gustavo and Tomás made a couple of trips to Ovalle to sell the remaining cordero to a middleman buyer there and to sell the skins from the sheep and goats. They chopped off the hooves and feet and carried them to a rack where they would dry in the sun before giving them to the dogs. This year the quality of the skins, or *cuero*, was not as good because of the animals' poor diet. When there is good pasture for the year the buyer will pay up to two thousand pesos per goatskin and a thousand per lambskin. This year they could only get about half of that price.

At this time in September they were selling about 30 liters of milk a day, or about 900 liters a month. They were receiving about 250 pesos per liter from a buyer who was coming by in a refrigerated truck to take it to a place near the town of Socos about twenty kilometers away on the main highway. From there the milk was transported to a factory in Santiago to be made into cheese and sold under the "Chevrita" brand.

In early November they began to mull over the idea of moving the animals to the cordillera between Chile and Argentina. They could stay in San Julián and just maintain the animals. They were then producing and selling up to about forty liters of milk a day, still about half of what they were producing and using to make cheese last year at this time. If they could produce enough milk to make the move worthwhile, they would do it, but they would need three trucks to move the animals to a place in the vicinity of Vicuña. From there it would take about four hours by horseback to shepherd the animals into the mountains.

One afternoon (which happened to be the second birthday that I spent with them), brother-in-law Enrique, who sells automobiles in La Serena, engaged Gustavo and Pablo for about an hour in a discussion of the pros and cons of keeping the animals and just "getting by" versus selling the animals and getting a steady income from a job in the city. Enrique spoke fervently about the benefits of knowing that he will get a certain amount of money every month from a job. Here, he argued, Gustavo and Pablo are too much at the mercy of the weather, availability of pasture, and other factors outside of their control. They listened but disagreed with him. Gustavo took a somewhat sentimental approach, emphasizing how this lifestyle works because people help each other in times of need. Pablo was more pragmatic about weighing the costs and benefits. Although their monetary income is cyclical now, he did not believe that he would be any better off working for low wages in Ovalle where living expenses would be much higher. He, too, became more sentimental as the discussion went on and more wine was consumed. It became clear that he did not really want to change his life. Happiness is the most important thing, and you cannot put a price on it, he said. His argument was that being your own boss and having control over your work is invaluable. He asked me if I agreed with this, and I said that I did wholeheartedly. I thought back to a discussion that I had with their mother in her kitchen, during the wheat harvest of the previous year.

Elena told me that she has often told Pablo that he could sell the animals if he ever feels like giving up. He tells her that he understands this, and that if he ever gets fed up and has had enough, he may do so. But he likes the freedom and being his own man. She described him as both dedicated to carrying on what his father and others before him had done while nonetheless having "modern thinking," a willingness to adapt to the modern world. We talked about how mathematically inclined Pablo is, and I told her how Julie and I had commented to ourselves on occasion that he seems to have the mind of an engineer. In discussing the intricacies of successful farming and livestock raising, he delighted in pointing out that it is not as simple as it looks from the outside, and that there are many factors to be considered. (He especially took pleasure in observing that plans to turn crianceros into commercial producers was much more *complicado* than many government officials and development agents realize.) Elena told us that Pablo had excelled at the *liceo agrícola* (a kind of agricultural vocational high school). She said that he had been offered a job working in a vineyard when he was younger, but that he had turned it down.

"Campo Lindo" and "Pueblo Limarí"

The next time that I saw Pablo and Amelia was in December after they had relocated with the animals to land that they were renting in the "Campo Lindo" sector, not far from San Julián. They had stayed in San Julián for four months until the pasture ran out. In Campo Lindo they were renting six hectares of open land, but because this place was more isolated than the previous one—several kilometers down a rutted dirt road—they were far away from the route of the Chevrita milk buyer, and they were back to making cheese on a full-time basis.

I spent my second Christmas in Chile with them here. By the early afternoon on Christmas Day the entire family (with relatives coming from Ovalle, La Serena, and Loma Seca) had converged at this one-room shanty to spend the day with Amelia and Pablo, who could not leave the animals unattended. Their workday was festive but proceeded with little interruption. Pablo and Amelia pressed six medium-sized cheeses as people took shifts eating at the small table. A new young goat wandering in and out of the house throughout the day generated a good deal of amusement, particularly because they were calling him "Marcello," as he was of a special French race that produces twice as much milk as the other goats. Pablo had paid 29,000 pesos for the artificial insemination. He said that Marcello could be worth a thousand dollars as an adult because of the amount of milk that his offspring would produce. He hoped to gradually upgrade his livestock in this way, the investment paying off in more milk made with fewer animals.

By this time the decision had been made to stay in the Limarí valley rather than to take the animals to the cordillera. Amelia said that there were not enough people available to help with the trip. She needed to be with Marcos now that he was of school age and not yet living in an internado. I got the impression that Pablo had been voted down by the lack of enthusiasm for the idea. Gustavo could not see leaving the job at Hotel Venecia, which allowed him to make a little steady money while still contributing to the care of the animals. Also, the elderly bachelor uncle Osvaldo's worsening asthma prevented him from making the journey into the mountains. Because of his poor eyesight, Eduardo, the youngest brother, could never have made such a demanding journey. There was also the cost of transporting the animal, which Pablo figured would have cost up to 400,000 pesos. This would have to be paid all at once in a lump sum, with the hope that they would be able to make this back from the sale of their products, which would, of course, be more difficult there.

They also spent about a month between January and February near "Pueblo Limarí," a small town that is only about a fifteen-minute *taxi colectivo* ride from Ovalle. The pueblo is a modest village with two, or three small stores and an aggregation of some small but nice houses with small yards in the center of town and some ramshackle structures on the perimeter. Just beyond the outskirts of town a path leads across a field through a cluster of trees and across a shallow but rushing canal over some slippery rocks, leading to the tiny house lacking basic amenities where they lived for this month.

"Parcela 48"

In mid-February they moved again. As with the three previous places, this one was a short ride from Ovalle. "Just tell the driver to let you off at Parcela 48," I was instructed. The owner here lives in a well-built house on a hill above where the family was living. There was a grape vineyard between Amelia and Pablo's house and several large fields of tomatoes and onions. This house was also adobe with a dirt floor, but with the added conveniences of electricity and an indoor bathroom.

It was much more difficult work pasturing the goats here. At the previous places the animals were more or less free to roam. Here, with the help of a couple of the dogs someone, usually Amelia, had to stand in the field whenever the goats were not in the corral and make sure that they did not cross over into the onion or tomato fields. The pasture was divided by a canal. I spent a good part of many days standing out there talking with Amelia and Pablo. Whenever the goats would stray she would make noise, walk toward them, or throw rocks in their direction. The dogs would also chase and herd them back to where they were supposed to be grazing. This work was not strenuous but required unflagging diligence.

At that point they were producing five to six cheeses per day. They were not selling any milk now because it was more profitable to make cheese, as the price was high. They were getting 1,500 pesos for an 800-gram cheese, selling them to a woman who has a stand on the highway near Socos where the road to Ovalle splits off from the Pan-American Highway. Because there was plenty for the animals to eat here, Pablo and Amelia were producing cheese at a time when the season would have stopped if they were only feeding the animals with natural forage at home. Here because they had increased production and easier access to markets, they could take advantage of the higher price. The trade-off was that they were renting this land and would be happy just to break even. Green tags on the ears of some of the goats showed that a sample had been tested for illness, primarily the infectious disease brucellosis, by an agent from the governmental assistance organization Servicio Agricultura y Ganadería (SAG). As the blood tests showed that the animals were healthy, Pablo and Amelia were permitted to sell milk and cheese until the end of the exemption in the cheese law on May 15. Amelia then believed that there would be yet another exemption granted because of the controversy that had been generated and because of the number of families dependent upon this as a source of income.

Last Parcela

At the end of March they moved yet again, their fifth and final relocation during my stay. This place was much farther away from Ovalle and not easily accessible by bus or colectivo. I usually caught a ride with Gustavo, leaving Hotel Venecia in the morning. Other times Tomás and I would share a taxi with Amelia's sister's family who visited frequently from Ovalle. The road that left the main highway turned very rough before it reached the large parcela where the owner had a field of artichokes, a field of tomatoes that had been harvested, two large sections of grape vineyards, and a green field of clover. The family believed that they would stay there for several months because there was plenty for the animals to eat there.

Although less convenient to Ovalle, it was better than the other areas where they had stayed because good irrigation from the Limarí River watered the green fields. When the goats finished with one section, they were moved to another field. Pablo was very careful in dividing it up this way. He told me that clover is second to alfalfa as the best pasture for his animals. If rain came by June Pablo thought that he would be able to take the animals back to El Arroyo. At the moment Uncle Osvaldo and Brother Eduardo were staying with the sheep at an area a solid two hours away on horseback and waiting for a friend of Amelia and Pablo's from Loma Seca to bring his sheep so that they could pasture them under the grape bowers once the owner has harvested the grapes. The sight of goats and sheep grazing under the grape trellises is a common picture as one drives through this part of Chile. Another advantage to this parcela was that the owner allowed Pablo to feed the leafy top stems of the harvested artichokes to his animals. They were his for the taking for clearing out the field. I spent a good part of one morning helping him and Tomás with transporting the many heaps of cut plants to a vacant field where the goats enacted a feeding frenzy upon the salubrious greens.

They were averaging about four cheeses per day and selling them every day to a bodega in Ovalle, as the price was up to 1,700 pesos per kilo. Like the other places, they were paying 120,000 pesos a month for the house and pasture, but they could stay longer here because the owner had more land so there would not be extra moving expenses. When they move, they use Gustavo's truck, but have to make many trips, and this uses much gasoline. Once again, there was talk that selling the animals was an option that they had considered. But since times were tough everywhere, there was no other work, and their best option was to sit out the hard times.

Still maintaining their twenty-six horses, Gustavo said that they often sell them, but this year would not be a good year to do so because the price was very bad. As with many other things, the reason was the general lack of money in the region as a whole. The best price that they could get at the time would only be about 60–80,000 pesos for an adult horse. Since it costs about 10,000 pesos a month just to feed them, the price would not even cover their costs for one year, so the best thing to do was to wait. They would have liked to have sold six or eight of them at that point, but not until the price was better. I was told about some wealthy speculators in the area who would take advantage of this dire situation and buy up horses for the rock-bottom price, then wait and sell them for much more once the local economy had improved.

Two days before Mother's Day, they slaughtered a pig that they had been raising and fattening at their various residences. Like the chancho sale described in the previous chapter, Amelia and Pablo sold about twenty portions at 3,000 pesos each. Their customers were people living in the parcelas and community nearby. The advertising to these neighbors was by word of mouth, and because it was Mother's Day, holiday business was good.

CONCLUSION: *LA GUERRA BRUTA*

Despite their hardships, Elena's plans to purchase a derecho in Loma Seca for daughter Isabel, and Pablo's investment in replacing his ordinary goats with more productive ones, demonstrate investments in this livelihood and a commitment beyond the trite description of "tradition." Pablo occasionally would joke that I was interested in understanding their fight in *la guerra bruta*. Before asking him to explain what he meant by this, I tried to think of various literal translations. The stupid war? The crude war? The hard war? *Bruta* or "gross" as in overall total? Perhaps a reference to the slang term for the "dirty war" of Pinochet's secret police? Pablo was (once again) playing with the language. He told me that he meant a little of all of these things. Yes, he meant the gross costs and profits of their various means of making a living. But this, he said, doesn't take into account the many sacrifices required to keep going, sacrifices that are not easily assigned a monetary value. Life is hard. The "war" is an uphill battle. At times it seems futile, an irrational, foolish endeavor for little gain. Though he joked that it is best to "work like a burro without thinking too much" (for one who thought too much would surely give up), throughout my time with his family he often discussed his careful consideration of the costs and benefits of these *sacrificios*. I would discover later the dark humor and personal meaning of his description, as he struggled to maintain the animals during the dry year, contemplating the pros and cons of various moves and even considering strong suggestions from some family members that he sell the animals and take a job in the city.

At no time are these sacrificios greater than during times when drought necessitates an itinerant lifestyle. In my second year in Loma Seca, Amelia and Pablo lived away from the community the entire time, moving their animals to various parts of the Limarí valley almost monthly from parcela to parcela, small landholdings from whose owners they rented idle, irrigated fields of pasture for their animals and modest dwellings from which they produced and sold their products. The sale of milk, cheese, and lamb varied depending upon the time of the year and their accessibility to buyers. The best that they could hope for was to offset the cost of moving the animals and renting the land with the hope that they could return to live in Loma Seca next year, provided that the drought ended. Although it was a struggle to meet this modest aim, by the time that I left Chile at the end of May 1999, it seemed as if they had succeeded. They had made it to the brink of winter, when they prayed they'd see rain.

My intention in this study is neither to valorize the community struggle in la guerra bruta nor to minimize the severity of the problems that they face. Had my fieldwork been limited to the drought year, my interpretations would have been biased toward the "elimination of the peasantry" perspective, as I would not have seen the positive results of the comunidad system. On the other hand, had I only been present for the "year of rain," in which the community was bustling with activity and productivity, I would have certainly leaned heavily on the "internal stability" view of persistence. Along with this temporal vicissitude, there was another dual nature to my work—to study both community culture and development policy. My goal was to identify specific social relations of production and to examine whether or not they conformed to the interpretations and recommendations of regional development agents. The assessment of the "success," "failure," or "rationality" of a particular form of production is relative to one's judgment criteria. In an area such as the Norte Chico, an economic model that does not go beneath the deceptively "nonproductive" economic veneer of rural poverty and fails to consider local culture, fails to get the whole picture.

To avoid such limitations, it is important to realize, as Godelier insists, that the rationality of any economic system (or the seeming "irrationality" of la guerra bruta?) is embedded in cultural life and social relations (1972, 317–18). Also, as Roseberry argued (in his example of Venezuelan coffee producers), continued production of a low-profit commodity "may fit within the reproduction strategy of the peasant household even when it makes no sense as part of a larger model of development" (1989b, 190). In the following chapter, I will describe the mode of production in Loma Seca, outline the production cycles that I have described here, and compare this family's economic strategies and individual resources with those of others. Understanding these individual strategies and how they are integrated with community relations will go a long way in understanding the "logic" of their toil. Within the context of community it can make sense as one part of something that is larger in the same way that within the context of a spirit of unity, that a single branch can be a Christmas tree.

7

Economic Strategies in a Peasant Community

INTRODUCTION

THE PREVIOUS CHAPTER PROVIDED A DETAILED ACCOUNT OF ONE family's extraordinary resiliency in maintaining its way of life and means of livelihood across drastically different climatic and economic conditions. Such adaptability is of particular importance in the unstable environment of the Norte Chico, but diversity in income and subsistence sources and flexibility in attaining them are keys to the persistence of peasant culture in general. Although these general characteristics describe what makes peasants unique, it is also important to recognize heterogeneity within communities in order to draw out what particular mechanisms make some families more successful than others. I will demonstrate in this chapter that in Loma Seca there is much variation in terms of individual livelihood, and there are considerable differences between households in terms of success in earning a living from the land. Available labor and flexibility are key factors of these differences. A good deal of this success depends upon the ability to adapt to environmental changes. As I have shown, in this part of Chile this often entails moving away from the geographic boundaries of the community during times of drought. Ideally, families have members remaining in the community while other members are engaged in income-generating activities in other areas.

In my last field season in Chile I conducted a household survey in Loma Seca, accounting for 39 households and 136 people. I present the data from that survey in this chapter. A previous community census taken in 1991 enumerated 196 residents living in 48 households. My survey was designed to record household size and makeup and the resources possessed and utilized by each family for both subsistence and income-generating purposes. Amount of family lluvia (rain-fed dryland) used for wheat production, number of family members participating in the group harvest, size of irrigated goce singular individual possession and use, livestock holdings, and sources of external income earned by family members were all recorded.

In order to put forward some general statements about prevalent productive strategies among families in this community, I have grouped the households into six categories based on family size and variety of resource possession and use. In order to put flesh and blood to these numbers and concepts, I will discuss variations in wealth and details of interfamily cooperation, and begin by briefly reviewing the family efforts described in the previous chapter.

FAMILY LIVELIHOOD (NOVEMBER 1997–MAY 1999)

Making use of a wide range of productive activities, Pablo and Amelia are among the most successful of the families in Loma Seca. A chronology of their actions during the time that I spent with them between November 1997 and May 1999 is represented in figure 7.1 Part a shows the changes in production and the movement of the family in response to rainfall and availability of pasture over the course of nineteen months. The period of November 1997 through June 1998, in which they all lived in Loma Seca and took advantage of the benefits to which they are entitled as members of the comunidad, is designated in the shaded area in part a. The primary advantages are free access to the campo común and shared production costs through their participation in group labor projects such as the group harvest (referred to here as la trilla) and the baño de ovejas. Part b of figure 7.1 shows the changes in costs and profits (in Chilean pesos) at these changing locales. The two greatest production costs—the renting of the machinery during the wheat harvest and the renting of pasture in the Limarí valley during the drought—are represented by the dotted line and shaded boxes.

From November 1997 through March 1998 they made cheese in the El Arroyo sector of Loma Seca. Over the course of the six-month production season they sold approximately 300 kilos of cheese. The market price fluctuated from 1000 pesos per kilo during the high production months of November and December to 1,800 pesos in March when production was down to just one or two cheeses per day. At an average price of 1,250 pesos per kilo, they made about 375,000 pesos (at the rate of 450 pesos per dollar, $833 U.S.) during that season.

They also periodically sold secondary products from their livestock. During the course of a year they sell about three truckloads, or *camionades*, of sheep and goat guano to farmers for use as fertilizer. Amelia reported earning about 120,000 pesos ($266 U.S.) from these sales. When he had the time to prepare them, Pablo occasionally

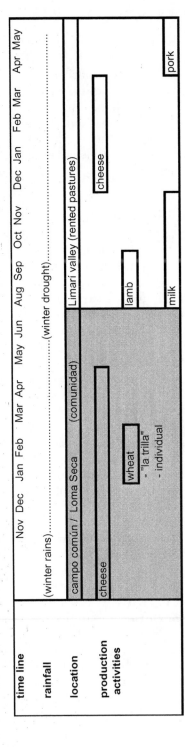

Figure 7.1a. Family production time line. (*Source:* Alexander 2004, 44.)

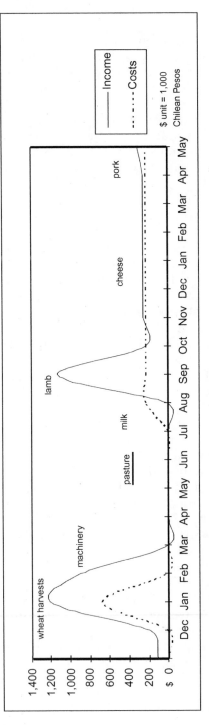

Figure 7.1b. Changing income and production costs. (*Source:* Alexander, 2004, 44.)

sold fine *artisano* sheepskins for 2,000 pesos to a leather dealer in Ovalle. After the Independence Day cordero vending, they sold the remaining lambskins and goatskins (cuero) for 500 to 1,000 pesos per skin.

Pablo, Gustavo, and Eduardo contributed labor to the group harvests in Nogales and La Mesa in late January. They each received fifty sacks of wheat. After depositing thirty sacks from this into the family bodega, they sold the remaining 120 sacks for 1,080,000 pesos ($2,400 U.S.). For their particular family harvest in early February, after storing another 3,600 kilos of wheat (another thirty sacks) for household consumption, they sold 13,974 kilos at 75 pesos per kilo for a total of 1,048,050 pesos ($2,329 U.S.) The cost of operating the combine harvester for forty hours at 18,500 pesos per hour was 740,000 pesos ($1,645 U.S.). This was taken out in wheat by the trillador (the harvester) who promptly sold it to the comprador (the buyer).

Since they were able to contribute three shares of labor to the group projects, the family could offset the extremely high cost of the harvester and more than double the money that they would have received had they only harvested their family lluvias. Figure 7.2 illustrates how their participation in the group harvest greatly increased both the amount of profit from sales and the amount of wheat that they could consume and keep as increased protection against upcoming lean years by stocking their bodega more heavily. As shown, the family harvest alone would have amounted to 27,441 kilos. Thirty-six percent of this, or 9,867 kilos, went toward the cost of the machinery. Thirteen percent of this, or 3,600 kilos, was designated for family consumption. Only the remaining 51 percent would have been sold. Combined, however, the family and group portions amounted to 45,441 kilos of wheat. The trillador's share only represented 21 percent of this total. The amount to go into the bodega doubled and represented 16 percent of the total. The amount sold for cash more than doubled to 28,374 kilos. It is easier to absorb the cost of production working together as a large group than as an individual family. Access to communal land and shared labor allowed them to considerably increase their individual production and reduce their individual net cost.

In addition, they harvested 2.5 hectares of barley in their lluvias. This was used primarily as feed for their livestock, principally for their twenty-two horses. They possess about one hectare of irrigated goce singular land. Most of this is used to grow alfalfa. A small portion is used to grow beans for the family's consumption. Along with the horses, they have five mules or burros, about twenty chickens, ten geese, and two pigs. Chickens were eaten on special occasions and kept the family supplied with eggs. None of the horses were sold

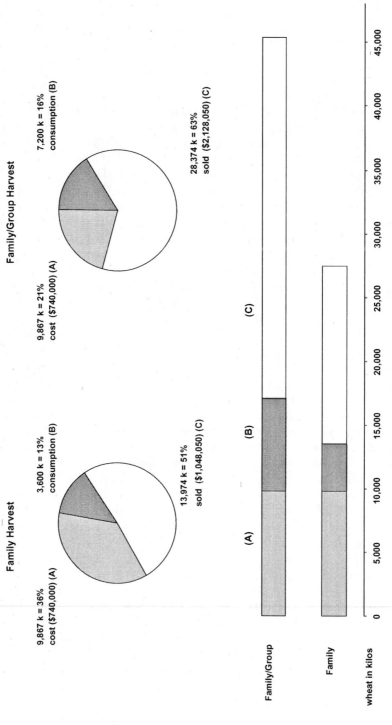

Figure 7.2. Comparison of family and group harvest strategies. (*Source:* Alexander.)

because of the low market price that year. One of the pigs was butchered and sold as the spicy delicacy chancho during Mother's Day weekend in 1999.

Wage labor income was primarily brought into the family by Gustavo. He worked for six months during 1997–98 on the highway construction project. After mining, highway construction is the most common employment for rural workers in this area. The widening of the stretch of Pan-American Highway between Los Vilos and La Serena was a major project and provided jobs for many people. As with any large construction job, it is the type of work making use of available menial labor, and there is a high turnover of employees. As it is a long-term project, it is there for people who wish to intermittently return to their homes to work for periods of time. Gustavo worked on this project for four months in 1997/1998 earning about 100,000 pesos ($222 U.S.) per month as the operator of a road grader. The job that he subsequently took as the night doorman at his aunt's hotel in Ovalle paid far less, but it provided him with a place to sleep and, most importantly, proximity to the various places where they were pasturing animals during the dry year allowed him to contribute labor to the family every day. During the previous year his construction job only allowed his return home on weekends.

The parcelas in the Limarí valley where they rented pasture between August 1998 and May 1999 cost them about 120,000 pesos ($267 U.S.) per month. They also were responsible for the expense of moving their animals to five different locations over the course of these nine months, as each move took many trips by truck. These added costs were ameliorated somewhat by their improved location to markets for their products. In September they made about $2,000 selling cordero during Independence Day. At San Julián they sold milk to the comprador who came by in the refrigerated truck. They averaged 900 liters per month from September to December. The price for milk fluctuated somewhat but was generally around 250 pesos per liter. This amounted to a cash intake of around 225,000 pesos ($500 U.S.) each month. They returned to focusing on cheese production for the remainder of their time away from the community because the subsequent places they rented were not easily accessible to the milk comprador and because the market price for cheese was relatively high because of the low regional production brought about by the drought. From January to March they produced an average of five kilos of cheese per day. Their own consumption of cheese was estimated to be about five kilos per month.

Family production earnings over the course of the nineteen months are broken down in figure 7.3. The brief period of wheat sales in late January and early February 1998 made up 41 percent of what they

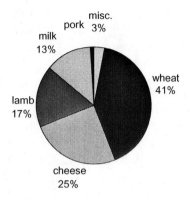

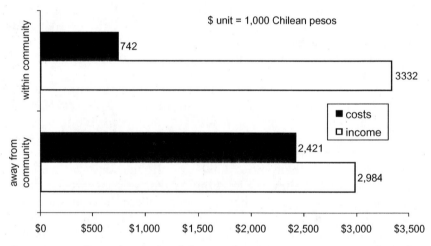

Figure 7.3. Family production breakdown and cost comparison. (*Source:* Alexander.)

earned. Cheese and milk sales made up much less, 25 percent and 13 percent, respectively, but were critical as constant sources of income for meeting the expense of renting land in the Limarí valley. Miscellaneous production made up 3 percent of the total, including things like the sale of guano and sheepskins. The large amount of Independence Day cordero sales represented another spurt of intense economic activity, but coming near the beginning of the long drought the income was steadily eaten away by the duration of the expense of living away from home. Figure 7.3 also illustrates the differences in costs and income between the time in which Pablo and Amelia lived in Loma

Seca and the period during which they migrated with their mobile means of production from parcela to parcela. From November 1997 through June 1998 they earned an estimated 3,332,000 pesos—the greatest part of which came from wheat sales. Their major expense was 742,000 pesos for paying the trillador. From July 1998 through May 1999 they earned an estimated 2,984,000 pesos from sales of lamb, cheese, and milk. Their major expense was 2,421,000 pesos for the renting of land. Thus, their real earnings were approximately 2,600,000 pesos (in Loma Seca) and 560,000 (in the Limarí) for a total of 3,160,000 pesos, which breaks down to about 166,300 pesos a month (or around $370 U.S. dollars) over the course of nineteen months. While their time in the Limarí allowed them easier access to markets for their products and a higher and prolonged production season for milk and cheese, the higher and prolonged production costs meant that they were just keeping their heads above water. Their resolve to return to the community as soon as they were able never faltered.

HOUSEHOLD SURVEY

In the following six sections, I present the results of the household survey. I have divided the thirty-nine households in Loma Seca into five groups based on amount and variety of resources and production activities over the course of the two years. Groups 1 and 2 are labeled "mixed production households" meaning that they both harvested wheat and possessed goats and/or sheep. Group 1 is made up of mixed production households harvesting individual lluvias of more than ten hectares. Pablo and Amelia's family is represented as Household 1 in Group 1. Households in Group 2 harvested ten hectares or less. Group 3 consists of households that harvested wheat but possessed no goats or sheep. Group 4 families are strictly crianceros (raising goats and sheep) who harvested no wheat. Families in Group 5 are labeled "nonproductive" households in that they earned neither money nor subsistence from the land. The final category, Group 6, is made up of families with no permanent residence in Loma Seca but which exercised their rights as comuneros to harvest wheat in 1997–98.

Group 1: Mixed Production Households Harvesting Lluvias of More than Ten Hectares (Table 7.1)

There are ten households in this group, with an average size of 4.9 people per household. The range of hectares of individual wheat harvests ranged from 8 to 40 hectares, with an average of 22.5 hectares of wheat per family. Six households harvested between less than one to

Table 7.1 Group 1: Mixed production, more than ten hectares of wheat

	household: total no., sex/age	wh	gr	b	gs	a	c	be	g	s	h	m	o	external income
									97–98/98–99	97–98/98–99				
1	7 m/37 f/32 m35+ m/30 f/70 m/13 m/8	30	***	2.5	1	1		f	140/120	185/195m	22	5	20c 10g 2p	+ highway construction, hotel doorman Ovalle
2	3 m/82+ f/69+ m/42	29		f	.5	.5f			70/72		3	3	Ico	+ pension
3	9 m/75 f/55 m/37+ m/36+ m/34 f/28 f/12 f/6 f/2	8	***	3	.5	.5			12/12	120/100m	6	4	30c	+ copper mines in Talca during week in '97; migrated to northern mines in '98
4	4 m/84 f/67 m/15 m/33	30	*		1	.5		f	80/80	70/70				
5	2 m/65+ f/61	20	*	20		10		10	160/150	60/70m				+ pension
6	5 m/70+ f/70+ m/40 m/38 f/8	15	**	f	1		f	f	15/15	40/40	3	1	10c	+ pension
7	5 m/67 f/65 m/37 +m/32++ m/25	12	***		1		f	f		110/110m	5		12c	+ laborer in Ovalle ++ miner, returned for harvest in '97
8	3 f/76 f/32 m/38	21	**		1					30/30	2	3		
9	9 m/69+ f/58++ f/48 f/39 f21x f/18x m/11af f/10af m/6af	20	*	12	2	1	1			260/280m	10	2	20c	+ pension; ++ cook in school; x clerks in Ovalle, send money home
10	2 m/65 m/58	40	**						150/20	140/140m				

key

af = assignación familiar
(cultivation. in hectares unless designated f = small amount for family consumption)

wh = family wheat

gr = shares in group project

b = barley

gs = goce singular (permanently irrigated possession)

a = alfalfa

c = corn

be = beans

(no. of animals)

g = goats

s = sheep, m = moved goats and sheep away from the community during winter 1998

h = horses

m = mules or burros

o = others, c = chickens, g = geese, p = pigs, co = cows

twelve hectares of barley. Nine of the families participated in group harvest projects. With five of these families having more than one member participating, there was an average of two members per household contributing to the group projects. Eight households possessing irrigated goce singular land (ranging in size from .5 to 2 hectares) used it to grow corn and beans for family consumption, alfalfa for animal consumption, or some combination thereof.

Six of the ten households kept both goats and sheep, with the average size of the holdings being 111 goats and 123 sheep in 1997. Of the four households with either goats or sheep, three kept sheep (with an average size of 133 in 1997) while one (Household 2) kept 70 goats during that year.

All have at least one member bringing income from an external source into the family. Six of these are solely in the form of pension benefits, while four families received money from wage labor earned during the year. These jobs include Gustavo's work on highway construction and at the hotel in Ovalle (Household 1), work in copper mines (Households 3 and 7), general labor in Ovalle (Household 7), clerical work in Ovalle (Household 9), and as school cook in Loma Seca (Household 9). Household 9 received the most external income with the male head of household receiving the small state welfare retirement pension (*jubilación*), his wife working as the school cook, and two daughters working as clerks in Ovalle during the week. In addition, an unmarried daughter received *assignación familiar* (state assistance) for the care of three young children. Households 3 and 7 benefited from the return migration of males in the copper mines. Two brothers in Household 3 worked at a copper mine near the city of Talca (five hundred kilometers to the south) in 1997, returning to Loma Seca in the summer to assist in the wheat harvest. In 1998 they relocated to a northern mine and did not return home since their labor was not needed. A thirty-two-year-old male in Household 11 who also worked in the same northern mine did the same.

Group 2: Mixed Production Households Harvesting Lluvias of Ten Hectares or Less (Table 7.2)

There are eighteen households with an average size of 2.6 members per household, considerably less than the previous group. This reduced size is because of the permanent emigration of household members. In turn, this diminished number of laborers within the household— either full-time residents of the community or those working at jobs that permit trips home to contribute labor at key times—precludes the harvesting of lluvias as large as those of Group 1. Two individuals—a

Table 7.2 Group 2: Mixed production, ten or less hectares of wheat

household	wh	gr	b	gs	a	c	be	g	s	h	m	o	external income
								97–98/98–99	97–98/98–99				
11	5 m/49 f/42 f/21+ f/18 m/21	5	*							60/60	1	2		+emigrated for work in '98
12	4 m/54 f/54 f/20 f/17	4	*							50/45	2	6		
13	2 m/74+ m/36	5	**						30/30	1/1	10	6	3c	+pension
14	2 m/35+ f/34			.5	.5		f	f	5/5	3/3				+school construction
15	1 f/82+	5	*	.5	.5	.25			15/10					+pension
16	5 m/42 f/46 m/20+f/18f/6	5	*	.5	.5	.5			55/30	16/10		3	10c	+emigrated for work in '98
17	3 m/49 f/80+ f/54	4	*	.25	.25	.25			20/15	20/19	3	1	10c	+pension
18	4 f/66+ f/47 f/21 m/11	3	*						30/0		7	7		
19	2 m/60 f/61	10	*	.25	.25	.25				150/150m	2	7	20c	

(continued)

Table 7.2 (*continued*)

household	wh	gr	b	gs	a	c	be	g	s	h	m	o	external income
20	1 m/38			.5	.5	.5				14/14				
21	2 f/78+ m/58	4	*						35/35	30/30				+ pension
22	2 m/38 m/12	5			.5		.5		95/80	195/72m	8	4	8c	
23	1 m/58	10	*						140/97	79/87m		1	1c	
24	2 f/85+ m/50	4					.5		45/40	45/35m		2	2c	+pension
25	5 m/37 f/31 m/9 m/5 m/3 f/1 f/ i	10							40/37		2	4	4c	
26	1 m/58	5	*	1.5	1.5	1	.5		60/80	125/150m	5	2		
27	2 m/58 m/43	10	**							30/30	8	3		
28	2 m/51 m/66+	8	**	.5	.5	.5				36/31	2	1	7c 4co	+pension

twenty-one-year-old female in Household 11 and a twenty-year-old male in Household 16—left in 1998 to begin lives in the city. Six families received income from members' pensions. The only wage earner in Group 2 is a thirty-five-year-old male in Household 14 who worked in Loma Seca on the school construction project.

The size of individual wheat harvests ranged from 3 to 10 hectares, with an average size of 5.4 per family. Seven households grew some barley, between .25 to 1.5 hectares. Thirteen of these families participated in the group projects, with only three families contributing more than one member and none more than two. Nine households possessing irrigated goce singular land (ranging in size from .25 to 1.5 hectares) used it to grow corn, beans, and alfalfa for domestic use.

Nine of the eighteen households had both goats and sheep, with the average size of the holdings of these nine families being 54 goats and 57 sheep in 1997. Of the nine households with either goats or sheep, only six kept sheep (with an average size of 57 in 1997) while only three had goats (with an average size of 28 in 1997).

Group 3: Households with Lluvias but without Goats or Sheep (Table 7.3)

There are five households in this group. The average size is 4.4 members. With the exception of Household 29 (which harvested forty hectares of wheat), the amount of lluvia utilized per household was between five and ten hectares. Three of the five households participated in the group harvests. These families grew small amounts of corn, beans, and barley for family consumption. External income plays an important part for these groups with seven (five males and two females) of thirteen working-age adults receiving wages from outside sources. Three of these worked within Loma Seca. Their jobs include schoolteacher, laborer on the school construction project, and temporary work as a carpenter. The other four worked in Ovalle and returned home periodically. Three brothers in Household 30 were general laborers in Ovalle, leaving their widowed father and younger brother to work at home. During the first year the three worked for wages sporadically, returning home for the wheat harvest. They turned to full-time employment during the next year. A thirty-two-year-old female in Household 31 worked in Ovalle as a domestic servant during the week, returning to Loma Seca on the weekends.

The next two groups represent the most impoverished households in the community. They are people with no comuneros living in the family. Though not entitled to lluvias or the right to pasture animals on the campo común, they may pay a fee in order to rent land for this

Table 7.3 Group 3: Wheat, no sheep or gotas

	household	wh	gr	b	gs	a	c	be	h	m	o	external income
29	5 m/41 f/31+ f/75++ f/6 m/4	40	*		.6	.3	.3		1		40c 9co	+ teacher in Loma Seca ++ pension
30	5 m/58 m/25+ m/23+ m/19+ m/17	10		1			.5	1	5	2	10c	+laborers in Ovalle, returned for harvest in '97; full time employment in '98
31	8 f/64 f/32+ f/24 f/20 f/18 m/16 f/11 m/16 f/2	10	*								20c 10t	+domestic servant in Ovalle, lives in Loma Seca on weekends
32	1 m/58+	5										+school construction
33	3 m/54+ f/40 m/1	5	*	f		.25			1	2	18c 6t	+'maestro de construcción," temporary work

r = rents lluvia from community

privilege. Six of the 39 households (comprised of 19 of the 136 people accounted for) fall into this category. These are people who have been excluded from getting a derecho—often women who have been abandoned by their husbands or their families or younger children of comuneros who were not entitled to inherit the title but have chosen to stay in the community and for whatever reason are estranged from their families. They pay the nominal fee of 5,000 pesos a year for the right to live here, and they give 10 percent of their goats and sheep to the community. The animals are sold and the money goes into the comunidad fund. Elena described this as a form of charity from the community to the poorest and derecho-less families, a way of taking care of those who lack the valuable right and title of comunero.

Group 4: Criancero Households without Lluvias (Table 7.4)

Four households make up this group. Only one, Household 36, had livestock holdings of considerable size (70 goats and 55 sheep) while the others held 20 or less. This household did not harvest any wheat of its own but did participate in and receive a share of the group harvests. They did not report receiving money from any external sources, relying solely on the products of their livestock. The other three households depend almost solely on small wage incomes. Households 34 and 35 produced small amounts of milk and cheese for self-consumption. The male head of Household 35 participated in the construction of the new schoolhouse in Loma Seca. Household 37 consists of a single male who reported earning about two hundred dollars a month herding sheep for others while paying the nominal fee to pasture his own small flock. Household 34 is headed by a single female. Her eldest daughter worked as a domestic servant in Ovalle during the week while she cared for the three younger children.

Group 5: Nonproductive Households (Table 7.5)

The two households in this group consist of a single retired woman living alone (38) and a spouseless mother of three young children (39). The widow receives the jubilación state retirement pension of 30,000 pesos ($66 U.S.) per month. The mother of three receives the assignación familiar state support for her children. She was also to be one of the beneficiaries of the Pro-Casa comités efforts to raise money for a house until the drought put their efforts on hold. People who are in financial need and do not have a separate house in the community, who are starting a family on their own, or whose house was destroyed by the earthquake or is in disrepair may petition the state for money to

Table 7.4 Group 4: Goats or sheep only

	household	gr	g	s	h	m	o	external income
34	5 f/36 f/18+ m/13 m/10 f/8		20/20r		2	1	3c	+domestic servant in Ovalle
35	4 m/46+ f/29 m/6 f/5		20/15					+school construction
36	4 m/35 f/30 m/55 f/93	* (4h)	70/70	55/55	1		10	
37	1 m/48+		20/20#					+herds sheep for others

Table 7.5 Group 5: Nonproductive households

	Household	o	external income
38	1 f/71+	10c	+ pension
39	4 f/35 f/7 af f/5af m/2af		af = assignación familiar

construct a simple dwelling. As with the other projects, the comité stages events to raise money for these people and the government provides matching funds. In the meantime the mother was living in various available spaces in and around the community. Estranged from her family because of her out-of-wedlock children (she had not been married to any of the children's fathers), she was dependent upon state support and the charity of others. For a while she was our neighbor in the campo común with Amelia occasionally babysitting for her children when she had to make trips to Ovalle.

Group 6: Households Living away from the Community Harvesting Lluvias (Table 7.6)

This table represents the families of three comuneros who do not live in Loma Seca, but who harvested wheat as an income supplement. Since they have emigrated permanently from the community, I did not give them a numerical designation. The head of the six-member household living in Ovalle is the full-time owner of a fishing pier (a *muelle micro-empresa* or small-business pier) renting to tourists and others for recreational fishing on a tributary of the Limarí. A single sixty-

Table 7.6 Group 6: Households living away from the community harvesting lluvias

Household	wh	b	external income
6 m/38 f/35 m/15 m/12 m/6 m/6	10	10	"muelle" or small business in Ovalle
1 m/68	20		mechanic in Ovalle
2 m/66 f/60	4		retired, living in Santiago

eight-year-old mechanic also living in Ovalle supplemented his income by exercising his right as a comunero by working twenty hectares of lluvia. A retired couple living in Santiago maintains a house in Loma Seca where they occasionally visit and where they spend the summers. They participated in the harvest in a limited fashion, harvesting and selling the products of four hectares of lluvia. Houses, like the goce singular land that they often adjoin, are "owned" and are "private property" in all respects except that one could not sell it to someone outside of the community without community approval.

Group Comparison

The breakdown of the five group categories within the community as a whole is shown in figure 7.4. The great majority of families (72 percent, or 28 of 39 households) are involved in mixed production strategies utilizing both livestock and wheat cultivation (Groups 1 and 2). Of the remaining 28 percent, the five families comprising Group 3—those households harvesting wheat but having neither goats nor sheep—are the most engaged in earning a living from the land. Tellingly, each of these five families is also, to varying degrees, dependent upon outside sources of income. Seven of thirteen of all adults of working age (both male and female and here between the ages of eighteen to fifty-eight) earned wages either in the community or in

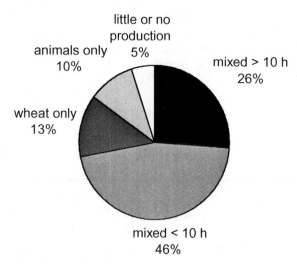

Figure 7.4. Production category distribution within the community.

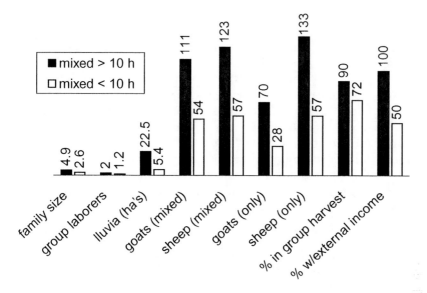

Figure 7.5. Comparison of Groups 1 and 2.

Ovalle. This is possible because while livestock need daily attention, cereal cultivation only requires large amounts of labor at key times. The six families in the remaining two groups are economically marginal households without rights as comuneros. As the most impoverished in the community, they rely heavily on the charity of the community and state assistance.

Since they represent nearly three-quarters of the households in Loma Seca, and because they rely on the traditional means of combining economic strategies, the twenty-eight households in Groups 1 and 2 warrant comparison. In addition to size of family wheat harvest, figure 7.5 demonstrates that on average families harvesting more than 10 hectares of wheat in 1997 greatly exceeds families harvesting 10 hectares in eight other indicators. The ten households in Group 1 harvested an average of 22.5 hectares per family lluvia, while the eighteen households in Group 2 harvested an average of 5.4 hectares. In terms of major livestock holdings per family, Group 1 leads in size of goat herd for families owning both goats and sheep (111 to 54) size of sheep herd for families owning both goats and sheep (123 to 57); size of goat herd for families only owning goats (70 to 28); and size of sheep herd for families only owning sheep (133 to 57). In terms of family size and extent to which they participated in the group harvest, families in the first group naturally hold a distinct advantage. The average size (that is, the number of members who live in Loma Seca full-time or adults who work away from the community but frequently return to contribute labor) of the household in Group 1 was 4.9 in 1997. For Group 2 this number was 2.8 per family in 1997. Ninety percent of the families in Group 1 contributed labor to and received shares from the group harvest, while 72 percent of the families in Group 2 did so. For those families who participated in the group harvest, the average number of shares per family in Group 1 was 2, while the average in Group 2 was 1.2. Finally, in addition to having a larger available supply of labor for family farmwork, all of the households in Group 1 received income from external sources while only 50 percent of those in Group 2 had at least one family member bringing in money via wage labor or pension.

Comparison of Groups 1 and 2

The two charts in figure 7.6 and figure 7.7 show the household-by-household farm production activities for Groups 1 and 2. The charts correspond to the information presented in table 7.1 and table 7.2. For these small families in Group 2, cultivating small amounts of wheat and participation in the group harvest (for those with the available labor to contribute to it) is very important. Ten households in Group 2 received shares of wheat in the group project more than or equal to the amount that they produced in their individual lluvias. Producing at a reduced level their costs are relatively smaller and the amount that they can sell or consume is relatively higher.

For example, Household 11, in harvesting only 5 individual hectares would have taken on about one-sixth the production costs that my host family (who harvested 30 hectares) incurred. Therefore, although Household 11 only received two shares of the group harvest (while Pablo's family received three shares), only a quarter of this would go toward paying for the machinery for their individual production while for my host family nearly all of it was absorbed as production expense. Putting it another way (and extrapolating from the previously analyzed data from Pablo's harvest), 30 hectares of Pablo's wheat is reduced to 19.2 hectares once the trillador is paid (10.8 hectares is required to yield the price of renting the harvester). Adding the 6 hectares per share yield of the group harvest almost doubles their total to 37.2 hectares. For Household 11, 5 hectares of wheat in their lluvia is reduced to 3.2 hectares after paying the trillador. Adding 12 hectares for two shares of the group harvest nearly quintuples their total to 15.2 hectares.

For Pablo and Amelia's family, like most other families in Group 1, access to communal land and participation in the group harvest

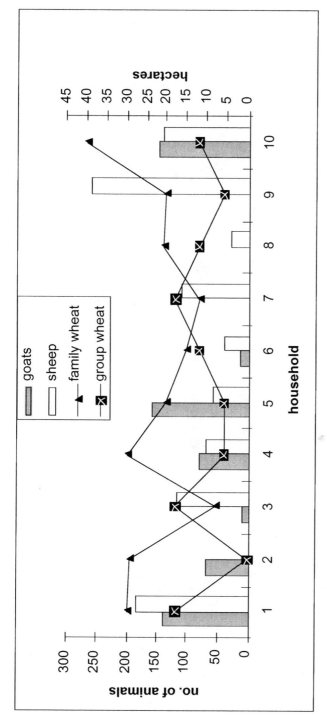

Figure 7.6. Diversity of production breakdown by households havesting < 10 hectares. (*Source:* [Alexander 2004, 45].)

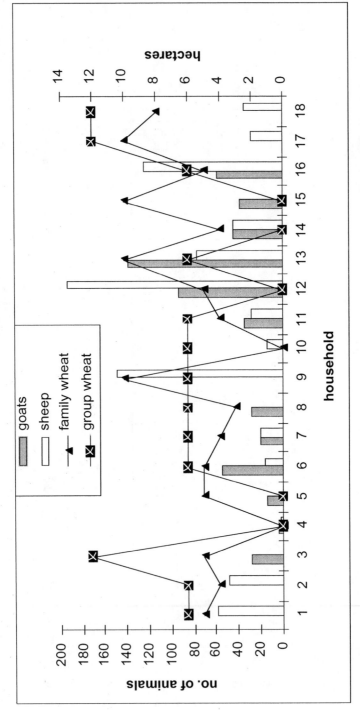

Figure 7.7. Diversity of production breakdown by households harvesting > 10 hectares. (*Source:* [Alexander 2004, 45].)

allowed them to make the most of their available labor and increase their production of wheat. The work in the wheat fields in Loma Seca is an almost exclusively male activity (although women play an important role in providing food for the laborers; women and children tend to be more heavily involved in herding goats and making cheese). With three adult males living in the household, they maximized their production to a relatively high output during the year of rain. For Household 11, access to communal land and participation in the group harvest allowed them to similarly make the most of their available hands. This labor was far less than that of Pablo's family and was somewhat tenuous in nature. Only two adult males were living in the community during the harvest, and one of these, a twenty-one-year-old son, emigrated along with a twenty-year-old daughter to the city in 1998 in search of a permanent job.

In general, households in Group 2 are smaller and have a diminished labor supply affected by out-migration of younger members looking for paid employment. Households in Group 1 are larger, and having attained a kind of "critical mass" of available labor and greater production levels for all major activities (wheat, sheep, goats) produce more for external markets. (Another indicator of this greater supply of labor is that the average number of male members between the working ages of 15 and 65 in Group 1 is 1.8 per household, with an average age of 35 years. In Group 2, the average number per family of male household members in this age group is 1.05, with an average age of 42.7.) Both groups benefit from community membership but in different ways. The households in Group 1, in combining group resources, with individual resources produced more with more. The households in Group 2 in combining group resources with individual resources produced more with less.

INTERFAMILY RECIPROCITY

As mentioned at the end of chapter 5 the collaborative efforts of different households is recognized by insiders and outsiders alike as one of the keys to Loma Seca's success in comparison to other comunidades. My survey shows that only a handful of families with a critical mass of working members living at home did not participate at all in any interfamilial exchanges of labor via the group wheat harvest. What accounts for such widespread involvement? First of all, there are different kinds of reciprocal bonds that are established. As to be expected, there is kin-based reciprocity between blood or affinal relations living in separate households. Such family bonds are typically both strong and informal, entailing exchanges and obligations that individuals can both expect to receive and are expected to contribute. Other bonds are kinds of working partnerships between particular families that have been built up over time. Some of these successful relationships have lasted over generations. Both of these bonds of support and trust are the primary informal connections that an individual will rely upon during times of need, with the family usually being the first line of assistance and obligation. Of course, in both relationships a measure of independence is valued as well. Anecdotally, I was told that individuals perceived as too needy and dependent upon the help of others are looked upon as suspiciously as those who are seen as miserly or untrustworthy.

At the same time, the comunidad structure provides a framework by which agreements to work collectively are formalized. Records are kept of participants and their expected contributions, pretty strict bookkeeping is maintained, and many prefer this arrangement as a protection against unmet obligations. Grievances over reneged payments are adjudicated through the Directiva in the same way that disputes over boundaries and land issues are settled.

Informal social sanctions are also effective means of mediation. Individuals who are exposed as dishonest or negligent in meeting their expected contribution, in terms of providing labor or sharing surplus, are ostracized and will undoubtedly not be invited to participate in future efforts. As in most rural communities, one's reputation is everything, especially when interfamily reciprocity is so crucial for a family's well-being. Some of those few households that were not part of the group project were excluded—or opted not to participate—because of such strained social relations. However, as it was described to me, considering the increasing need for farmers to work together and the unpredictability of success from year to year, there is much pressure to abide by the consensus and to put aside such differences. Now more than ever the cosecha is a critical complement to household income. Years in which such harvests are even possible are few and sometimes far between, making them special events in which rivalries and disagreements—petty or otherwise—are more likely to be dropped in favor of working together.

Neither a "Tragic Commons" nor a "Limited Good"

There are several areas that, I was told, had led to competing factions in the past. When those families who have achieved a higher level of productivity and who have a large number of workers living at home or nearby can save enough money to buy additional derechos from others, concentration of rights within households can be a problem. This can cause resentment from or public sympathy for the individual who decides that he or she no longer can or no longer wants to try to make a go of it and opts to cash in the right to use the land for a sum of cash now. When there is more than one successful individual competing to buy this derecho, factionalism can ensue and can be especially acrimonious when a family or group of households representing the interest of a family group holds a large portion of voting rights in group meetings. Access to the naturally irrigated plots located near water sources can also be a sensitive topic due to the fact that water is scarce and these plots are small in size and number. These possessions are set, with the oldest most established households generally claiming hereditary ownership of them.

Such competition in the Directiva can also arise over decisions regarding the development of common land for group projets, with families arguing over which commodities to produce for market and the relative costs and benefits of each. It is not uncommon for those groups who have experience in producing a particular crop or who have connections at the markets in town to try to make a case that is advantageous to their interests. The Directiva works to build a consensus, but with all such compromises, hard feelings can die slowly. Along these same lines, since development agencies for the most part work with individual families, not with communities as a whole, the more successful families are the ones likely to solicit and receive the assistance. As I will discuss in the next chapter, such favoritism can be an issue, and can aggravate among the "unfavored" feelings of suspicion toward state intervention in community affairs. This is something that is particularly painful in a country only recently emerged from dictatorship. There is certainly lingering resentment from the priveleged treatment that favored individuals and families in the countryside received during the military regime, and the government is now wise to be sensitive to the ways in which such divisiveness can hinder the success rates of their projects.

In general, factionalism did not appear to be a major problem in Loma Seca at the time of my fieldwork, but it is important to recognize such differentials in wealth and influence. All of this is relevant to the thesis of this book, as coverd in the first two chapters. Recognition of this differentiation in the community is important so as to avoid romanticizing or giving unrealistic representations of communitarian "otherness"—the inward-focused, persistent view of peasantry from chapter 2. At the same time, there are distinct, important aspects of the community structure that modify and shape such potentially destructive differentiation in ways that the capitalist-centric "proletarianiza-tion" or "elimination" of the peasantry perspective from chapter 2 also cannot account for.

Additionally, in their assessments of the problems of the com-unidades, many rural economic development and environmental re-source management experts seem to rely, explicitly or indirectly, on assumptions about peasant culture and common property that were put forth and debated in the social sciences beginning in the 1960s. To me, two theories that first expressed these assumptions upon which much policy in the region appears to be predicated are Foster's "Image of Limited Good" (1965) and Hardin's "Tragedy of the Commons" (1968). The suppositions of both seem to place limits on sustainable economic development and growth within peasant communities: the first "ideologically" or "cognitively" by stereotyping peasant "cogni-tive orientation" as individualistic and fearful of risk and progress; the second "structurally" or "materially" by assuming that there are in-herent elements in common property that prevent it from being effec-tively managed and conserved. Such positions, it seems, justify state intervention. As peasants reproduce their domestic economy through their relationship with external capitalism, they also reproduce, among other things, their specific community forms of resource conservation and mutual assistance. These local institutions, whether explicitly "economic" (in a conventional sense) or not, are key components of the mode of production. They are important parts of the culturally specific "how (not why)" in Nugent's rephrased question in chapter 2.

The appearance of communitarian ideals and practices contradict much prevailing thought about the nature of the peasantry. In *The Eighteenth Brumaire of Louis Bonaparte,* Marx explained the inability of the mid-nineteenth-century French peasantry to develop a revolu-tionary consciousness of its own as a corollary to the conservatism, near self-sufficiency, and lack of internal cohesion inherent in the mode of production of smallholders (1994, 123–24). Forgetting that Marx was writing about a specific peasantry with its own particular historically created inventory of limits, choices, and possibilities, oth-ers have extended his observations to construct general explanations as to why peasants are ill-suited to act together as a group. In Foster's "Image of the Limited Good," peasants are reluctant to accept leader-ship and maximum cooperation aimed toward collective change be-cause the harsh realities of scraping out a living engender a supposedly shared cognitive orientation that ironically favors, through cultural institutions that control behavior, extreme individualism over orga-nized shared responsibility (1965, 304–15). Foster believed that he had identified a "cognitive orientation" based on poverty and subordination (specific to peasants but applicable to any group under the same restraints) that regards the world as one in which wealth and opportunity are "always finite and in short supply" (296). This worldview patterns peasant behavior as individualistic, uncooperative in areas outside of the family, and afraid to upset the balance of wealth in the community because of local institutions that maintain the equilibrium through negative sanctions against those who change economic position. This equilibrium creates a static economy and resistance to programs of economic development (Foster 1965, 293–95; 303–5).

As I have recalled a number of times so far, the "mentality" of "the comunero" is frequently described by outsiders (and some insiders!) as selfish, hyperindividualistic, and stubborn. Drawing upon this characterization of resistance to change and suspicion toward outsiders, one might add the word "paranoid," and considering their historical marginalization and treatment during the Pinochet regime in particular, one could scarcely call suspicion unjustified. This is the reality that those set on bringing structural changes to the comunidad system are up against. Others have compared, without irony, the set number of titles to shares of stock in a privately owned corporation (Rosenfeld 1993). From the outside, they appear to hold a monopoly on something of little value, but I have attempted here to show otherwise. It is also important to recall that Foster himself said that for those in this structural position of marginalization "the good" in actuality probably *is* limited. With improved access to education, health care, and the benefits enjoyed by other segments of society, Foster observed that the "image of limited good" diminished.

Leveling mechanisms in which individuals willingly engage might suggest the community forms of wealth redistribution present in Foster's "Limited Good" model, however, rather than born of suspicion of individual success, it is more a result of a cognizance of the *shared* good of life improvements at the community level. Also, because of the ability to rely upon group labor at key times, individual production is enhanced. This is why I call this community a mixed mode of subsistence, individual, and communal production. At the family level many, of course, include wage labor as a key part of this mix. Finally, and critically, this casts doubt on "stasis" and "equilibrium" as a final cause, as these group efforts maximize capital accumulation in the countryside rather than work against it.

While many outsiders seem to believe that something like the "Image of the Limited Good" works to impede capitalist development in these communities, another common misconception deals with the incompatibility of common property and resource conservation. In the "Tragedy of the Commons," Hardin, who was primarily interested in understanding overpopulation, used the allegory of a common-property pasture to express his belief that uncontrolled freedom to produce children is ushering the world toward disaster. As the parable goes, initially there is little damage to the pasture, but as more animals are added overgrazing results. Even so, it is nevertheless still "rational" for herders to continue to add animals. This is because each herder individually gains the profit from additional animals, while the cost in erosion and soil depletion is shared by all. Ultimately, "freedom in a commons brings ruin to all" (Hardin 1968, 1244). Ironically, Hardin's theory was picked up by the environmental movement beginning in the 1960s to advocate government control of resource use, as opposed to Hardin's belief in the individualization of rights.

Acheson demonstrated how anthropology has shown that the assumptions that (1) all common property users are individualistic profit maximizers who overexploit resources at the expense of society as a whole, (2) all people have the technical capacity to surpass the resource renewal rate, (3) communities are unable or refuse to establish institutions to sufficiently protect resources, and (4) government intervention and private property are the only way to halt the inevitable outcome of the "tragedy" do not hold up under cross-cultural comparison. Communities are capable of creating effective conservation institutions and rules that limit rates of exploitation. In this respect, Acheson makes the distinction between communal property as either an "open-access" or "controlled-access" resource (1989, 357–58). In Acheson's terminology, the land of the comunidades is a controlled-access resource. The comunidad structure engenders a restricted number of use rights and sets limits upon its use. In generating such rules or institutions to manage resources, they are creating what Mancur Olson called a "public or collective good" (1965, 15). As Acheson points out, rational individuals will join a collective effort only when there are what Olson identifies as "selective incentives" that negate the "free rider problem" (1989, 373). McCay and Jentoft remind us that although Hardin is often attributed (by opponents of his view) with revealing that the irony of "the commons" is that there really is no "community," what he is really saying is that in the context of common property the individual is faced with the "double-bind of being condemned for not being a responsible citizen, on the one hand, and for not being a rational individual on the other" (1998, 22).

The suppositions of both the "Image of the Limited Good" and the "Tragedy of the Commons" seem to justify state intervention and suggest a selective reading of the history of the articulation of peasant production with capitalist development. In the examples that I provide, this reading entails (1) the ascription of ethnicity and identity based on local economic practice (chapter 8) while ignoring (2) the important role that this form of production has historically played and continues to play in regional development (chapters 3 and 4), (3) the part that detrimental capitalist development has played in creating environmental problems (chapters 3 and 4), and (4) the part that articulation with the capitalist mode through labor migration has played in reproducing the specific social relations of production (chapter 5) at the community level. To restate, while theories such as "The Image of the Limited Good" and "Tragedy of the Commons" are largely discredited in cultural anthropology, their assumptions are nonetheless implicit in a good deal of development and environmental policy. Still, since as social theory they are outdated, I may risk the accusation of setting up a "straw man" in making my argument, yet in practice in the development milieu I contend that they persist. Perhaps a "tin man"— or "heartless"—accusation would be more accurate in an assessment of some of the harsher policies.

RISK MANAGEMENT BEYOND THE INDIVIDUAL/COMMUNAL DISTINCTION

In chapter 5 I described functional relations between comuneros and non-comuneros via the group efforts of the comités. Just as many development workers have told me that Loma Seca is, in their words, unusually "forward thinking," the director of the organization in Ovalle to which the communities solicit projects spoke very favorably about the success of the Loma Seca comités. In many communities, I was told, there are often conflicts and differences between the *junta de vecinos* (the organization of residents not possessing rights as comuneros) and the Directiva (the community political body of comuneros). The *vecinos* tend to be younger and more "progressive" and are more likely to make proposals and solicit projects than "comuneros." For example, in the comunidad of Salala (one of the "Punitaqui System" comunidades), there had been recent conflicts between the Directiva and the vecinos over the placement of a community reservoir. On the other hand, I was assured, people in Loma Seca have had much more success in collaboratively coordinating their projects than in many other places.

If this is true, why is it the case? I contend that there is a reciprocal articulated relationship between "community" and "individual" ideals in the community of Loma Seca. As demonstrated, individuals can maximize their productivity during good years by combining group efforts with individual efforts. It is in their individual interests, then, for the community to function as a community. At the same time, the non-comuneros benefit from the success of individuals because the value that is gained from this availability of human resources is reinvested into the community in the social welfare projects of the various comités. Just as there is a mutually formative dialectical relationship between communities and agents of development (domestic production is articulated with copper mining via labor migration; petty commodity production is articulated with regional markets via development policy), there is an internal dialectical relationship within communities between comuneros and non-comuneros. The common ground is the community structure, which (1) subsumes opposed interests into manageable positions while (2) making both individual and communitarian goals possible. As discussed previously, such a process makes both the supposed deficiencies of "tragic commons" and the "limited good" (as argued, based on shaky cultural assumptions) untenable in my example from Loma Seca. Many observers feel that at times the state's use of intermediary entities to distribute assistance to the comunidades is a divisive process that serves to disperse resistance against state policies. My argument is that potential rupture between the comuneros and the vecinos based upon conflicting interests in the community that I have described is tempered by a reciprocally beneficial tension that spawns institutions of assistance. This bond between "the community" and "the individual" is best understood as one of the many risk management tools available to families in Loma Seca and other communities like it.

Such management of both environmental and human resources are outcomes of what I will define in the concluding chapter of this book as "Mutable Mobile Modes of Resource Maximization." Spatially expansive and flexible and made up of integrated elements of both community and individual rationality and motives, such a system has the capacity to adapt to changing economic and resource-use opportunities so as to maximize the productivity of the unique human ecology it comprises. Community members frequently engage in group activities whose benefits are shared by all, and the community has its own particular institutions and rules for conserving and distributing resources. On the environmental side, this includes limits to the number of derechos, restricted access to common land by both insiders and outsiders, and decision-making processes dealing with the use of natural resources. On the human side, group projects get the most out of available labor power for productive families and, importantly, traditions and structures that disperse wealth and bolster common good projects from which non-comuneros and less advantaged families can benefit temper the negative effects that such limits to rights and access naturally engender. The comunidad system, like many other peasant societies, I contend, is situated beyond the individual/communal binary distinction that, in Levi-Straussian terms, is to the Western, capitalist mind so "good to think."

FORMS OF DIVERSITY

Diversity is the key to survival in this unforgiving environment. Although the households in these two groups have different internal characteristics and therefore different production goals and activities, they are each part of and participate in a common structure that, it might be said, allows one to get from it what one puts into it. The majority of the families in Loma Seca satisfy, in different proportions, a certain percentage of their own food needs. Almost every household designates at least some part of its efforts toward producing food for itself. This includes the cultivation of vegetables (primarily beans and corn) in the small parcels of irrigated goce singular land. Alfalfa is also grown there to support livestock. The primary products of these animals are goat cheese, goat milk, goat carne, and lamb cordero. To a lesser extent, sustenance also comes from the products of chickens, turkeys, geese, pigs, and cows. The land and climate is insufficient for complete subsistence production for an extended period of time. Nevertheless, subsistence production plays an important role as a supplement during good times as well as during the leanest of times. The majority of the families in Loma Seca also produce, to varying degrees and depending upon environmental conditions, farm commodities both large-scale (wheat) and petty (goat cheese) for external national and regional markets (the wheat buyer came from Santiago; most cheese is sold in Ovalle or La Serena; Pablo sold milk to a factory in Santiago). Most households also have members who periodically engage in wage labor away from the community or who earned a pension from wage work during earlier years. Finally, this community, like all of the comunidades agrícolas in this part of northern Chile, suffers from restricted access to capital. This was most evident in the significant portion of the wheat harvest that was exchanged for use of the harvesting machinery. Geographic isolation of these communities also restricts access to markets for their products.

I have shown in my example of this community that there is much variation in terms of individual livelihood, and there are considerable differences between households in terms of success in earning a living from the land. Available labor and flexibility are key factors of these differences. A good deal of this success depends upon the ability (or willingness) to adapt to environmental changes. In this part of Chile this often entails moving away from the physical confines of the community during times of drought. Ideally, families such as Pablo and Amelia's have family members remaining in the community while other members are engaged in income-generating activities in other areas. Evidence of such "differentiation" in economic and social position and power within communities is a meaningful topic of debate within peasant studies.

SOCIAL MEMORY OF DICTATORSHIP

Differences between households in terms of levels of market production (and differences in income earned from selling these commodities) are important. At the same time, the practice of basic subsistence production (or lack thereof for the more "successful" market-integrated families) at a particular given moment is also notable. Both of these activities, however, should not divert us from noting the dormant ability to either increase subsistence production or to rely more heavily upon selling commodities in times of need. When there are extreme sociopolitical changes in the wider society, geographic isolation (or even political or social isolation through neglect) may serve as a kind of shelter. This shelter and the capacity to produce food have served families in the comunidades agrícolas during hard times. One of these extended periods was during the "shock therapy" following the Pinochet coup that precipitated a swift change from heavy state involvement in the economy to neoliberal economic policies (today, such radical changes are almost always referred to benignly in the conventional parlance of global economy observers as "reforms"). During the initial phase when state assistance was abruptly withdrawn and the comunidades were isolated and their more outspoken leaders persecuted, the communities were an uncertain shelter of sorts— Loma Seca was briefly occupied by military police forces in search of socialist and communist political leaders from nearby towns. Also, during the prolonged period of state indifference to poverty in the countryside when policy objectives strove to develop export agriculture, campesinos in all parts of Chile found themselves relying more heavily on producing food to feed themselves (Castro and Bahamondes 1986, 114).

After the coup, prices for farm goods plummeted, and costs that had been reasonable during the Unidad Popular rose dramatically. Even among those who emphatically stated that they themselves were never "socialists" or "communists," many, such as Elena, still feel that Allende did good things and was the only Chilean president to have concern for the poor. She also echoed the belief of many others that the rich were in collusion to expedite the coup by faking the massive shortages that plagued the last days of the Allende government. Stories are still told of locked warehouses full of goods that were reopened after Pinochet took over.

I was told that there was a military presence in the community for three months after the coup. Everyone—men, women, and children—were interrogated. Pablo, who was a young boy at the time, remembers being questioned. Elena told me that after the coup times were so hard that her husband was forced to hunt for rabbits and birds to feed the family. This lasted until the police came and took everyone's guns away, she told me. She said that they would arrive unannounced, searching houses and ripping up mattresses in search of hidden guns. Buses on the road to Ovalle were frequently stopped and searched.

During the military government the freedom to hold community meetings came to a halt. In order to hold a meeting, the comuneros would have to petition the local government and a policeman was required to be present. The Directiva could no longer be freely elected. Officers were appointed by the government. Group activity stopped, and since the economic times were so hard, many of the men left the community to work in the mines in the north. In the popular discourse going to the mines was perceived as a dangerous choice: One elderly woman solemnly reported that men worked in the mines for ten or fifteen years, became sick with lung problems, and often died within a year or two after returning home. Again, mining was described to me as a dangerous, undesirable way to make a living.

When talking to people about these times, I was told an amazing story. It is believed by some that the mayors of many of the nearby towns hid in Loma Seca, finding refuge in the church and in the school. The military police found them, took them off, and killed them, and their dismembered bodies were found in a quebrada in El Arroyo, near where we lived in the campo común. After checking the United Nations human rights report and talking with knowledgeable people, I found no one else who could confirm this, yet it is interesting nonetheless that this is to some extent part of the community's social memory of the Pinochet era.

The first book of the *Libro de Actas,* the minutes of community meetings, is missing because the man who was president of the comunidad at that time fled. He sold all of his machinery and animals and, in Elena's words, "stopped being a comunero." He disappeared, taking the book with him, because it could have contained "incriminating evidence." Elena said that she was afraid at the time because the secretary who was a communist often wrote in the book "my comrade said this . . . my comrade said that . . ." She feared that people referred to as "comrade," regardless of their political beliefs, would be arrested. Along with the people who left to work in the mines, many fled Loma Seca in fear after the coup. Two of Elena's brothers, one a socialist, left for Argentina immediately after the military takeover. She told me that one of them set off by foot to walk across the cordillera. It took seventy days. Most people who left took horses, at much risk, she said.

MODE OF PRODUCTION

The peripheral nature of peasant communities has inspired vigorous debate over the years, mainly over what have been the consequences of this peripheralization. As we have seen (chapter 2), for some theorists, isolation gives rise to specific cultural and economic characteristics that reflect this balance between insularity and domination as a kind of adaptive stasis (Chayanov 1996; Reinhardt 1988; Shanin 1987). For others, the efficacy of the relationship between peasant society and external capitalism is one that always benefits and is determined by the latter because the subordinate position of peasants fills a functional niche in the reproduction of inexpensive labor (de Janvry 1981; Meillassoux 1981; Stavenhagen 1978). For still others, the more salient part of this relationship is the means and style by which peasant communities propitiously reproduce not only their ways of life and their ways of making a living, but also a form of resistance against both economic and cultural domination (Kearney 1986a; Nugent 1993). Despite these varying views, each of these positions assumes—either directly or indirectly—that peasant production is something distinct from capitalism (a "mode of production") and yet linked to capitalism in a mutually formative dynamic relationship ("articulation").

To what extent does the work of the comuneros in Loma Seca represent a distinct mode of production? It is my contention that in both the material "forces of production" (land, labor, and resources) and the ideal "relations of production" (reciprocity, communitarian ideals, cultural institutions and values that regulate and shape land, labor, and resources), they possess characteristics that are unique and configured in distinct ways. How is the community of Loma Seca articulated with the wider economy of the outside world? The two primary ways are through the market for the commodities that are produced there and through the wage labor migration of workers.

There seems to be a symbiotic relationship between the most common means of employment for wages in which people from Loma Seca are engaged away from the community and the livelihood that they seek to maintain at home. As mentioned, mining and highway construction are frequent sources of work. Both are types of jobs that do not require formal education and in which information on openings is spread primarily through word of mouth. Work in the mines was invariably described to me by people in the community as low paying, sporadic, and dangerous. Highway construction jobs are similarly low paying and temporary in nature. Desire for such employment and the shift to wage work suggests the familiar processes of proletarianization in the peasantry. However, both of these jobs permit workers to return home, either on weekends if the workplace is nearby or for longer periods during downturns in employment. For the families that are most heavily invested in the comunidad system, this work is not an end in and of itself, but is a necessary means toward the ends of keeping the family's production going at home. This is demonstrated in the commitment to the rural life and livelihood shown by Gustavo and the other participants in the harvest who also work away from the community. Other common jobs, such as general day labor in Ovalle or work for young women as domestic servants there, permit such frequent returns home on the regularly scheduled bus service, which is necessary since very few people own vehicles.

On the one hand, it might be said that in the absence of opportunities for better wage work of a more permanent nature, these people are simply "making do" with the limited kinds of jobs that are available to them, and in some ways this is true. The flight of youths lured by the prospect of urban life and jobs in the cities is a problem frequently expressed by both people in the communities and those agents and advocates who work with them. Many of the smaller-sized families in Group 2 are reduced because of members who have made the decision to migrate permanently. For those who choose to stay, however, there not only is the satisfaction of being a comunero and having greater control over one's life and labor (the priceless satisfaction debated eloquently by Pablo and Gustavo with their brother-in-law that spring afternoon at San Julián), but also specific material benefits that make it preferable over wage labor (here I recall the frustrated development worker who complained: "They have jobs, but if they see that there is going to be rain, they quit and go back home"). What makes this choice preferable to comuneros and confounding to outsiders?

The market prices for the staple commodities that are produced in the community are low. For the most part, wheat production and handcrafted goat cheese are activities seen from the outside as trifling endeavors taken on only by those who have no other means of scraping a living from the land. Those crianceros, such as Pablo, who are able to maintain a sizable herd of sheep are in a somewhat better position because of the relatively higher price of cordero during the seasonal market in September. For Pablo, of course, this influx of cash was a buffer that kept the family going during its extended period of living away from home. While the market prices for their products are undeniably low in comparison to other commodities produced in Chile, the costs of their production are also small in comparison. In the example of harvesting wheat, when the capital required to control a means of production (the harvesting machinery) is beyond the reach of the individual family, that cost is extracted directly in the commodity itself, and this expense is further reduced by expanding production of the commodity in a group effort. As I have discussed, production costs would probably be prohibitive without the comuneros' capacity to work together en masse. Furthermore, it is also obvious that the cost of living itself is much less in this community than in areas in Chile where wage laborers live. Producing a significant amount of their own food and living in a dwelling and on land where they are not obligated to pay rent affords community members the luxury of living on less cash than the urban poor. As was evident in Pablo and Amelia's months in the Limarí valley, community members experience their most serious problems in making ends meet when they are forced to live away from home.

As the time line in figure 7.1 illustrates, the life of the comunero, like that of the miner, is marked by cycles. The articulation between the worlds of peasant production and mining traverses time as well as space. This is evident by the fact that many of the retired male *jubilados* are former miners. Migrants also provide economic support for the community, either directly through support of family members or indirectly through attendance at community events. As shown in chapter 5, the celebrations and the horse races staged by the various comités act as leveling or redistribution mechanisms that take cash from individual pockets and put it into funds that benefit the community as a whole.

Life in the community can serve as a temporary cushion when the external economic environment is inadequate or as a shelter when the political environment turns hostile. Individual families—both large and small—looking to maximize production can get a leg up on poor market conditions through reduced production costs at home. For the community as a whole, an improved standard of living at home is made possible by organized efforts and contributions reflecting these

"The individual/group articulation: Mobilizing labor during good years." Photo courtesy of the author.

same values and practices. The community can also be a place to go to live once one's life in the mines is over. When all of these things are considered, it is inaccurate to think of the continued participation in this traditional lifestyle as a "Hobson's choice"—an apparently "free choice" when there is no real alternative. Neither is it accurate to think of the people being drawn back to the community by some strange magnet, mystifying and attributable to that confounding realm of "culture." In what follows, we shall see that when community ideals and lived relations encounter development policies, differences over what constitutes "rational behavior" may not simply be differences in perspective or differences in degree, but are often differences in kind and, when livelihood is put under pressure by these policies, these differences are freighted with consequence.

8

Standardization of Rural Livelihood and Market Integration Policies

IN THE PREVIOUS THREE CHAPTERS WE SAW THAT SELLING THE PRODUCTS (primarily hand-pressed cheese) from their goat herds is a key source of income for many families in Loma Seca, as it is in most comunidades. In many ways goats are a symbol for this traditional livelihood. In a positive sense, goats stand for freedom of movement as they function as a kind of "mobile capital," a portable tool of production that can be relocated during drought years. Others emphasize the negative aspect of this symbol. Goats graze incessantly and they will seemingly consume anything. Like mining, goat herding is viewed as an unsustainable "extractive technology" that depletes the land and makes it unusable. As discussed in chapter 3, there are competing theories about the origins of the comunidades agrícolas and differing ideas as to the ethnic and cultural identity of the people who live in them. Their way of life was at times described to me by outsiders as a backward indigenous system and their selfish attitude toward the land as a "mining mentality," both of which need to be changed for the comuneros' and the region's economic betterment. In this chapter I examine a law that is having a drastic impact on the lives of crianceros (people who raise goats) and the "policy environment" (Weaver 1996) from which this law originates. In doing so, I think about how images of origins and ethnicity are implicit in the development ideology and consider how they differ from the self-image and self-identification of the comuneros with whom I lived and worked. I contend that "Policy-Positioned Ascriptions of Ethnicity Identity and History" is a useful designation for such naturalization of ethnic difference via the economic development apparatus of the state. I will also argue that consideration of petty commodities—such as the home production of goat cheese—is important in understanding both the nature of campesino livelihood and the relationships between peasant and nonpeasant economies and cultures.

"The State": Weighing In on Standards and Measurements

The government of the military dictatorship was more concerned with elite interests than with rural poverty, but the state's influence was still felt in the countryside. Foreign investment was courted while government spending was slashed as, in theory, government intervention took a backseat to market-driven export-oriented "agents of growth" (Hojman 1990, 1–3; Kay 1993, 19–20). Portes has emphasized the duplicitous and ironic nature of this guise of laissez-faire economics pointing out that "Chile's neoliberal experiment did not so much 'free' markets as to create them from scratch using the resources of the state" (2000: 360). Typically, neoliberal agendas espouse nonintervention in the economy while simultaneously making concerted offerings to transnational interests in the form of investment enticements and the removal of trade barriers. While certainly more attention is paid to rural poverty in postdictatorship Chile, the channels through which much of this assistance is given are firmly positioned in the familiar "free market" model. In addition, the discourse of economic development with regard to the comunidades agrícolas at times draws upon imagined ethnic traditions positioned in opposition to the model and ideals of "modernization."

Any state may control the actions of its citizens through law so as to explicitly circumscribe what actions will not be tolerated. This restraint of individual will via punitive means is overt and easy to identify. Any state may at the same time authorize specific ways of "doing business" or participating in particular activities. This creation of consensus—"inclusive" rather than "exclusive"—can in the final moment serve the same function as the wielding of coercion, but it is achieved through ways that present themselves as benign or even benevolent.

Beyond the judicial domain, at the level of nationalist discourse and ideology, a familiar practice of exclusion by way of defining inclusion emerges through the fashion by which the modern nation-state, to quote Anderson's famous phrase, "imagines itself" (1991). Having developed into complex political structures through conquest, colonialism, boundary redefinition and migration, state society has always been comprised of diverse cultures. But although constituently diverse, they are never genuinely pluralistic in terms of equal participation and representation for all segments. The political elite must maintain an order of authority that is in agreement with the legitimizing social pact or moral charter and at the same time create or conserve efficacious practices that ensure the survival of its ability and perceived right to rule. To secure the continuance of its dominion, it is often necessary for the state to differentiate between those who are and who are not judicially under its sway, and it is through such processes of inclusion and differentiation that ethnic antagonism arises. Dynamic interethnic relationships are thus part and parcel of the continuous process of state formation. Although ethnic variation is a quality attributable to all populations under the rule of a state, the essence of that diversity is specific to the ways in which an individual state operationalizes its particular construction and maintenance (Toland 1993, 2–5). Nationalism has come to connote loyalty to the state rather than loyalty to the nation. In a world rife with ethnic antagonism within state borders, it should be clear that this is not simply a matter of quibbling over semantics. Perhaps incognizant of this instability, policy makers and some scholars who insist that the state is the political extension of the nation must either believe that ethnic group loyalty corresponds with state loyalty or that it will fade away through the modernizing advances of state society (Connor 1994, 97–98).

The abstraction of "nation" as the defining element of "nation-state," then, is fraught with contradictions surrounding the questions "which nation?" and "whose state?" Some social theorists have complained that many political scientists, Marxist and non-Marxist alike, have overdrawn and mystified the state as an object of analysis, confusing what states *do* with what they *are* (Abrams 1988; Corrigan and Sayer 1985). This should not be surprising because the modern state presents itself in an overdrawn and mystified form, hiding the incongruity of its declaration that it speaks for a diverse mass of people. The illusion of the history of the modern capitalist state as a singular history of successive laws, which separates law from its empirical relation to material conditions and is incognizant of its actual historical struggle to seize and maintain power, is what Marx and Engels call the "specific illusion of lawyers and politicians" (2001, 148). This illusion involves both memory and amnesia. Anderson's contention is that, like all communities, states imagine themselves as cohesive, legitimate, and sovereign through *classificatory* practices and *selectively constructed* historical narratives (1991, 3). In a similar vein, Corrigan and Sayer contend that the history of state formation is a continuous cultural revolution, centuries spent manufacturing a *standard* of national identity by which oppositional cultures and behaviors are measured. These authors argue that the state acts as the moral regulator of society by "stating"; that is, imbuing normative meanings into what are actually "ontological and epistemological premises" about acceptable behavior through sanctioned societal institutions: "schooling" equals "education," "policing" equals "order," and "voting" equals "political participation" (Corrigan and Sayer 1985, 4). "Measured" is the operative word as Corrigan and Sayer assert that upholding the state depends to some extent on the "moral regulation" of its citizens through standardizing and classificatory practices. In addition, privileged historical narratives of a national/cultural past are given currency while others are ignored as nationalist discourse obscures the inherent contradiction that it speaks in a single voice for what are in reality diverse groups of people living within the country's borders. In the course of forging a consensus among these groups as to what makes up a national identity, a unified history, and a common heritage, cultures, behaviors, and values that do not "measure up" to these standards are identified and, to a large extent, defined (via the insider/outsider binary) in terms of "what they are not."

"Measurement" is also a consequence of economic development policies that promote the integration of peasants, or other "peripheral" groups, into new markets. Development agencies in establishing the outlets through which aid is given and setting standards by which progress is measured play an important part in this process. Standardization and regulation—purportedly value-free and objective measurements—may serve to construct oppositional identities and difference in measurable terms. Failing to meet these standards naturalizes this difference as something autonomous and "real" rather than one part of a binary in a modernizing discursive construct. Images of identity and ethnicity may spring from the contested ground where "national" comes to mean "modern" and "traditional" becomes a euphemism for "backward."

Reglamento Sanitario de los Alimentos

On May 13, 1999, the sale of hand-pressed artisanal goat cheese was placed under the regulation of a national law in Chile that fixes standards for the sanitary production of food items for sale to the public (Reglamento Sanitario de los Alimentos). The initial legislation (which regulates the sale of many other items, such as cakes and sandwiches) was passed in 1993, but cheese producers (queseros) were given an exemption until a plan could be developed to ease the impact that the restriction of this source of income would have on families like those in Loma Seca. Throughout the course of my work I heard the widely varying points of view from herders to public health officers to development agents. They voiced opinions and reactions running the gamut from fear to optimism to uncertainty. Government officials assured the public that the central objective is to establish improved levels of hygiene that will both protect the public health and help producers reach new markets with an improved and well-marketed product. The development agencies involved emphasized that their primary goal is the integration of small-scale local producers into national and, eventually, international markets. By the time that I left Chile in May 1999, many others in the countryside still did not share this confidence.

What development specialists have devised is a multiple sector plan of subsidies and credit extension for improved irrigation and animal forage. With these two needs met, it is hoped that ecological resources can be stabilized so as to allow consistent production of milk and a production of cheese that complies with the requirements of the law. They anticipate that state support will yield actual progress in the creation of locally owned small factories and milking centers. However, many small producers worry that their inclusion in the law represents a targeting of their previously unregulated activities and that it will ultimately eliminate a critical productive activity for those who simply cannot conform to the new guidelines and standards. They do not believe that they can compete with big commercial factories because of their limited production season, their lack of start-up capital, and their continued dependence upon natural forage. They also fear becoming vulnerable to credit institutions should they take out loans to finance this enterprise.

In response to the grave problems of drought and erosion in Region IV, recent Chilean governments have vowed to address rural poverty through development projects that are environmentally sound. These efforts include: (1) transfer of appropriate modern technology and management practices demonstrated through pilot programs; (2) the growing of animal feed such as alfalfa and planting reforesting plants such as *Atriplex nummularia* and *Acacia* shrubs to reduce dependency on the depleted natural forage and to help maintain the animals year-round; (3) irrigation projects for such plantations; and (4) support for small-scale commercial enterprises, including the creation of small cheese factories and milking centers. All of these projects are funded through a combination of state subsidies and easy term loans.

Initially a public health issue, the project to improve the quality of cheese soon came under the management of economic development and environmental policy. But even proponents recognize that this is only the beginning of a long-term plan that may take a number of years before the necessary elements are in place. Now clandestine production in the informal market continues but under a cloud of enforcement as venders now must show that they purchase their cheese from registered cheese makers. As discussed earlier, in times of

"Milking goats in the corral." Photo courtesy of the author.

drought, those who can afford it rent pasture outside of the community, and many still move their animals to the cordillera, the Andes mountain pastures that Chile shares with Argentina. (Recall that for several months, Pablo and his brother Gustavo seriously considered this move during the drought.) Even in adequate years, those who depend on natural forage can generally only expect to produce sufficient milk between the months of August and January. This short production season is the reason why small producers skeptically view their ability to compete with large factories and why they feel that they should not have to conform to the same production standards. To produce year-round requires cultivation of food for animals to get them through the winter, and most producers simply cannot do this as adequate water and forage are the first elements needed for compliance with the law.

MODERNIZATION AND LAW

Region IV is one of the poorest regions in Chile, and it is here where the majority of goat and sheep raising is practiced, so there was much concern about the impact of the application of the new law. Health officials became alarmed over the public health risk of contamination in artisanal cheese with an outbreak of food poisoning in Santiago in 1990. A subsequent study revealed the frequency of microorganisms from samples purchased in public markets, roadside stands, and from venders boarding buses on the Pan-American Highway. The conditions under which milk is collected and cheese is produced were identified as the cause for this contamination. In the last few years, public awareness has been raised about sickness-causing microorganism contamination in this cheese. Subsequently a large part of the market for this product has been reduced. Families like Pablo and Amelia's have long sold goat cheese as a means of supplementing their incomes. Small stands are scattered along the coastal highway. Cheese produced by such families sells at a price that is about a quarter of what cheese produced under sanitary industrial conditions costs in the grocery store. The people living in the communities of the producers themselves seem to have no problem with eating the cheese because they have been doing so all of their lives. A health official offering an explanation to me said that having had the cheese as part of their diet for a long period of time, many people are resistant to the bacteria. Beyond the communities themselves, the internal market is seen as negligible and the result is low production and low profit. However, as in the example of wheat production that I offered in the previous chapter, a seemingly low-profit, low-cost commodity can be a crucial piece to an integrated system of production.

A 1991 study argued that such local commercial production in the hands of the small producer could be viable provided that there was government assistance in terms of credit, proper forage, donation of building materials, training in sanitary manufacturing of cheese, access to market, and the employment of community labor resources (Ramirez 1991, 146–48). Following such recommendations, a program was created to help producers improve the milk coagulation process by using chemical enzymes. So far there are ten factories in the Limarí province, with plans for five more in the near future. In March 1998 the initial construction of one such factory in the rugged interior between Ovalle and Loma Seca was garnering a good deal of attention. Located near Punitaqui, in the heart of a concentration of comunidades in the "interior arido" sector, the factory at Ajial de Quiles is owned by forty-nine socios from the community. It will serve about 200 crianceros in the area, and there are plans to build two milking centers (*centros de acopios*) to serve them. The factory is organized as a Sociedad Agro-Industrial, a small business cooperative eligible for special loans and partial government subsidy of building the factory. The total cost for the plant at Ajial de Quiles was 55 million pesos

($122,000) of which the government subsidized 20 percent and the socios borrowed the rest.

The Department of Rural Development (Departamento de Desarrollo Rural, or DDR) is a large government organization that is directing projects throughout Region IV. This group's primary job is to coordinate the efforts of those organizations providing specific assistance. These organizations include the Corporación Nacional Forestal (CONAF), which provides assistance with reforestation; Instituto de Desarrollo Agropecuario (INDAP), which offers small loans to producers for strictly commercial enterprises; and the group Proyecto de Desarrollo Rural de Comunidades Campesinas y Pequeños Productores (PRODECOP), which makes loans to the rural poor who would not otherwise be eligible for them. Most comuneros fall into this latter category since corporately held communal land is unavailable for use as collateral. PRODECOP is especially proud of the development projects that they have sponsored and funded in the comunidades. Other assistance-giving groups include Servicio Agricultura y Ganadería (SAG), which provides veterinary medicine and technical assistance with livestock and the Instituto de Investigaciones Agropecuarias (INIA), which carries out research projects at experimental stations and promotes the transfer of technology to small-scale producers. While the Ministry of Health (Ministerio del Salud) in Ovalle is responsible for enforcing the law in the Limarí province, they prefer to emphasize their role as a provider of education and assistance in helping cheese makers meet the new standards. There are also private consulting companies, such as IPD (Inversiones Producción Desarrollo), which has an office in Ovalle and is the group directing the cheese factory in Ajial del Quiles. This firm focuses on developing small-scale businesses in the countryside, providing such new entrepreneurs with technical and legal assistance to help them make it through the critical early years when many endeavors fail.

This assistance is needed because it is difficult for small community-based factories to make it on their own initially because they lack the resources to be entirely self-sufficient. It also is important that cheese be produced under acceptable conditions and in quantities that a viable market can bear. It is acknowledged that care must be taken to prevent overproduction and market saturation. Some opponents feel that this is where the "sacrifice" of the majority of small producers under the new regulations comes in. While many see two paths to development for crianceros—to either produce and sell milk or produce and sell cheese—other paths go uncommented on: to sell on the black market or to stop producing altogether.

"Making goat cheese at home." Photo courtesy of the author.

The law requires that all sites of production have potable water, showers for workers, sterilized equipment, special corrals with concrete floors or rooms with milking platforms and sterile rooms where cheese is pressed and set out to mature. As I have described, crianceros like Pablo and Amelia milk their goats every day in their corrals, press the cheese by hand in their kitchens, and leave it out to mature on shelves in cool, dry rooms in the backs of their houses. Most of these homes have neither running water nor electricity.

Since the average family cannot comply with these standards, there was great apprehension among the crianceros, and many saw the law as a form of persecution. In 1997 it was calculated that there were 308,000 goats in the region, while before the devastating drought there were more than 500,000. It was also shown that there were more than 5,800 families dependent upon this form of production (PRODECOP 1997). The word "persecution," perhaps, assumes a malicious intent that may more likely be a blind spot of faith in market-oriented development to solve all problems. It is ironic that state intervention is limiting the market access of many producers participating in what is sometimes called the "informal economy"—"informal" indicating that which operates outside of the purview of state control. The market here only appears "free" for those who can participate in the costly sanctioned style of production. Many producers believe that state control of this activity will bring an end to a crucial part of their traditional livelihood.

It is very difficult for administrators to reliably estimate the number of goats in the region at any particular point in time. Herders, wary of government interference in their lives, will often underestimate. With the scarcity of forage and degradation of the land that excessive herding brings, development agencies would prefer that the same amount of production be obtained from two or three hundred thousand. Sometimes administrators are frustrated with what they see as a family's desire to own as many goats as it can. (Recall a similar frustration described in chapter 5 over the status symbol of owning many horses in the countryside.) State agents, however, realize that in light of drought and little access to more efficient productive methods, a large number of animals is often seen as a means of economic security, allowing the flexibility to either thin the herds or keep the animals depending upon changing climatic conditions. The more goats a family owns, the more that will survive the dry season. There will be a larger pool of animals available to sell, to use in cheese production, or if times are very bad, to eat. The latter option was said to have been chosen at an alarmingly high rate during the time of my initial fieldwork when the first phase of the drought was at its peak. This backup plan, in which hungry people eat the scrawny meat of hungry goats, is a truly depressing scenario. (However, during that time I also heard this described to me by urban academics in Santiago unfamiliar with the life ways of rural people in the north as simply, "Things are so bad that they're *eating* the goats." Only during my fieldwork in the community did I learn that male goats are eaten regularly and are meat staples during both good and bad years.) For Pablo and Amelia a large number of goats was necessary in their attempt to balance income and expenditure in the time spent away from the community.

When I left Chile in April 1998, the status of the exemption was undetermined. When I returned in September of that year, I found that indeed the exemption had been extended. Throughout that year and into 1999, as the deadline approached, the controversy became a hot-button issue in regional elections, and the government attributed much of the fear of the law to opposition parties' propagation of confusion and myths concerning the state's real intention. Although some figured that after granting a twelve-month exemption the previous year the authorities would yet again give in to popular sentiment, the line was held this time, and the law went into effect. Portraying the hard-line position as a short-run sacrifice for long-term progress, press statements used language recognizable to applied anthropologists familiar with classic Rostowian modernization rhetoric and evolutionary metaphors (stages of growth, the "precondition" runway leading to "flight" [Rostow 1960]): "We are taking the more difficult road for the sake of future producers . . . "Our intention is to make sure that the majority of the producers are part of the 'take-off' [el despegue] plan, which will eventually place their products in international markets" (El Día 1998, 16; translation mine).

My first indication of the extent of the acrimony that was developing over the end of the exemption came toward the later part of my second stay in Chile when I went to visit an animal husbandry specialist in La Serena whose institution was working closely with comuneros on improving goat production. I had interviewed him twice during my previous visit, and I felt comfortable in telling him what I had been doing that year in the countryside.

I was taken off guard when he incredulously questioned me, "You've eaten this cheese?"

After informing him that Julie and I had not only eaten it regularly but that we had participated in the making of it for a good part of the last two months, he looked at me as if I had just told him that we had been handling plutonium.

"And you've never gotten sick?" he continued the interrogation.

Still unsure as to exactly where this was heading, I cheerfully bantered back that not only had we never gotten sick, but also that we both found it to be delicious. He was still smiling, but the edge to his sarcasm became sharper: "And where did you make this cheese? In the shade? On the kitchen table? . . . Under the kitchen table?"

Realizing that my careless disclosures were coming off as an affront to his authority and to what his organization was trying to accomplish, I hastily began to backtrack.

"But would you trust it to give as a gift to a friend in the United States?" he asked, "Would you let your professor eat it?"

"No, no, of course not," I assured him. I told him that I saw his point and that Julie and I had been very lucky indeed to have never taken ill.

There is a critical element of "image" implied in the modernization discourse. Statements by officials in the press often claimed that, cloaked in illegality, clandestine production has long depressed the product's price, has cut off access to new markets, and has hurt the region's image as a whole. Words like "traditional" and "artisan" (which the crianceros especially hold as a source of pride) have contested meanings in this public debate of a free market development ideology that is seeking to control, through standardization, livelihood strategies that have articulated peasant production with market economy but outside of state control. These contested meanings appear to me to represent a struggle over the image of a modernizing Chile and the role that "peripheral" or "marginal" sectors of society play in this national image.

I do not intend here to write off the real and serious issues of food contamination and illness. Nor do I mean to cast doubt on either the motivation of the people working to solve the problem or the desire of the crianceros to bring a safe and desirable product to market. What are relevant, I believe, are the differences in perceptions of the product among different public sectors. These perspectives became polarized as the deadline grew nearer. Opponents of the law saw the declaration of a public health risk as alarmist and unfairly assigning blame to the local producers. (This resembles Julia Paley's description of the Chilean government's discourse on the threat of cholera in the early 1990s—see chapter 5 on "The Paradox of Participation " in her book *Marketing Democracy,* in which the health issue was framed in terms of individual responsibility and behavioral changes regarding cleanliness, thus delimiting the government's role as restricted to an educational function [2001, 159–60].) In the rural areas almost everyone eats this kind of cheese, while many in the city, especially those with ties to the countryside, praised its distinct taste, a preference that endorsed the crianceros and their position. On the other hand, many urban residents do not trust the rural product and will only buy factory-produced cheese in the supermarket. For my eighty-year-old landlady in Ovalle, who owned a house and was solidly middle class, Pablo and Amelia's cheese was a guilty pleasure. She seemed to believe the dangers as reported in the media, but could not resist eating it when I brought it in from the countryside. Once during his family's transient period in the Limarí valley, Pablo aptly expressed the feelings of most people in the area who had eaten this product their entire lives. Holding up a cloth sack stuffed with a number of cheeses that Amelia's sister was taking to Ovalle to sell, he pointed to the contents inside, winked, and said "contrabando." The product was the same as the ones that we had made together the previous season and that his family has been crafting for generations, but the market for it had turned from informal to black.

Such patterns recall Arjun Appadurai's groundbreaking ideas on "the Social Lives of Things," or how commodities and their demand are socially constructed and bear cultural dimensions and how their consumption create meanings in our lives in ways that tie local producers and consumers to "larger regimes of value" (1986). In the capitalist economy, this is accomplished through processes of "commodity fetishism" and "reification" whereby in the exchange of commodities the social relationships between human beings are masked and subsumed in the commodities themselves. They assume the appearance of relationships between "things," as producers and consumers only come into contact with each other through the market. Their products, which are in actuality subjective, unique, and qualitative (that is, they are produced by social labor), are transformed into objects that are purely quantitative via a system governed by exchange-values appearing to be inherent to the commodities exchanged (Marx 1976, 167–77). This intrinsic sleight of hand (of masking "a relation concealed beneath a material shell" (Marx 1976, 167) from a Marxist perspective is an ideological mechanism serving to reproduce class relations.

In the case at hand, a kind of microlevel "development-of-underdevelopment" effect can potentially divide producers into the "haves" who can fill the market niche and the "have-nots" who cannot. This differentiation, in a sense, is disguised in the transformation of the product itself. On the market shelf, the consumer sees only the replacement of an unsafe product that is symbolic of backwardness with a safe, modern commodity that many are told and many believe the region as a whole can take pride in.

¡COMO LOS INDIOS!

Pablo and the other queseros are always quick to stress the word "artesanal" in distinguishing their product from other types of cheese in the market. (The word is also used to describe other petty commodities that they sell as supplemental forms of income, such as the handworked lambskin that Pablo occasionally makes.) These products are considered to be of high quality (*fino*) because they are handmade (*hecho a mano*), which means that they are unique, they take a certain amount of time to produce, and they are representative of long-practiced local cultural traditions. The goal of the cheese factory is to continue to make the product by hand but under sterile conditions. The *maestros de queso* in these factories are local people who are skilled at pressing cheese, but by making their product within state guidelines, it is hoped, their cheese will bring a price that queseros making cheese the traditional way cannot get.

Others see mainly negative connotations in the word "artesanal." One official at the Ministry of Health in Ovalle with whom I spoke said that to advertise the factory cheese as such would be "bad advertising" (*mala propaganda*) and would tell the consumer that the product is of poor quality (*falta calidad*). He, like many other officials in many of the other agencies, spoke of the difficulty in getting the "stubborn" crianceros to abandon their "antiquated "backward" system (*sistema rustico*) of letting large numbers of poorly producing animals forage on rapidly deteriorating land so as to make an inferior product under unsanitary conditions. He boasted that he saw a product from one of the Limarí factories selling for $6 U.S. (he did the currency conversion on a calculator) recently at a supermarket in Region V. Slowly the habits of the crianceros will be changed, and they will learn that they can, under the right conditions, produce milk (in his words) "HERE in this sector without having to go to the cordillera." Their resistance to change is unfortunate, he said, but their fears are understandable. He stressed that this is why enforcement of the law was going to be "flexible." He, like others with whom I spoke, also corrected me when I referred to the Reglamento Sanitario de los Alimentos as "the new law." The law was passed several years ago and the producers of other manufactured food commodities (candy, baked goods, etc.) have been adhering to it all along. The cheese producers, he reminded me, were generously given an extension of the deadline while the Plan Caprina (the integrated plan for helping crianceros comply with the law and integrate external markets with their products) was being worked out.

While "artesanal" may be a "dirty" word to some, others are using images reflecting public perceptions of tradition and ethnicity to their advantage in the marketing of this product. On the wall of his office was a poster demonstrating possible labels and advertising for one of the cheese factories. The image on one of these labels was a drawing of a generic "Indian" with a single feather in his hair, sitting cross-legged on the ground and pounding a drum with his hands. Behind him a goat peers from behind a mountain, and in the valley are cacti and rows of grape vineyards. While farcical in its representation of the ethnicity of the people who make this product, the company is nonetheless playing upon outsiders' perception of who they are.

The three largest producers of pisco in Region IV are making use of a similar trope. Pisco, a kind of jam brandy, is the national drink of Chile. Most of the special grapes used to make it and most of the factories that produce it are in Region IV. Pisco Capel advertises its product as "El Autentico Pisco del Valle Elqui." Pisco Control bills its product as "Full of History" (*Lleno de la Historia*). Tres Eres makes an expensive premium brand of pisco under the label "Los Artesanos de la Cochiguaz." The Cochiguaz is a famous valley with a mystical and romantic reputation not far from Vicuña. My friends there laughed at this claim as it is no more made "by hand" than it is made by elves.

Claims to authenticity and appeals to tradition, of course, are common themes in advertising worldwide. Sparsely populated, poor, and distant, the Norte Chico (and most certainly the regions of the Norte Grande to the north) contrasts strongly in the public mind with Santiago (where one-third of the nation's population lives) and the fertile Central Valley of Chile (the agricultural heartland whose bounty is the nation's patrimony). Living in the northern desert and mountains and making a living from the land in traditional ways makes them seem more vaguely "Andean." The other important image of the north is that of copper mining. Unlike the "indigenous history," however, the history of copper is that of the nation. The northern frontier was settled because of copper. Copper has always been the main reason for Chile's relative wealth in comparison to other countries in Latin America.

Seeing the advertising mock-up in the health official's office reminded me of two instances during the previous year's wheat harvest in Loma Seca. I used sixteen rolls of film that year, but afraid of being intrusive, I was always a little self-conscious in photographing people. Most of the time people were happy to be photographed and eager to show me where they lived and how they did things. At two different times during the trilla when I was photographing Pablo and the other men working together to separate the newly cut wheat with the wooden shovels and whisk brooms made of tied sticks, he stopped to pose. Holding the broom rigidly to his side, he said, in mock-solemnity to the delight of his friends: "¡Como los Indios!" His ribbing was good-natured, but he was responding not only to the awkwardness of being photographed but also expressing his self-consciousness over using a rudimentary technology that is perceived by most outsiders in his country as a "backward tradition." He was also more than likely responding to what he knew about the interests of most anthropologists. The only other time I can recall Indianness being invoked in the community was in a similar situation in which the objective was to ridicule. I had been expressing my frustration at my inability to penetrate the thick accent of an old man in Loma Seca. This frustration was increased by the fact that he was warm and genial, ever present at community functions, and almost always eager to talk to me. His articulation was impaired by the fact that he was toothless and sometimes intoxicated, and I could scarcely discern from his utterances more than a word or two at a time. My friends agreed that even they had difficulty with his accent. They laughed and said, "Don't worry. No one understands him. He speaks Mapuche."

Chile is known as one of the most ethnically homogenous countries in Latin America. The largest Indian group is the Mapuche, who live in the southern part of the country. As previously described, the members of the comunidades do not consider themselves to be any more "indigenous" than anyone else. They are not ethnically distinct from the majority of Chileans. As also discussed, in terms of self-identification, the predominant image for most of the men is that of the historically romanticized huaso, the Chilean cowboy. This identification is seen in the style of everyday life, but is especially evident in their fanaticism for horsemanship, rodeos, and horse races. Public events such as the carreras and the rodeo Chileno where huaso culture is strongly expressed and where money is raised by the various comités, I have argued, play a key part in reproducing the local economy and promoting group cohesion (see also Alexander 2006).

Petty Commodities and Peasants

What of the commodity itself? What is the significance of cheese in both material (the money it brings in for family producers) and ideal (the images and identifications associated with its regulation) terms of economic production? These are important questions for other commodities and producers outside of north-central Chile.

A literature review of recent studies of petty commodities and artisan production in peasant communities in Latin America reveals some important themes relevant to the impact of the law regulating goat cheese in the Norte Chico. These include the importance of petty commodity production as a meaningful unit of analysis in understanding: (1) the *diversity* of income-generating activities in impoverished areas, (2) the *linkages* between subsistence-oriented and market economies, (3) the effects of uneven *capitalist development* in the countryside, and (4) processes of class *differentiation* within peasant communities. The study of petty commodities, like the "peasant" category itself (see chapter 2), comes with its own particular set of contradictions that have inspired rigorous debate stemming from the "in-between" nature of their participation in different economic spheres. In the case at hand, the Reglamento Sanitario de los Alimentos is the dividing line in this differential access to the requirements of standardized production.

In many ways, peasant culture by its very nature defies easy categorization, as is evident in Kroeber's archetypal definition of peasants as people who "are definitely rural—yet live in relation to market towns; they form a class segment of a larger population which usually contains also urban centers . . . They constitute part-societies with part-cultures" (1948, 284). This definition has understandably proven controversial in recent decades as many analysts, for good reason, take issue with the condescending bias in the term "part-culture." Yet differential access to material resources remains an important element of any peasant analysis and, as Gavin Smith has pointed out, even those who distance themselves from Kroeber's definition still acknowledge peasant culture's "Janus-faced propensity . . . to relate both to the characteristics of the larger society and to those of the local, face-to-face community" (1989, 18). Discussing new meanings of the peasant category in the late twentieth century, Cancian noted that peasants "have long been partly market dependent and partly subsistence producers, partially autonomous and partially controlled from the outside" and even though subsistence production is no longer the primary activity for the majority, there is still something expressly distinct about, as Cancian described, "people who have some ability to produce their own food, or have a close kinship connection to people who have some ability to produce their own food, or interact in a local economy with people who have some ability to produce their own food" (1989, 164). Cancian's expansive category includes not only (1) "traditional" peasants substantially involved in subsistence production, but also (2) "petty commodity producers" who sell goods made with a low level of capital investment and little or no hired labor and (3) "semiproletarian" wage laborers whose survival depends in part upon the production of food or petty commodities by themselves or their families (1989, 165).

Thus, production of petty commodities for local and regional markets has been for a long time considered a defining feature of the peasant mode of production. As Plattner points out, petty commodity production in peasant households is both similar to and different from commercial forms of market commodity production. Competitive markets may exist for petty commodities between specialized producers who for the most part "control their own means of production," but such "owners" do not extract "significant surplus value" from wage labor in the process of production. Even though individuals in peasant economies own or have exclusive rights to land, they are often impoverished (from a monetary "standard of living" viewpoint) and they frequently supplement their incomes with wage work and the manufacturing of goods for sale (Plattner 1989, 392–93). Roseberry extols the potential that research on petty commodities has for giving us a complete picture of how rural livelihoods are reproduced in the countryside. Too often, exclusive focus on land and farming in his words "precludes a more sophisticated understanding of the *actual* reproduction strategies" (1989, 123; emphasis mine). Along these same lines, Estellie Smith notes the usefulness of studying petty commodity production as a means of clarifying linkages between peasant modes and the "developed" economy, since the emergence of economic practices in this so-called "informal" sector is largely a response to conditions in the "formal" sector (1989, 306–7).

Recognizing the subaltern position as a response to uneven development, however, is not an acceptance that economic relations in peasant communities will operate by either the "rationality" of the "universal" laws of neoclassical economics or the orthodox Marxist position on the inevitable impact of capitalism in the countryside. Carol Smith's landmark study of weavers in western Guatemala describes several generations of successful manufacturing that did not produce permanent class differentiation through the "inevitable" (by capitalist logic) expansion of business and the hiring of outside labor for low wages. Her argument is that this was neither the result of scurrilously attributed "cultural inertia" or hidebound "peasant tradition," but rather a consequence of the shared feeling of Indian solidarity in response to domination by Ladino society. In this way, the dynamic integrity of the community is recognized and represented as an active response to their engagement with capitalism and not in terms of "timeless customs" or an ambiguous "moral economy" somehow separate from the modern world (C. Smith 1984, 1990). Binford and Cook's exploration of peasant differentiation in Mexico's Valley of Oaxaca, however, eschews descriptions of small producers as subsistence-oriented, petty commodity producers that function outside of capitalism. Their framework is a complexly differentiated capitalist system that organizes even the smallest and most isolated of producers. Primarily a rejection of "functional dualist" (see chapter 2) analysis, which sees things such as markets for petty commodities as the exploitative links between "connected but distinct" relations of production, this aspect of their work is heralded by Kearney in his "reconceptualization"/rejection of the "peasant concept" in the contemporary world (1996), even as he mildly chides them for lumping such subaltern sectors into a singular "other" position through their insistence that the penetration of global capitalism determines this differentiation (1996, 96–97). More recent work in the Valley of Oaxaca by Clarke (2000) adheres to a conventional category of "peasants"—that is, they are small-scale farmer/artisans historically geared for self-sufficiency but struggling in the modern world—yet avoids criticism of producing "timeless," "romanticized," or "essentialized" ethnography by emphasizing processes of change and dynamism in the petty commodity sector of maize, mescal, and coffee.

Some recent studies of the results of the market expansion of artisan goods produced by peasant groups in South America offer surprising and complex views that transcend the well-worn "developed-underdeveloped" binary. Colloredo-Mansfeld documents a cultural renaissance among Octavalo Indians in the Ecuadorian Andes spurred by the global marketing of textiles from peasant villages known for their weaving. This economic success has ushered in many other remarkable transformations, including the invention of new and strongly marketable "traditions," the abandonment of traditional farming practices, and new ethnic and class division within communities that are expressed in the conspicuous consumption patterns of what Colloredo-Mansfeld identifies as a globe-trotting "native leisure class" (1999, 2002). Healy's *Llamas, Weavings, and Organic Chocolate* (2001) provides numerous case studies of grassroots movements in Bolivia from recent decades that likewise challenge both Western models of development and essentialist views of peasant culture. Relating oral histories of small-scale projects that promote active expressions of indigenous culture, Healy gives voice to associations of indigenous artists and weavers in the Andes valleys and the eastern lowlands whose success has not only generated substantial income for poor communities but has also revitalized indigenous identity, increased outsiders' respect for their craft traditions, and even worked to improve the status of women (2001, 267–326).

Success of this exact nature may not be feasible in ecosystems like the Norte Chico where the limited and erratic availability of natural resources make multiple and flexible survival strategies necessary. In a case study from Sardinia, Vargas-Cetina shows how the market expansion of handcrafted pecorino cheese resulted in a commoditization process that spawned a roller-coaster trajectory of development resulting in great disparities of wealth and differential access to economic opportunity. A diversified subsistence economy of which handicraft production was one component was ultimately eliminated in response to rising demand for the product. A short-lived prosperity resulted from the expanded market, but once the market was saturated by the product, an ensuing crisis culminated in rural development and a critical need for alternative sources of income (Vargas-Cetina 2000). These transformations in the lives and livelihoods of Sardinian pastoralists may be seen as a cautionary tale for the development of artisan goat cheese in northern Chile.

"Policy-positioned Ascriptions" in the Development Milieu: From "Spatialization" to "Practical Political Economy"

At times development literature and policy materials present representations of comunero culture that reflect assumptions of ethnicity and identity. As I have argued elsewhere, frequently "these assumptions conflate *where* these people live and *what* they do to make a living into a representation of *who* they are ethnically" (2006, 153). Instructional manuals on cheese production and land regularization are very revealing in this way. In a 1988 publication by the NGO Juventudes para el Desarrollo y el Producción (JUNDEP) entitled "A Brief History of the Comunidades Agrícolas" (Una Breve Historia de las Comunidades Agrícolas) (JUNDEP 1988), the development of the community system makes use of strikingly exaggerated illustrations of race and ethnicity. In depicting the evolution of the communities over several hundred years, the drawings show: (1) Diaguita Indians idyllically living the simple life of communal land, subsistence farming, and terrace irrigation; (2) the rude introduction of the concept of private property by the conquering Spaniards as a question mark hovers above the confused Indian's head; (3) the rise of the institutions of slave labor and the encomienda system as gold-crazy Spaniards drive marginalized Indians (*indígenas arrinconadas*) up into the peripheral lands; (4) sons of a conquistador whose estate has fallen into disrepair deciding that it would be in their best interest to work and possess their hijuelas (the predecessors of the irrigated goces singulares) individually while leaving the inferior quality land intact as common property to be worked together; and (5) mid-nineteenth-century pirqueneros feeling the exploitation of royalties and rent deciding to abandon the copper mines and throw their lots in together to work the unused land as farmers.

A composite drawing of the land tenure system in a typical comunidad that is often used in research publications shows pre-Columbian artwork etched into the stratigraphy between the sloping communal land and the individually possessed irrigated plots, a faint indicator of the indigenous history. Ethnic caricatures in illustrations that appear in "Training and Consultation for the Constitution of a Comunidad Agrícola" (Capacitación y Asesoria Jurídica Para la Constitución de una Comunidad Agrícola), also published by JUNDEP (n.d.) are more obvious. This handbook gives basic information on the 1967 law (Ley de las Comunidades Agrícolas) (and its 1984 revision during the Pinochet era), which enacted the legal means by which comunidades may standardize (*sanamiento*) their boundaries and set the number of internal use rights. As mentioned, nearly 180 comunidades have registered themselves in this way with others in the region in the process of doing so. Again, recall that the legal definition of what constitutes a comunidad agrícola is that they are comprised of lands held in common in which the number of people holding use rights exceeds the capacity of the land to provide adequate subsistence. Other aspects that distinguish comunidades agrícolas from comunidad indígenas (primarily Mapuche reducciónes) include the three particular forms of land tenancy within their boundaries and the fact that they are "communities" comprised of different families rather than the smallholdings of single kinship groups. While the JUNDEP publication does not mention comunidades indígenas the subjects in the illustrations are caricatures of perhaps Mapuche or Aymara people. The manual also outlines procedures for electing a Directiva. Here, the stereotypical representations in exaggerated physical characteristics and Andean dress and their slumping body language contrasts strongly with that of the modern dress and upright posture of the ethnically neutral figures of a lawyer and official with the Registry of Property (Conservador de Bienes Raices). In the final panel, having achieved legitimate recognition, the body language of the comuneros is then rendered as upright and serious as they conduct a community meeting. Along these same lines, pamphlets providing instruction on how to make goat cheese according to the law's sanitary standards convey a similar transformation (Comisión Regional de Ganado Caprino 1993). In these illustrations, a disheveled, careless cheese maker working in filthy conditions is changed into a clean and conscientious quesero, proud to be getting the stamp of approval from a paternalistic figure of the health inspector. Both the commodity and the producer are essentialized as "clean" and "correct" subjects imbued with legitimacy via the state.

In this discourse of development, "indigenous" acquires a meaning analogous to "noncapitalist" and "backward." "Mining" becomes synonymous with an "individualist" and "extractive" way of life. "Comunero" is externally identified as a kind of conflation of the two meanings: antiquated and backward, selfish and obstinate, carrying on an environmentally damaging extractive livelihood, and committed to radical political and social organization. Constructed in opposition to images and ideals of modern, ethnically neutral Chile, I have coined the term "Policy-positioned Ascriptions of Ethnicity, Identity, and History" (2006) to describe such attributes in that (1) they have meanings that are generated via public policy and the state apparatus and (2) they can be corrected through conforming to authorized standards of production and participation in sanctioned programs and forms of organization. The message is that collective action and organization in itself is not a "bad thing." Sociedades are cooperatives, but they are seen as forward thinking and with an entrepreneurial purpose, while comunidades are usually seen as obstacles to development because they represent a rigid monopoly on worthless undeveloped land as well as resistance to change.

Identifying comunidades with "indígenas arrinconadas" based on where they are located and the poor quality of their land suggests the discursive use of both "spatialization" and the "backward other" (Alonso 1994, 393–96) in development ideology. Brackette Williams notes how such state control of the mechanisms by which group and individual identities are brought into existence as positioned subjects in a power hierarchy is a process by which subaltern societal segments bear the stigma of racial difference in relation to an "unmarked" homogenous mainstream category (1989, 429–39). All of this suggests that race as a category is just a fiction playing against a nationalist identity. Balibar tells us that through "social normalization and exclusion" such categories carry meanings not of "group x as group x" but "group x as . . . criminals, degenerates, etc." (1991). In the case that I am presenting here, it is the presumed attribute that signifies the ethnicity: "noncapitalist" or "backward" *as* "Indian." Gupta and Ferguson, reflecting on the construction of such "spatialized culture through both state policies and anthropological inquiry and state policies" warn that "Associations of place, people, and culture are social and historical creations to be explained, not given as natural facts. . . . whatever associations of place and culture may exist must be taken as problems for anthropological research rather than the given ground that one takes as a point of departure . . . cultural territorializations (like ethnic and national ones) must be understood as complex and contingent results of ongoing historical and political processes. . . " (1997a, 4).

In the quote above, they are insisting that such a recognition is a preliminary step toward moving beyond naturalized conceptions of "spatialized cultures" (such as "indígenas arrinconadas") and toward exploring the "production of difference within common, shared, and connected spaces" (Gupta and Ferguson 1997b, 45). To reiterate my contention, these ascriptions via public policy only fully "make sense" within the particular development context, and they are by necessity not static. They function to naturalize as "common sense" categories such difference even while they promote prescriptive measures to change them. This may seem paradoxical, but Hannerz for one emphasizes that even though such ideologically positioned common sense may be ubiquitous, it is not comprised of a crosscutting uniform content. Genuinely geared toward securing a stability of meanings, one form of common sense may appear dominant, but it is never exempt from change (1992, 128–29).

Once race or ethnicity becomes an objectified principle, it is propelled by forces quite different from those forces that were working to bring about its rise. This is Comaroff and Comaroff's dialectical model of ethnicity as a historically specific process that includes control over various modes of production in seemingly uncontested ways.

These modes are simultaneously symbolic (cultural) and material (structural), and principles of ethnicity can work as both the tool of exploitation and the ideology of nationalism. And, importantly, the particular "set of relations" (or "mode of consciousness") that constitutes ethnicity often has an influential power over the social organization from which it emerges, an illusion of autonomy that may define cultural boundaries and determine social action (Comaroff and Comaroff 1992). As such identities come from specific histories and political economies, their meanings are not fixed for all time. With regard to meanings of "rurality," Ferguson shows in an interesting example from Zambia that popular discourses shifted over the course of that nation's economic development from idealized images of country life to negative images of "selfishness" following an economic crisis (1997).

While the orthodox Marxist model and the sociological split-labor market theory of race (Bonacich 1972; Farley 2005, 265) view racial categories and relations as serving the needs of capitalism and empire-building (see, for example, Wolf on the "New Laborers" created by the expansion of European capitalism into the Western Hemisphere [1982, 379–80] and Worsley on the "situational" nature of racial identity via exploitative labor relations [1984, 242]), it is important to also recognize that once split from their material genesis, ascriptions may act upon and alter these relations of production. Recall my discussion in chapter 2 of Kearney and Nagengast's research on the incorporation of Mixtec labor from southern Mexico into the economies of northern Mexico and the United States. Substantively drawn along similar theoretical lines as those suggested by Comaroff and Comaroff, they observe that while institutionalized racism is one of the forces that pushes the Mixtec from their homelands and is reproduced in the severe working conditions in the northern fields (that is, racism is articulated in the social formation with capitalist expansion), the resulting resurgence of Mixtec ethnicity as a result of the labor migration process has led to union organization and inroads into the improvement of these conditions. In a dialectical class struggle played out across cultural and national boundaries, the instruments of domination—including racial distinctions that support dual standards of wages and treatment—bring forth modes of resistance and opposition (Nagengast and Kearney 1990).

Policy-positioned ascriptions can also work to the advantage of the subjects of development. Much recent work focuses on the positive aspects of ethnicity and identity as shaped by state policies within the development milieu. In the field of applied anthropology, it has been recognized that development initiatives may be improved, accountability increased, and trust in the government earned when states acknowledge the pluralistic makeup of their societies (Carroll and Carroll 1997); construction of collective identity as a means of uniting small producers that transcends traditional ethnic boundaries can be used successfully to make demands upon the government (Medina 1997); and subaltern groups can make essentialized representations work in their favor via the "vocabulary with which to defend the rights of communities vis-à-vis states" in what Li terms "practical political economy" (1996, 501). There is little doubt that renewed expressions of comunero identity via comunidad advocacy organizations in the post-Pinochet transition era have produced positive results. Unfortunately, as the sample cheese label described previously shows, representations in advertising that reinforce and give legitimacy to stereotypical images may be another manifestation.

From Clandestine Artisans to Integrated Producers

Many critics feel that the program to develop small factories has drawn disproportionate attention in the public eye than the problems associated with the plan and the negative impact of the policy on people who do not have the resources to participate in the project. The government has maintained all along that soft credit will be available to small producers who form the commercial associations and show that they are willing to do what it takes to make a viable factory. A combination of subsidies and credit has also been extended in order to convert arid land into sustainable pasture called *praderas* or *empastadas*. It was expected that the majority of small producers who participate in this new system of regulated production would fill the niche of selling milk to the factories, however, so far only a few of the authorized milking centers (*centros de acopio*) have been built. To reasonably expect these crianceros to meet the sanitary law's standards, there will have to be a large number of such production sites in operation over the entire region and into remote areas like those that I have described in which roads and infrastructure are inadequate and undeveloped. It is unrealistic to think that those producers living in the most rugged parts of the interior could make use of these centers. Recall that for a couple of months when they were living away from home in a part of the Limarí valley near the main road between Ovalle and the Pan-American Highway, Pablo sold milk to a buyer from a cheese factory in Santiago. When they had to leave the accessible spot on the highway, they simply returned to making their own cheese. When living in Loma Seca selling milk is not a viable option but making and selling cheese is. For Pablo and Amelia and the others living in the El Arroyo sector in the campo común, such accessibility is not in the near future. The 1997 earthquake caused further damage to the already unsound road (the "burro trail" in the words of my friend from Vicuña), and because the comuna of Ovalle has limited funds for repairs, a road that serves as few people as live in El Arroyo is far down on the list of priorities. They and many others in Loma Seca understand that funds are limited, but many are resentful that the location of the community puts them in an untenable position for complying with the new production requirements.

Again, authorities acknowledge that this is only the beginning stages of a long-term plan that may require eight or more years before all of the elements are in place. In the meantime, clandestine production and the informal market continues as before but at a much reduced level because of the year's devastating drought. Likewise, milk and cheese production at the new factory has been minimal. During times of extreme drought, a 75 percent drop in milk production in Region IV can be expected. Enforcement of the law occurs at the place of sale, where vendors must show that their cheese is made by registered producers. The drought had temporarily made the controversy a "nonissue," as those noncomplying producers who are dependent upon rain-fed natural forage struggled to keep their animals alive, to prevent the natural abortion of the fetus that occurs under starvation conditions, and to produce enough milk to feed the newborn animals. At the time that I left Chile in May 1999, the plant at Ajial del Quiles was producing a small amount of cheese, but because of the drought the milk used to make this cheese was being brought in on trucks from Ovalle, a distance of more than forty kilometers each way over rough roads. This reaffirmed the skepticism of the crianceros in Loma Seca with whom I spoke. The socios were becoming restless while the consultants were telling them to "stay the course."

Concerns over the problems associated with state assistance and the special needs of the communities are voiced by representatives and advocates in public meetings and workshops, and in newspaper interviews. I discussed the general response to the Reglamento with the president of the Limarí Asociación de Comunidades Agrícolas. A bright and animated woman who views her vocation as a combination of advocate and educator, she is responsible for organizing regional meetings to inform comuneros and community residents of their rights and of the assistance that is available. She also works to educate the public on the cultural importance of the comunidades and to raise consciousness regarding their particular challenges. We first met on a Sunday afternoon in February at a big agricultural exposition at the municipal soccer field in Ovalle. The exhibit where she and another woman in the association were stationed was creatively built as a kind of composite picture of a typical comunidad dwelling, featuring adobe construction, a stone corral, and a cactus fence. A few days later I met with her in the office of the Asociación, a simple single-room wooden structure on a backstreet in Ovalle, makeshift in design and surrounded by ongoing postearthquake construction. A couple of days after that, an interview with her appeared in the local newspaper in which she discussed issues dealing with the termination of the exemption.

The president repeated the complaints that I had heard from the crianceros in Loma Seca: Credit is still difficult to come by for the poorest of the rural poor; there is favoritism for the commercial farmer over the individual producer; and the state's requirement that crianceros form commercial enterprise associations as a stipulation to receiving loans and subsidies is a dangerously divisive force within communities because it furthers the concentration of wealth in the families who can afford the legal fees and take on the risk to borrow money. She went on to note that there are problems in the coordination of assistance, that projects are sometimes redundant with many organizations working in one community while others in need go neglected. She inferred that there is preferential treatment in the selection of the communities to receive services.

Development officials see many of these problems but counter that due to limited budgets it is a healthier risk for both the government and the producers to form sociedades. Additionally, they point out that because sustainable development requires input from a variety of economic, environmental, and technological transfer agencies, it makes more sense to concentrate efforts in particular communities as initial steps toward overall regional development. They defend the use of selected communities as pilot programs of "demonstration," the strategy of giving full technical support to a few selected households as a means of dispersion of technology and practices in order to show others "the way." This is a method that has been used in this region on many other projects in the past. In the short-run, it is cost-efficient in terms of administering aid, but critics say that it potentially provokes counterproductive resentment and factionalism.

The program emphasizes the inclusion of those producers who can conform to these standards set down by the law and assures that those who do can expect a higher standard of living as a result. What often goes unexamined, however, is the exclusion of those unable to abide and participate and their projected loss of a crucial means of support. Albeit under the auspice of development, ultimately poverty in an already poor segment may be exacerbated and the decline of a traditional livelihood that is already in decline may be hastened.

Such potential effects are insightfully examined in an investigation by Ciadella (2003) that provides an overview of the great diversity of campesino production relative to access to pasture and ability to comply with the new law and the resulting varying impact that the sanitary law will have on these groups. Drawing upon information from three different zones in Region IV, she identifies several representative types of producers, the disparity between their income and quality of life levels, and the relations and conflicts of interest between them. At the top is the big entrepreneur (*el gran propietario*), owning large tracts of irrigated land in a prime spot near the coast and engaged in various agricultural and livestock activities, including a cheese factory. The study notes that this producer was aligned with other industrial and semi-industrial producers in putting pressure on political institutions to enact the prohibition on artisan cheese (Ciadella 2003, 347). At the bottom and in a dependent relationship with the big proprietor is the milk-selling landless producer (*el sin tierra vendedor de leche*) renting irrigated pasture. Also in a designated "marginal" position is the "traditional comunero" (*el comunero tradicional*) who is dependent upon the insufficient dryland of the campo común and who produces hand-crafted cheese and the non-comunero landless producer of cheese (*el sin tierra productor de queso*) renting pastureland. Faring somewhat better is the "specialized comunero" (*el comunero especializado*) who has entered into a cooperative with others to build a cheese factory. However, the ensuing debts, the poor yield of milk and cheese, and competition with the big factories places him in a precarious position. Maximizing production via freedom of movement to the veranada pastures in the Chile-Argentina cordillera is the "transhumant producer" (*transhumante*) who fares far better but also finds himself in competition with the *gran proprietario* and at the mercy of the new law. Utilizing this complex production mechanism ecologically adapted to arid lands, possessing a deep knowledge of the land and the seasons, and enjoying a modest livelihood and higher status, Ciadella and Dubroeucq (2003) note that the future of the transhumant pastoralist is uncertain as their critical mobility of production is threatened by the sanitary law.

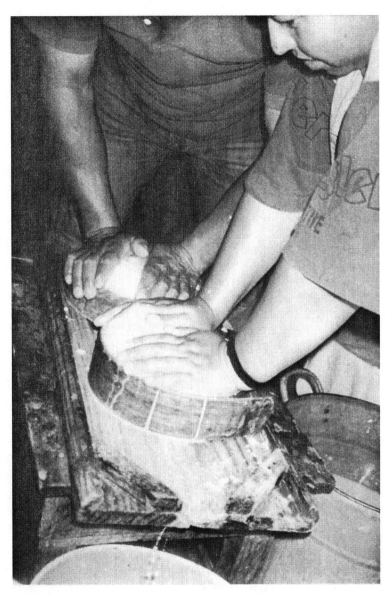
"Pressing cheese by hand." Photo courtesy of the author.

"Natural Truths": Of Mushrooms and Goat Cheese

> Philosophers do not spring up like mushrooms out of the ground;
> they are products of their time, of their nation . . . Philosophy does
> not exist outside the world, any more than the brain exists outside
> man because it is not situated in the stomach.
>
> (Marx 1989, 5)

> Idealists, in contrast [to materialists], place more emphasis on what
> goes on in human minds than on what goes into human stomachs.
>
> (Peoples and Bailey 1988, 98)

The first passage above is a barb aimed at both those who produce
and those who consume ideas about "economy" and "history" as
natural, neutral "things." It encapsulates Marx's historical materialism
in appropriately alimentary metaphors. Such "ruling ideas" should be
exposed as "ideal expressions of dominant material relationships"
(Marx and Engels 2001, 92) that have been detached from the social
relations of production that produced them and that have given them
credence as seemingly objective "truths" ready-made to be swallowed
whole. Once this is understood, Marx says, "history ceases to be a
collection of dead facts, as it is with the empiricists . . . or an imagined
activity of imagined subjects, as with the idealists" (Marx and Engels
2001, 69). For Marx and Engels, social structure and the state are not
imposed from above, but emerge from the "life-process of definite
individuals," not as they are imagined by others or imagine themselves
to be but as "material producers under definite material limits, presup-
positions and conditions independent of their will" (2001, 68). This
notion of "limits" is crucial because within limits or "boundaries" is
space. Within this space people live their lives. They may comply with
some conventional ideas, reject others, or come up with their own
unique ones throughout the course of their pursuance of a material
means of support and subsistence.

The second passage is taken from a popular introductory textbook
in anthropology and frames materialism/idealism into a familiar
"either/or" debate. Here the subject is contrasted in exemplary fashion in opposing explanations of religious prohibition against the eating of pork. In the book *Case of the Unclean Pig*, Mary Douglas's
idealist categorical disorder argument (1966) is pitted against Marvin
Harris's materialist cost/benefit analysis (1977) of the pork taboo. In
this book I have made a case for the historical materialist method in
understanding the mutually formative material/ideal factors involved
in the rural development policy environment in Chile—one manifestation of which I have described here in what might be called "The
Case of the Unclean Cheese."

The revealing of the false dichotomy between the material and the ideal is the greatest strength of the historical materialist method. This is contrary to what many critics of Marx claim and to what many reductionist "vulgar proponents" (Friedman 1974; Post 1978) of Marxism *do*. (In a famous correspondence in 1890, Engels himself complained that many young Marxists of the time misunderstood historical materialism and myopically regarded the economic base as the master determinant in society despite the fact that these spectra of social, historical, and cultural elements interact to shape the organization and style of production [Engels 1890/1978, 761].) This is a practice that Raymond Williams says came after the ironic "transition from Marx to Marxism" (1977, 75), or the leap from ideas and methodology of historical materialism to the orthodox dogma of the determin*ing* economic base and the determin*ed* superstructure (culture, ideology, etc.). This is ironic because this is exactly the kind of reductionist dualism Marx was rejecting, and that a dialectical approach strives to correct.

Although in the course of "making history" human agents make use of "time-honoured disguise" and "borrowed language" (Marx 1994, 15) taken from the material and ideational toolbox left for them by previous generations, the ways in which they use these tools are neither predetermined nor predictable. This is because of the dynamic reciprocal action between (1) people and the parameters of environment and social structure, (2) between "ideas" and material limits, and (3) between alternative forms of production and the limits set by the capitalist mode with which they are articulated (R. Williams 1977, 81). Such a structurally limited but open-ended approach to history and human agency, while still maintaining an articulation of modes of production framework (a dialectic of "structures in process"; see Comaroff 1982), allows breathing space for local culture and addresses the concerns of those who find the extreme structural and ahistoric elements of Althusser unpalatable if not impossible to digest. (In Althusserian terms, development and policy could be described as "Ideological State Apparatuses": those seemingly "nonpolitical" institutions of civil society that "naturalize" as custom, routine, and spontaneous behavior action that ultimately works to the advantage of those in power.) For applied anthropology, in terms of operationalizing political economy toward goals of development policy, it is necessary to take into account the history of capitalist expansion of large-scale commodity production in order to understand how this past has shaped present-day relations between local communities and agents of development. In the example of the comunidades agrícolas of Chile's Norte Chico, copper mining and wheat production were the major areas of export production that impacted regional environment and economy (the material), the formation of both capitalist and non-capitalist social relations of production in specific communities (the ideal). The mutually formative historical relationship between these two realms has produced the political economy of today, the differentiated structure that has revealed itself in the form of this controversial law.

Laws and policies, unlike then "lived" and seamless forms of state ideology, must work harder to cover the tracks between themselves as ideal expressions and the material relations upon which they are based. They must disguise or "make natural" their stated goals as things that are separate from the class interests they represent. State coordination of laws and policies serves to maintain particular structures of power through the creation of new political subjects and the maintenance of old ones with the sanctioned and outwardly nonpolitical institutions or intermediaries between the political and the civil or between the individual and the state (Gramsci 1971, 3–23; 105–20). The state often presents aid and assistance in objective and neutral ways even while it is controlling the means and setting the requirements through which this assistance is given. Standardization, in a sense, creates a problem and then presents itself as the solution. This process echoes what Escobar calls the state's creation of "victim subjects" (1995, 155). The stimulus for much recent criticism of development can be found in his book *Encountering Development: The Making and Unmaking of the Third World,* in which he challenges conventional thinking by asserting that in targeting marginal or minority groups—including peasants, women, ethnic minorities, and so on—a new style of rhetoric has formed around an emerging paradigm that co-opts these groups via language that constructs them as passive recipients whose needs are defined by and can only be solved by the apparatus of development (1995, 155–59).

In general, this seems to be what is happening in Region IV as the government's new attention to poverty is not just guided by faith in the free market, but its drive toward market integration at times writes the viability of nonmarket production and communalistic conservation practices completely out of the story. The observation that the state's use of intermediary entities to distribute assistance is a divisive process resonates with the point that Escobar is making. This process recalls the more sophisticated aspects of Gramsci's concept of hegemony: in times of political stability the state must constantly try to maintain the balance of power through the creation of new political subjects and the upkeep of old ones within the sanctioned and ostensibly nonpolitical institutions of everyday life. Institutions like the ones that usurp power from the traditional comunidad political structure (albeit in the capacity of providing support) promote the agenda of the construction of consent for the free market model policies through a deceptive democratizing of authority: communal class interests are divided and, through necessity or otherwise, these subjects, receiving both assistance and ideology, participate as or place their faith in the intermediaries between the political and the civil. In Gramscian language, the "organic intellectuals" (directly informed by their class position) of the comunidades both experience and perceive the negative results of policies that impede their ability to sell their products. (This stands in contrast to the modernization discourse of the "traditional intellectuals" of the free market cure-all tradition [Gramsci 1971, 3–23, 105–20; Hall 1988, 53–54].)

In the law that I have described, many of the "peripheral people" who it purports to help are negatively impacted. The socioeconomic structure of unequal access to resources and power is not precisely reproduced, however. There are some whose lives will be improved by these policies, but there are others, at least in the short run, whose lives are being made worse. Still, as we will see in the final chapter, there are organizations in Chile with a better understanding of the particular needs, values, and social relations of the comunidades who are working with the communities to help them solve their problems in more appropriate ways. Many comuneros with whom I spoke emphasized that working *with* them is the key to success.

Marx sought to clip the wings of the "natural truths" of major epochs in world history: his mission was to expose the fallaciousness of "philosophy" in general and "natural economy" in particular descending from heaven to earth by showing it rather as entailing the ascent from earth to heaven (Marx and Engels 2001, 68–69). He held that Aristotle's "man is a political animal" reflects the political economy of ancient Greece's "town-citizen" fixation, and that Benjamin Franklin's assertion that "man is a tool-making animal" reflects "Yankee industriousness" (Marx 1976, 444). The political economy of "The Development Project" (McMichael 2004) in Chile, one might say, produces a set of material and ideological limitations codified in law as to the correct way of doing business where it is cheese, rather than politics or tools, that is being made.

CONCLUSION: THE LAW'S IMPACT ON LOMA SECA

As shown in chapter 6, over the course of the nineteen months leading up to the beginning of the official restriction on artisanal cheese, Pablo and Amelia earned 25 percent of their income from the sale of the product. While this percentage is considerable by itself, it is the mobility and supplemental role of this income-generating activity that is even more important. In the five and a half months that they produced cheese in El Arroyo—the traditional "short season" within the community—they earned more than $800 U.S. During the drought months away from home, during the "prolonged" production season made possible by the rented pastures, they expediently switched from selling milk to selling cheese when they were no longer able to continue living near the route of the milk buyer. Both in and away from home, the income is relatively small, but it is a steady source that keeps the family going during the long "valleys" between the brief income "peaks" of wheat and lamb sales.

There are three other families in Loma Seca with at least as many goats as Pablo and Amelia. (Recall that the community sets a limit to the number per family.) There are seven other families with at least forty goats. The sale of cheese, then, could be considered a significant source of income for at least eleven of the thirty-nine households in the community. These eleven households contain thirty-eight people and harvested 188 hectares of wheat in the individual lluvias (or nearly half of the 392 individual hectares harvested). Eight of these eleven households also contributed a total of eleven laborers to the group harvest, the benefits of which were received by non-criancero participants in the cosecha. As mentioned previously, the community as a whole benefited that year from the bountiful cosecha in terms of the money raised by comité-sponsored events. Seen in this way, production of the petty commodity of cheese is in many ways a keystone to both family and community success. It is no wonder then that crianceros were granted exemption for several years, that enforcement of the law was expected to be lax, and that authorities and crianceros alike agree that the "black market" (mercado negro) could scarcely be controlled. Still, there is no doubt that the law will only make a difficult way to make a living more difficult and make poorer and further stigmatize those who cannot conform to it.

The comunidad continues to not only provide security in indivisible land that cannot be lost on the open market, it engenders relations of mutual assistance, and it provides a safety net where the government's social welfare system is lacking. In the case of the comités it is encouraging that the state is working with the human resources and communitarian ideals that the comunidad system engenders. Rather than implementing change from above, policy should enhance local level structures already in place. Peasant forms of cooperation and mutual assistance are not incommensurable with capitalist aims.

In 1998 as part of this market integration plan, the government subsidized the cost of a project in which twelve comuneros from Loma Seca (referred to as "socios" or "associates" when they are members of such an organized project)—including Pablo—took out loans and contributed labor to convert a few hectares of land previously used for wheat into an irrigated alfalfa field. Each socio's share was about a quarter of a hectare. As with the funding for cheese factories, the unsubsidized portion was paid for with money borrowed through soft loans. For the pradera of alfalfa, the twelve individuals pay around 300,000 pesos (about $670 U.S.) taken out in long-term credit paid back over a period of four to five years at 7 to 8 percent interest after a two-year grace period. The irrigation for this pradera cost about 1,790,000 pesos (about $4,000 U.S.) of which the state subsidized 75 percent. The twelve socios shared the cost of the remaining quarter, which comes out to about $80 U.S. tacked on to each individual loan. Eduardo, who lives in Loma Seca most of the time with Elena, contributed to the labor project. I monitored the progress of the project from time to time when I made trips to the community. The men were proud of their work and quite optimistic. The finished irrigated field was very impressive. For Pablo, who has more than one hundred goats and nearly two hundred sheep, it will be important but will only serve as supplemental food for animals. Alfalfa is the highest-quality forage and important for good milk production. Pablo is very slowly replacing his animals with breeds that produce a higher rate of milk, but the cost is prohibitive.

As I stated in a 2004 article in *Culture and Agriculture:*

> These are only small first steps, and the prohibition on the sale of cheese is here now. Meanwhile families wait for stable animal forage, the creation of milking centers, and improved transportation to bring this commodity to market in a way that meets the new standards. Mainly, however, they wait for rain. When the winter rains return, they will plant wheat again. They will clandestinely sell cheese on the informal market because for the poorest of them, the "step-by-step" process of standardized market integration has a few steps missing. (Alexander 2004, 49)

9

Rural Development Beyond the Neoliberal Model

INTRODUCTION

THERE ARE A HOST OF GOVERNMENT AND NONGOVERNMENT ORGANI-
zations offering assistance to rural people in the Region IV. More than
twenty work specifically with comunidades agrícolas in areas such as
rural development, transfer of technology and training, and problem
analysis. Although many of them are involved in the various components of the plan to integrate criancero milk producers and artisanal
cheese makers as described in the previous chapter, they are far from
agreement as to how this process should be carried out. Some of them
bemoan the fact that even though Chile is an incredibly geographically
and ecologically complex and diverse country, the policy-making apparatus tends to be excessively standardized or "one size fits all" in
approach. This view was expressed by a project director at one of the
government organizations providing credit and assistance who told
me that sometimes decisions are made in Santiago to implement policies that are inappropriate in some parts of the nation. He said that it
would be better if each region had a greater hand in managing its own
affairs. If at the local level, the comuna took responsibility for its own
resources, then the results would be, in his words, more "socially
integrated." This is especially needed in Region IV, he said, because it
is among the poorest regions in Chile. With regard to the Reglamento
Sanitario de los Alimentos, I was still confused as to how queseros like
Amelia and Pablo could comply with the law that was to soon come
into effect. "They can't," he matter-of-factly answered and went on to
describe the law as a top-down decision from the Ministry of Health,
symptomatic of a centralized bureaucracy removed from the real interests of people at the local level. "More law," I was told, will create
"more clandestine production."

When I asked if the socios of the factory at Ajial were in a risky
position because of the low milk production, it was suggested that the

agencies involved, including the private consulting company providing managerial training, had sufficient subsidies and a strong rooting interest in nurturing the project through such initial difficulties. Others with whom I spoke repeated similar opinions, with one person remarking that the mayor of a local town was strongly pushing it for political reasons. Another recited a cautionary tale in reverse: Before there can be cheese, there must be milk; before there can be milk, there must be pasture; and before there can be pasture, there must be water. The factory should be the "last part of the chain" (*el último punto de la cadena*), but it seems as if this is the part that was paid for first.

Not to belabor the chain metaphor, it is easy to see that this policy is excluding or "de-linking" or "*dis*articulating" (in mode of production terms) from this chain the poorest segment of the crianceros of the Norte Chico. I chose to highlight chapter 8 as a set piece in this book because it is my hope that studying how and why handcrafted goods are made will help us to understand how peasants reproduce their distinct economic culture and to better appreciate the effects of their engagement with external economies. Regrettably, peasants are sometimes neglected by rural assistance programs because of their dependency on nonagricultural economic activities. With specific regard to Chile, Kay has termed this the "*minifundia* problem" of the post-Pinochet Concertación center-left governments, pointing out that state-mediated processes of *reconversión*—that is, replacing traditional productive activities with more profitable endeavors—often privilege those peasant producers judged "viable" or "potentially viable" while passing over household units with tiny landholdings. Since such land-poor households depend upon wage labor and the manufacture of various petty commodities for survival, they tend to fall through the cracks. State agencies faced with finite resources and dwindling budgets for rural development projects favor smallholders deemed better bets for market success while directing minifundistas to welfare services (Kay 1997). Here it appears that marginalization necessitates survival strategies that inadvertently "create" a poverty designation, and it is the failure of the state's categories that exacerbates poverty through a limited view of productivity.

In the closing pages of this book, I will conclude with two concepts that have emerged from my study of the resource-use practices of people in Loma Seca that would be useful to economic development and sustainability programs in Chile and beyond that aim to transcend such limitations: (1) "Mutable Mobile Modes of Resource Maximization" and (2) the "Subsistence-Stewardship Approach to Productive Diversity." First, however, I will highlight two recent development initiatives in Region IV as two good examples of projects that are attuned to the special qualities and needs of the comunidades agrícolas that aim to support—rather than supplant—the comunidad system's effective relations of production and community welfare.

Supporting the Existing Systems of Support

As we have seen, in the case of the comités, it is encouraging that the state is working with the human resources and communitarian ideals that such a system engenders. Instead of imposing change from above, policy should enhance structures already in place. Peasant forms of cooperation and mutual assistance are not, as is often believed, incommensurable with capitalist aims. Two such development and conservation projects under way at the time of my fieldwork were working in conjunction with the extant comunidad structure and cooperative practices in order to improve rather than radically change them. One was being coordinated by researchers in the Department of Agronomy at the University of La Serena at Ovalle and involves numerous government assistance agencies, including CONAF (forestation) and PRODECOP (credit extension). The two comunidades where the work is being carried out are Alcones and Divisidero (both are "Punitaqui system" communities [see chapter 4] like Loma Seca). One of the exceptional advances of this study is that it acknowledges that every community is unique in terms of how land and resources are used. Within these communities, the researchers are "clustering" the producers according to demographic, resource, and production patterns so that state monies can be allocated more efficiently and directed toward the specific needs of the community. The other important contribution of this study is that it acknowledges from the outset that although at the moment agriculture alone may not be sufficient to support households, family members who temporarily migrate to earn money still contribute to the domestic unit with remittances and by returning home to provide labor when they can. Thus, one of the goals of the study is to coordinate the work demands of proposed projects with the cyclical opportunities for wage labor so as to maximize available human resources.

As in Loma Seca, the government is working in these communities to recover soil through planting alfalfa and reforestation plants such as *Atriplex* and *Acacia*. The common problem that the development team faces is that they must convince the comuneros that setting aside a portion of the common land for reforestation does not mean "losing" the land but rather making it available to their animals in a more manageable and more efficient form. They are optimistic, however, because of the participative nature of this project. After determining the specific productive activities traditionally practiced in the communities, there will be an analysis of what types of support should be given taking into consideration the community members' needs and limitations. All of this will be done before they begin initiating changes that may prove to be inappropriate. The goal is still to assist the comuneros in finding alternatives to their traditional ways of making a living, but to do so in conjunction with them.

In Alcones, there is also a project to develop citrus production. Like the community of Loma Seca, they already work together on common projects. Individual producers will contribute labor, and the water from new irrigation projects will be distributed among them. The intention is not to eliminate the raising of goats as a means of subsistence but to diversify production with fruit plantations so that they can subsidize production from goats while sustainable pasture is being developed. In the community of Divisidero, the scenario is a little bit different. When the price of copper is low, many small mines that are owned by individual comuneros are forced to close. They then turn more heavily to herding or agriculture. The project's main idea is to have plantations (avocado has been suggested) available to them as an alternative.

In both projects, it is emphasized that the goal is to first understand the particular system of the comuneros, to grasp the limitations of it, and then to work together with them to implement decisions. I was told that this is very important because many projects in the past have failed because they did not have community consent. It was stressed to me that members must be involved from the beginning, that the projects have to "originate with them" (*nacio de ellos*). The goal is to maintain the traditional strengths of the comunidades and to address the problems that limit production while preserving the effective cultural adaptations of these systems.

SUBSISTENCE-STEWARDSHIP APPROACH TO PRODUCTIVE DIVERSITY AND MUTABLE MODES

Such projects are progressive and a far cry from the highly centralized "top-down" model (a bureaucratic legacy of the dictatorship as well as cookie-cutter neoliberalism applied indiscriminately) decried in the cheese law controversy. As part of a biodiversity and sustainable development research group, I initially came to Chile believing that any workable concept of biodiversity protection should not only incorporate subsistence production into its concerns, but a consideration of the ways that people bring forth livelihoods from the land should lie at the crux of its definition. I believed that any such definition of biodiversity conservation can better serve the aims of biodiversity programs by taking into account local methods of resource conservation and can better address the problems of rural poverty by strengthening the community structures of resource control that manage these conservation practices. While the protection of biodiversity is conventionally imagined as something separate from production and its transformative technologies that procure profit from the environment, the irony and injustice of the fact that most of the world's biological diversity is located in regions where people are the poorest is regularly noted as well. Taken together, these two precepts—the presumed separation of economic production and biological diversity and the observed coexistence of biodiversity and poverty—would seem to reinforce each other, but only if wider social and political structures of inequality and alternative definitions of "production" are ignored. Should not those whose livelihoods are most closely tied to environmental conditions—who have the most at stake—be in a better position to protect the environment? (Alexander 1997).

As I have demonstrated here, survival for rural producers in the Norte Chico depends upon productive diversity and flexibility of environmental use options. Earlier important research in this area was carried out by Grupo de Investigaciones Agrarias (GIA). In 1992 Bahamondes, Gacitua, and Rivas published results of a study examining three communities in the Guatulame valley. In each community certain "types" of household production units were most prevalent: (1) those in which farming and grazing provide the majority of productive activities, (2) units in which income from working of the land contributes to about half of the household income, and (3) units in which income from the property is only peripheral or partially complementary to income generated primarily through wage labor. (Referring to the differences between these types as degrees of "proletarianization", it is interesting to note that this study was published four years after the 1988 plebiscite that defeated Pinochet.) Able to distribute risk across multiple strategies, the first "type" of community was in a far better position when economic downturn occurs or excessive drought puts too much pressure on any one means of livelihood (Bahamondes, Gacitua, and Rivas 1992, 94–95). A 1994 follow-up report more specifically correlated the abilities of families to diversify income-generating activities in the reproduction of the domestic unit with overall sustainability of the valley in which these communities are located (Bahamondes, Gacitua, and Rivas 1994, 21). These findings indicate some important points: Wage labor alone is simply not adequate; reliance on any particular source is risky; the community mode of production is viable as long as there is environmental, economic, and productive diversity and, seen in this light, complete proletarianization (the "predestined" wage labor dependency foreseen by some perspectives in chapter 2) is far from inevitable.

Those who are critical of development anthropology sometimes charge that applied anthropologists are guilty of a blind faith in the neutrality of the language in the literature produced by development agencies. Such wholesale acceptance of an authoritative discourse obscures the power relations that are reproduced by way of the state's development apparatus (what problems are acknowledged; how are they imagined; who gets assistance, etc.). At the same time, it may also render us blind to the amount of control that the rural poor actually have over their own lives outside of the influence of the state (Gow 1996, 165). A subsistence production-oriented approach necessarily puts us *in the field*, developing original analysis that avoids reliance on limited types of information or on sources in which the flow of information is controlled by parties with vested interests. Focusing our attention on the space where, say, biodiversity and domestic production interact, we can discover key connections that are informed more by the fundamental relationship between nature and culture and less by particular political, ideological, or methodological biases.

Such fieldwork is necessary in order for biodiversity programs to achieve a mutually informative relationship between traditional and nontraditional technologies and production activities. This need for "complementary sources of wisdom" was beautifully laid out in Billie DeWalt's call for *mutable mobiles*, means of analysis that entail "contextualized, holistic knowledge that can be adapted and applied to similar phenomenon in other circumstances" (1994, 127). DeWalt firmly grounds idealism for such prescriptive mutualism in a pragmatic demand that these resource utilization solutions must be averse to the risks of both markets as well as climate (1994, 129). In Region IV, the local institution of communitarian property rights and the conservation methods within the communal structure must be part of this mutually informative process, and by working within and accepting the community as the legitimate entity of reference and negotiation, the problems of generalized knowledge, group identity, and legal status can be addressed in ways that are adequate and fair.

With this in mind, the biodiversity project attempted but did not succeed in establishing contracts to set up community trust funds in areas where collection was taking place. (Here I recall Dove's advice that "the best solution may be to make explicit in any intervention with intellectual property rights, that the intervention itself is prob-

lematic, and to develop means for addressing this" [1996, 61–62].)
Brush made clear in a later work that the success of contracts in
conserving biological resources is largely contingent on the ability of
local people to control and limit the collection and exportation of
these resources (1996, 17). It continues to be my recommendation—
whether the area of concern is bioprospecting for medicinal plants
or the promotion of market integration and resource conservation
practices—that the political and economic structure of the comunidades agrícolas must be given due attention in this negotiation and
compensation process. It is my hope that such inclusion would offset
"top-down," market-biased trappings by promoting equity, making
use of and perhaps strengthening the group identity and solidarity of
the "marginalized," and, most importantly, keeping the focus on the
protection and improvement of their livelihood and subsistence strategies. The government in Chile is taking steps through social welfare
programs to improve the lives of its citizens (rural people in semiarid
areas included), but these efforts will continue to be incomplete as
long as there is a lack of dialogue between the agents of free market
development ideology and these representatives of the systems of subsistence based on indivisible communal land.

MUTABLE MOBILE MODES OF RESOURCE MAXIMIZATION

Taking my inspiration from DeWalt's work, I have expanded the term
to coin my own, which describes the flexibility and resourcefulness I
have observed and analyzed in the preceding chapters: "Mutable
Mobile Modes of Resource Maximization." The unique principles of
this term can be broken down into the following four characteristics:

1. *A "mode" entails methods particular to a functioning arrangement of component elements.* The various components of the mode
that I have described here include individuals, households, and the
community itself, each articulated in varying ways with the wider
economy via markets, wage labor migration, and development policies. Productive activities are outfitted in a variety of ways toward a
variety of ends and entail a combination of subsistence agropastoral
activities for domestic consumption, petty commodity production of
artisanal goods for informal markets, agropastoral commodity production for formal markets, and wage labor. Means of production
include a combination of individually and communally held properties and land access traditions. Relations of production in the agropastoral area include a combination of unpaid household-oriented
contributions and arrangements of reciprocal exchange, including

pooling of community property and group labor. Individual families are supported by both products of subsistence and low-level capital accumulation, while at the same time, the wider community is supported by social-oriented mechanisms that direct a portion of individual capital surplus toward group needs and community improvements from which everyone benefits and has equal access to regardless of one's position as a comunero (chapter 5). Thus, the mode is an integrated system of individual/family/community, subsistence/ commercial, and capitalist/communalist methods, means, and outcomes of production, consumption, accumulation, and distribution.

2. *A mode is "mutable" if it is capable of changing form in relation to changes in the wider environment in which it functions and to which it is articulated.* In the Norte Chico, this is crucial for households like the ones in this study, because families need the ability to change from one type of production to another depending upon the relative abundance and scarcity of environmental resources resulting from seasonal and cyclical changes in climate, as well as seasonal fluctuations in prices for goods and access to markets (chapter 6). Indeed, as we have seen (chapter 3), domestic livelihoods have been articulated with large-scale capitalist production (commodities of copper and wheat) since the inception of the comunidades, with agropastoral activities becoming more important as commercial activities played out. In addition to resiliency in this delicate and changing natural environment, I have described the remarkable perseverance of these communities across wide swings in the political climate (chapter 4) during which subsistence requirements were more or less successfully met by the land and livelihood of the comuneros depending upon their relationship with the state. Today, as I have also described, economic policies in postdictatorship Chile provide challenges in the climate of rural development. One thing that has remained largely immutable throughout the changes in these various "environments" is the basic structure of land tenure and the security that it provides.

3. *A mutable mode is "mobile" if its adaptability includes the capacity to be migratory while maintaining its essential connection to "home."* Hostile environments require versatility, not only in what is produced, but in how and where livelihood activities are organized. Pablo and Amelia's family showed extreme resiliency and resourcefulness during protracted periods of drought in the time that I spent with them: shifting production sites from the campo común to the lluvia to the Limarí valley in their migratory search for pasture for their goats and sheep and markets for their cheese and milk during their "itinerant seasons of sacrifice," as well as in the preceding years when they moved with their animals hundreds of kilometers south to Viña del

Mar in order to access the summer tourist market. This is a fierce dedication to the preservation of what Pablo called their "mobile capital," but, of course, efforts like the two research and development projects described above, if successful, would eliminate the need for such extreme sacrifices. Such mobility requires (as I argued in chapter 1) an expansive concept of "community" in order to recognize the mode's unique cultural and economic adaptations: expansive (or beyond conventional boundaries) in terms of geographic space, time, and constituent membership. Migrants as well as family members at home (in varying ways and to varying degrees) participate in and benefit from community activities and express commitment to the comunidad (chapter 5). Within the property limits of the comunidad there is a microscale mobility (shifting cultivation and regeneration of the lluvias and shifting sites of production between the campo común and the lluvias) spawned by land tenure and resource use practices (chapter 3) that also makes the most of periodically scarce resources.

4. *Such mutable mobile modes are necessary in order to maximize resources in environments of cyclical instability.* Just as fixed notions of community need to be "unbounded" in order to grasp the complexity of rural livelihoods in the Norte Chico, resource maximization efforts should be conceived of in terms of human resources as well as environmental ones. Various family members engage in various types of petty commodity production and agropastoral activities at various locations, often simultaneously. Preferred wage labor jobs away from home allow workers to return to participate in important family and community work efforts. Group work projects (such as harvesting wheat on the common land) share costs and increase individual family profits by maximizing labor that is available during a "year of rain," and ancillary activities such as money-generating carreras, dances, and other festivities during good years similarly make the most of the presence of people in the community. Such crosscutting resource maximization blurs the distinction between social forms and work-focused forms of mutual assistance (chapter 5) and between our "working" and "nonworking" lives that we make in our highly individualized wage labor–based society. Also, that periods of scarcity are cyclical is key. "Cyclical" means that "down" periods are only transitory. When one's experience is marked by persistent periods of cyclical scarcity and successful productivity, there is a tendency to take both the "long view"—and be neither demoralized by times of want, nor incautious during times of plenty—and the "wide view," and engage in multiple productive strategies and avoid overinvesting in any one endeavor, both of which make the persistence of peasantry in Latin

America in general, and the resiliency of the comunidades agrícolas in particular, quite a bit more comprehensible.

The Subsistence-Stewardship Approach to Productive Diversity

Along with effective management of human resources, we have seen how the comunidad system generates management of natural resources (chapter 3) through the setting of "limits" on the use of "limited resources": limits to "use rights" (or "shares"), limits that discourage overuse of resources, regulation of access to arable land (use of "lluvias"), limits to privatization of land, and a democratic body that works to achieve consensus on how land should be used. Such control promotes environmental diversity in a similar way that diversity in production and income activities is the key to family success. Access to multiple sources in an area of unstable resources (environmental, economic, and, at times, sociopolitical) means not being overly dependent upon any one source. I contend that such a connection between economic subsistence and environmental resource stewardship is vital in areas of periodic and long-term scarcity. The "Subsistence-Stewardship Approach to Productive Diversity" can be an effective template in other parts of the world and is understood by the following characteristics:

1. *The meaning of "subsistence" is relative to particular environments.* From a capitalist perspective, the meaning of "subsistence"—activities that provide all or nearly all of the products required by a farming family without any substantial surplus for sale—usually bears a negative connotation that implies a minimum, inadequate return on the labor involved in the production. More generally, however, "subsistence" also means existence, continuation, and persistence; a set of essential characteristics or qualities of an entity's existence or "real being," as opposed to an abstraction. Beyond a negative evaluation of subsistence as a "minimum" meeting of the necessities of life (what is necessary to "just survive"), then, the word can also mean the character possessed by "what is possible." In this light, mere "survival" in the face of long odds is not a disappointing "minimum," but an inspirational "maximization."

Similarly, if local knowledge and environmental practice is not conceived of as a process, our analysis is overly deterministic and rooted in an extreme separation of Nature and Society that reduces the actions that people take to mere reactions against environment and state political and economic domination. This not only gives short shrift to representations of local culture, but also to our understanding of how the state apparatus works as well. The assumption of the dichotomy of Nature and Society is taken for granted by both materialist scholars concerned with empirical details and structuralist theorists determined to construct relational models. At their extremes, as Descola and Pálsson tell us, both deny that communities and their constituent households are "embedded" in the relationship between environment and culture (1996, 2–4). Within the parameters that environment provides, there are many possible combinations of actions driven by the human ability, through individual and collective decision making, to transform as well as adapt to the environment.

2. *Subsistence (conceived broadly in terms of such persistence) in fragile environments must by its nature entail environmental stewardship.* Stewardship—or individual responsibility in managing one's lifeways, livelihood, and property with proper regard to the rights of others—means to actively manage or direct the usage of resources in ways that are both equitable and sustainable.

The corollary to my assertion that communal landholdings and their means of self-regulation are appropriate strategies within the social and ecological context of Chile's Region IV is that development policies that fail to adequately address rural poverty issues do so because they are based on concepts of culture and environment, which are not appropriate in this region. The false separation of resource conservation and environmentally informed productive economic activities has been the subject of much debate over the relationship between environment and culture. The best models replace the culture and nature "dualism" with a kind of "mutualism" in which people procure immediate knowledge of their natural environment through everyday activities, which in turn act upon the environment. Production is not culture imposed upon an external reality of nature, but is involved in a mutually informative relationship with natural surroundings (Croll and Parkin 1992, Ignold 1992). Pálsson constructs a useful framework for thinking about the ways in which environment is conceptualized and engaged. When people from industrialized society think of the environment, we usually imagine something that exists either to be exploited ("orientalism," in which the environment serves to meet the needs of people) or protected ("paternalism," in which people are the guardians of the environment). The latter approach is modern and seemingly progressive when compared to the former, yet it holds on to the same certainty of the radical separation of Nature and Society, something that his third model, "communalism," rejects. Here the emphasis is on practice and generalized reciprocity in the relationship between people and environment (Pálsson 1996, 63–76). Much official environmentalism in Chile is, in Pálsson's terminology, paternalistic means toward orientalist ends. The dangers of resource depletion are stressed in terms of the loss of a precious commodity (potentially arable land that can be developed for market production), or biological diversity is promoted in terms of the market value, of a potential commodity (medicinal plants, for example).This privileging of market definitions of economy over domestic meanings, of exchange value over use value reinforces the position that environmental concerns are both a luxury of and tools for a healthy market economy. This conceptual disjunction has all too real consequences. It further separates the poor from their means of supporting themselves and severs local conservation practice from the social and environmental mode of production in which they developed. The rigid dichotomization of Nature and Society mirrors society's class stratification. It serves those who sit on top. Environmentalism in the impoverished margins is rendered as unthinkable an extravagance as environmentalism without profit in the capitalist sectors of society.

   3. *Since productive diversity is necessary in fragile environments, environmental policies in such areas will not only be more fair, they will be more effective if they are linked to subsistence production needs.* If biodiversity and sustainable development efforts are not coordinated with poverty programs and economic initiatives in which people regenerate or maintain resources in marginal areas for subsistence purposes, the rural poor will never be able to choose long-range conservation over quick-fix chaos. The relationship between biodiversity and diverse economic activities in places like the Norte Chico must be emphasized in order to help people maintain control over their environment and their means of livelihood. It has been shown that there is a direct correlation between the abilities of families in comunidades to diversify income-generating activities with overall ecological sustainability. Shiva is a prominent voice supporting the belief in interdependence of production and biodiversity at the community level. She argues against the implementation of centrally controlled environmental technologies and systems of production, or "monoculture," which are ultimately unsustainable and which increase risk by transforming people's means of livelihood into "raw material" commodities (Shiva 1993). By distributing risk across loosely connected multiple subsistence strategies, local systems like those in the Norte Chico have "room to heal" when catastrophe strikes. Conversely, a single-market blow or a single ecological disaster shakes from top to bottom systems of centrally controlled, homogenized, uniform, unsustainable production to which Shiva refers. (Forgive the distinctly North Amer-

ican example, but umpires remove from play baseballs that have become soft and battered during games. The fresh, tightly wound ones
go farther when they are smacked.)

In communities such as Loma Seca, which has a good reputation for
being open to change (as well as in the above-mentioned communities
of Alcones and Divisidero), comuneros understand the ecological
problems associated with many of their traditional means of making a
living and have shown that they will adopt corrective measures when
doing so does not threaten either individual livelihood or community
survival. The comunidades agrícolas of the Norte Chico present serious challenges to dualistic models. By looking at how communal
ownership of land and community social relations of production and
political association reproduce solidarity and identity even while this
cooperative style of production is closely linked with the capitalist
system, we see on the part of local culture an *active*, rather than simply
reactive, struggle over the use and management of resources.

Examining the fundamental relationship between natural resources
and livelihood requires original fieldwork at the specific site of this
mutually constitutive interaction. This type of fieldwork is less likely
to produce data and engender recommendations that privilege market-
oriented production at the expense of the needs of the rural poor. Such
fieldwork similarly provides empirical data on local culture that is
often missing from macrolevel theories of economic development and
underdevelopment. A program in which biodiversity is conceived of
in relation to subsistence production helps the rural poor maintain
control over their resources and means of livelihood. This is done by
acknowledging and protecting the varied and connected means of
resource use and conservation. In return, by utilizing or enhancing
local practices and structures, development agencies have access to
knowledge that has been researched and tested extensively by the
people whose lives are most directly affected by environmental policies. In the case of Region IV, this "testing" has occurred over hundreds of years in an area where drought and lack of arable land are
permanent features, in an area where resource maximization is critical.
Finally, this approach provides a means for understanding the persistence of modes of production that differ from, but are undeniably
linked to, Western capitalism. By bringing to light the tools of conservation and management and the ideological struggle over resources,
we better see the specific ways in which these rural modes of production reproduce themselves in the modern world economy. Agarwal,
for example, warns that it is critical that local communities be in
charge of management of their natural resources. This is not only
because it is fair, but also because they are the ones directly involved in

the reciprocal relationship with nature. They have the most intimate knowledge of management practices and the most stake in continued productive subsistence based on biodiversity (Agarwal 1994).

Environment and development should not be considered ends in themselves but rather as means with generative and regenerative connections between development and livelihood and between environment and productive activities. Those in Chile who advocate for the protection of the comunidades realize that there is both an ethical imperative and a practical basis to the preservation of community control. These communities are self-regulating systems that have been in place for hundreds of years and have developed as responses to the austerity of local ecology and the larger socioeconomic context. Even among those who want to treat the problems of the Norte Chico through replacement of tradition with technology and through complete integration into the capitalist economy, there is a "yet they are still here" acknowledgment of the ability of these people to survive. But does this persistence entail constancy and control or is it marked by adaptiveness, variability, and a complex interaction between stabilizing and destabilizing factors? The answer, it seems, depends upon one's definition of "resilience."

Throughout this book I have referred explicitly to the resilience of the families in Loma Seca in the face of extreme challenges and changing circumstances. Here, and elsewhere (2002), I have identified this persistence as resiliency across various shifting social, political, and ecological environments. I am using "resilience" as a descriptive term to describe their survival in light of the adaptability and complexity of the strategies they use to reproduce both family livelihood and community structure. I am also using it to describe the flexibility of these livelihoods and the structures themselves. I have argued that recognizing this requires scholars to use broader and more flexible models of concepts like "community" and for policy makers to take a closer look at the diversity of peasant livelihood strategies and the impact that laws and projects may have when they threaten or reduce this diversity. Dualistic models, whether in theory or in applied work, impoverish our understanding of peasant culture and diminish our capacity to facilitate appropriate assistance.

"Resilience" is currently associated most frequently with a new school of thought and area of research that envisions the dynamic relationship between societies and ecologies in cutting edge and exciting ways. Drawing upon the groundbreaking work of scholars like Holling and Gunderson (Holling 1973, 1996, 2004; Gunderson and Holling 2002; Gunderson and Pritchard 2002), this theoretical orientation moves beyond what it sees as outdated and ill-conceived cultural ecology models of equilibrium and homeostasis as the ideal and normal state in the relationship between humans and the environment. While stability had typically been limited to an understanding of resilience as the rate at which a system returns to a single steady or cyclic state after a major shock or disturbance—a view marked by constancy—from an ecological and evolutionary view, resilience may entail the wholesale reorganization of a system from one "stability domain" or "behavior regime" to another. Thus, rather than seeing efficiency and predictability as standards of measurement, a system's long-term success may in fact be marked by persistence, adaptiveness, and variability based on its ability to transform itself in response to major disturbances (Holling 1973). For issues of sustainability, the differences between these two aspects are profound. The first view, sometimes called an "engineering resilience" (Holling 1996; Gunderson et al. 2002, 4), imagines that status quo sustainability is possible since natural systems can in effect be managed and that the outcomes of the human-nature interface are predictable. The second view, sometimes called an "ecological resilience" (Holling 1996; Gunderson et al. 2002, 4) says that a recognition of the interaction between "stabilizing" and "destabilizing" features—including things like global climate change and the loss of biodiversity—must be considered in order to gauge the magnitude of trauma that the system can withstand before it "flips" or transforms into a different stability domain/behavior regime based on a different set of structures and processes. Gunderson and Holling (2002) have coined the term "panarchy" to describe and explain how "complex living systems both persist and innovate at the same time" as they "create and also benefit from crisis" (Holling 2004). Defined as a layered set of interactive cycles, panarchy is the process by which systems "grow, adapt, transform, and in the end, collapse." Occuring at different rates, the "back loop" of such transformations is a time of critical opportunity for innovation and discovery, when "resilience is tested and established." Holling and his colleagues warn that we "now see changes on a global scale that suggest we are in such a back loop" (2004).

Along with the works of Holling and Gunderson, a good place to start for the reader interested in learning more about this kind of research is the Web site for the Resilience Alliance (http://www.resalliance.org), an interdisciplinary organization made up of scientists and applied practitioners engaged in interdisciplinary collaboration exploring "the dynamics of social-ecological systems" around the world. Another good introduction is the electronic journal *Ecology and Society,* a multidisciplinary journal of "Integrative Science for

Resilience and Sustainability" that is committed to the "rapid dissemination of current research" in this field.

While the book that you have just read is not directly based on this kind of research, nor does it make use of the specific tools of this orientation, I see a good deal of crossover themes, concerns, and concepts that lend themselves to further research in this area. For example, in my considerations of the "Peasant Question" in chapter 2, I began this book with a rejection of homeostatic views of peasant culture as a system of self-regulated equilibrium that balances consumption needs, productive capacity, and resource availability in a kind of insular, inward-oriented steady-state system. Also, like the position that I have taken here, the field of the study of resilience moves away from the Nature-Culture binary by identifying the "social-ecological system" as a single unit of analysis, seeing the relationship between people and the environment as "an integrated system in which the dynamics of the social and ecosystem domains are strongly linked and of equal weight" (the Resilience Alliance).The Web site of the Research Alliance identifies other key research terms, including "resilience" defined as "the capacity of a system to absorb disturbance, undergo change, and still retain essentially the same function, structure, identity, and feedbacks" and adaptability defined as "the capacity of actors in a system to manage resilience, either by moving the system toward or away from a threshold that would fundamentally alter the properties of the system, or by altering the underlying features of the stability landscape" (the Resilience Alliance). In my exploration of the persistence of the people of Loma Seca, I have provided a detailed account of such adaptability and managed resilience through innovation born of ecological as well as economic and, at times, political crisis. It is my hope that the ethnographic data provided here will contribute to seeing social-ecological systems like the comunidades agrícolas as integrated systems, and that this will in some way make the persistence and variability of such systems less mystifying. Whether these innovations and future collaborations with external environmental and economic problem solvers will represent a short-term adaptation before a long-term collapse remains to be seen.

CONCLUDING REMARKS

I believe that the "Subsistence-Stewardship Approach to Productive Diversity" and the concept of "Mutable Mobile Modes of Resource Maximization" are applicable to the understanding of the persistence of and problems faced by many other peasant communities around the world. There are many common denominators between the comunidades agrícolas and other communities in dryland areas where people are—often against great odds—maintaining their traditions and reproducing their local economies while under similar ecological, social, political, and market pressures. Along with deterioration of fragile ecosystems and shortages of arable land, there are shared social characteristics: a near-exclusive use of family labor, low levels of external income, production oriented toward family consumption, rudimentary technology, and limited access to credit, technical, and social assistance. Another common denominator is the neoliberal market-integration development model through which assistance is administered.

Survival suggests strength and persistence of local culture, but it is still very easy to deny the unit of analysis its dynamic integrity when it exists in a "marginal environment." The comunidades agrícolas of the Norte Chico are situated between capitalist/noncapitalist oppositional categories. By examining how cultural understandings of the environment and diversified economic activities cross the boundaries of economic systems, we can better understand the persistence and resiliency of entities like the comunidades agrícolas of Chile's "Little North."

Works Cited

Abrams, Philip. 1988. Notes on the Difficulty of Studying the State. *Journal of Historical Sociology* 1 (1): 58–89.

Acevedo Diaz, Sonia, et al. 1968. *Rol de la Mujer Como Agente de Cambio: Memoria para Optar al Título de Asistente Social.* La Serena: Universidad de Chile.

Acheson, James. 1989. Management of Common-Property Resources. In *Economic Anthropology,* ed. S. Plattner, 351–78. Stanford, CA: Stanford University Press.

Agarwal, Anil. 1994. Local Control or Global Plunder. *Multinational Monitor* 15 (9): 15–20.

Alexander, William L. 1995. Land Tenure and Subsistence Strategies in the Norte Chico, Chile. Paper presented at the Society for Applied Anthropology Annual Meeting, March 30, Albuquerque, NM.

———. 1996. The Cultural Component of Biodiversity. Paper presented at the Bioactive Agents from Drylands Plants of Latin America Project Workshop on Biodiversity and Sustainable Economic Development, March 27, Buenos Aires, Argentina.

———. 1997 The Productive Diversity Approach to Sustainability: Examples from Northern Chile. Guest lecture at University of Iceland, Department of Anthropology, April 15, Reykjavik, Iceland.

———. 1999. Clandestine Artisans or Commercial Producers: Law and the Market Integration of Rural Livelihood in Northern Chile. Paper presented at Society for Applied Anthropology Annual Meeting, April 23, Tucson, AZ.

———. 2000a. Resiliency in a Hostile Environment: The Comunidades Agrícolas of Chile's Norte Chico. PhD dissertation, Department of Anthropology, University of Arizona.

———. 2000b. Cowboys and Indians and Miners: Mining History for Origins and Identity in Chile's "Little North." Paper presented at American Anthropological Association Annual Meeting, November 19, San Francisco, CA.

———. 2001. Itinerant Seasons of Sacrifice: Drought and Migration Patterns in Chile's Norte Chico. Paper presented at American Anthropological Association Annual Meeting, November 28, Washington, DC.

———. 2002. Organization and Advocacy in Rural Chile: Peasant-Worker Consciousness in the Transition to Democracy. *Anthropology of Work Review* 23 (3–4): 25–30.

———. 2004. Clandestine Artisans or Integrated Producers? Standardization of Rural Livelihood in the Norte Chico, Chile. *Culture and Agriculture* 26 (1–2): 38–50.

———. 2006. Cowboys and Indians and Comuneros: Policy-Positioned Ascriptions of Ethnicity, Identity, and History in Chile. *Social Identities: Journal for the Study of Race, Nation, and Culture* 12 (2): 139–65.

————, ed. Forthcoming. *Lost in Transition in Chile: A Critique of Neoliberalism from Pinochet to "The Third Way."* Lanham, MD: Lexington Books.

Alonso, Ana Maria. 1994. The Politics of Space, Time, and Substance: State Formation, Nationalism, and Ethnicity. *Annual Review of Anthropology* 23:379–405.

Althusser, Louis. 1971. *Lenin and Philosophy and Other Essays.* London: New Left Books.

Althusser, Louis, and Etienne Balibar. 1970. *Reading Capital.* London: New Left Books.

Alvarez Soto, Guido. 1987. Impacto de la Degradación y Desertificación Sobre el Medio Ambiente en Comunidades Rurales. In *Investigación y Desarrollo de Areas Silvestres Zonas Áridas y Semi-Áridas de Chile,* ed. Alvaro Rojas and Juan Franco. Santiago: Corporación Nacional Forestal Programa de las Naciones para el Desarollo de las Naciones Unidas.

Anderson, Benedict. 1991. *Imagined Communities.* 2nd ed. London: Verso/New Left Books.

Appadurai, Arjun. 1986. Introduc. to *The Social Life of Things: Commodities in Cultural Perspective,* ed. A. Appadurai, 3–63. Cambridge: Cambridge University Press.

Autumn, Suzanne. 1996. Anthropologists, Development, and Situated Truth. *Human Organization* 55 (4): 480–84.

Avendaño, Sergio. 1986. Las Comunidades Agrícolas de la Cuarta Región: Una Particular Relación Hombre-Tierra. Comisión Reginal Para El Desarrollo Integral de las Comunidades Agrícolas de la IV Region: Ovalle, Chile.

Aydin, Zulkuf. 1989. Household Production and Capitalism: A Case Study of Southeastern Turkey. In *The Rural Middle East: Peasant Lives and Modes of Production,* ed. Kathy Glavanis and Pandeli Glavanis. London: Zed Books Ltd.

Azócar, Patricio and Sergio Lailhacar. 1989. Bases Ecológicas para el Desarrollo Agropecuario de la Zona de Clima Mediterráneo de Chile. In *Terra Arida: Taller Interregional Africa/America Latina, MAB-UNESCO.* Coquimbo, Chile: Universidad de Chile Facultad de Ciencias Agrarias y Forestales Centro de Estudios de Zonas Áridas.

Bahamondes, Miguel, Estanislao Gacitua, and Teodoro Rivas. 1992. Una Aproximación Teórico Metodología a la Formulacion de Tipologías de Productores Agrícolas: El Caso de las "Comunidades Agrícolas" de la IV Región. *Revista Agricultura y Sociedad* 9:85–105.

————. 1994. Sistemas Agrícolas Campesinos y Medio Ambiente: El Caso de las Comunidades Agrícolas de la IV Región De Coquimbo, Chile. *Revista Agricultura y Sociedad* 10:7–51.

Balibar, Etienne. 1991. Racism and Nationalism. In *Race, Nation, Class: Ambiguous Identities,* ed. Etienne Balibar and Immanuel Wallerstein. London: Verso.

Batallán, Graciela. 1980. Las Comunidades Agrícolas del Norte Chico Chileno. *Revista Paraguaya de Sociología* 17 (50): 89–139.

Bauer, Arnold J. 1975. *Chilean Rural Society: From the Spanish Conquest to 1930.* Cambridge: Cambridge University Press.

Bernard, H. Russell. 1988. *Research Methods in Cultural Anthropology.* Newbury Park, CA: Sage.

Bonacich, Edna. 1972. A Theory of Ethnic Antagonism: The Split Labor Market. *American Sociological Review* 37:547–59.

Boorstein, Edward. 1977. *Allende's Chile: An Inside View.* New York: International Publishers.

Borde, J., and R. Santana. 1980. *Le Chili: La Terre et les Hommes.* Paris: Editions du CNRS.

Bravo Garcia, Anibal Mariano. 1989. Análisis Comparativo de Paramentos Productivos y Reproductivos de Caprinos a Través de dos Temporadas Comunidad Agrícola Alvarez de Valle Hermosa. Dissertation, Universidad Católica de Valparaíso, Facultad de Agronomía.

Brush, Stephen. 1977. The Myth of the Idle Peasant: Employment in a Subsistence Economy. In *Peasant Livelihood,* ed. R. Halperin and J. Row. New York: St. Martin's Press.

———. 1993. Indigenous Knowledge of Biological Resources and Intellectual Property Rights: The Role of Anthropology. *American Anthropologist* 95 (3): 653–71.

———. 1996. Whose Knowledge, Whose Genes, Whose Rights? In *Valuing Local Knowledge: Indigenous People and Intellectual Property Rights,* ed. S. B. Brush and D. Stabinsky, 41–67. Washington, DC: Island Press.

Calavan, Michael M. 1984. Prospects for Probabilistic Reinterpretation of Chayanovian Theory: An Exploratory Discussion. In *Chayanov, Peasants, and Economic Anthropology,* ed. E. Durrenberger. New York: Academic Press.

Cancian, Frank. 1989. Economic Behavior in Peasant Communities. In *Economic Anthropology,* ed. S. Plattner, 127–70. Stanford, CA: Stanford University Press.

Carroll, Barbara Wake, and Terrance Carroll. 1997. State and Ethnicity in Botswana and Mauritius: A Democratic Route to Development? *Journal of Development Studies* 33 (4): 464–86.

Castro Lucíc, Milka. 1986. Antropología y Mecanismos de Subsistencia. In *Ecosistemas Pastorales de la Zona Mediterránea Árida de Chile.* Vol. 1, *Estudio de las Comunidades Agrícolas de Carquindano y Yerba Loca del Secano Costero de la Región de Coquimbo,* ed. David T. Contreras, Juan C. Gastó, and Fernando G. Cosios. Montevideo: UNESCO.

———. 1988. Antropologia y Mecanismos de Subsistence. In *Ecosistemas Pastorales de la Zona Mediterranea Arida de Chile.* Montevideo: UNESCO-MAB-3.

Castro Lucíc, Milka, and Miguel P. Bahamondes. 1984. Un Aporte Antropológico al Conocimiento de los Mecanismos de Subsistencia de las Comunidades de la IV Región de Chile. *Revista Ambiente y Desarrollas* 1 (1): 143–46.

———. 1986. Surgimiento y Transformación del Sistema Comunitario: Las Comunidades Agrícolas, IV Región, Chile. *Revista Ambiente y Desarrollas* 2 (1): 111–26.

Castro Lucíc, Milka, and Marcela Romo Marty. 1996. *Los Habitante de Zonas Aridas del Norte de Chile y el Uso de Plantas Medicinales Informe Preliminar.* Santiago: Universidad de Chile.

Chayanov, A. V. 1966. Peasant Farm Organization. In *The Theory of Peasant Economy,* ed. Daniel Thorner, Basile Kerblay, and R.E.F. Smith. Madison: University of Wisconsin Press.

Ciadella, Nathalie. 2003. Diversidad de los Sistemas de Producción Caprina y Perspectivas de Evolución en la Region de Coquimbo. In *Dinámicas de los Sistemas Agrarios en Chile Árido: La Región de Coquimbo,* ed. Patrick Livenais and Ximena Aranda. Santiago: Universidad de Chile, Universidad de La Serena, Institut de Recherche pour le Développement.

Cialdella, Nathalie, and Didier Dubroeucq. 2003. La Transhumancia de Cabras en Chile: Un Modo de Gestión Adaptado a las Zonas Áridas. In *Dinámicas de los Sistemas Agrarios en Chile Árido: La Región de Coquimbo,* ed. Patrick Livenais and Ximena Aranda. Santiago: Universidad de Chile, Universidad de La Serena, Institut de Recherche pour le Développement.

CIPRES Consultores. 1993. Diagnostico para la Regularizacion y Sanearmiento de las Comunidades Agrícolas de la Region Metropolitana. Santiago: CIPRES.

Clarke, Colin. 2000. *Class, Ethnicity, and Community in Southern Mexico: Oaxaca's Peasantries.* Oxford: Oxford University Press.

Cohn, Bernard. 1980. History and Anthropology: The State of Play. *Comparative Studies in Society and History* 22 (2): 198–221.

Collier, Simon. 1993. From Independence to the War of the Pacific. In *Chile Since Independence,* ed. Leslie Bethell. Cambridge: Cambridge University Press.

Collier, Simon, and William F. Sater. 1996. *A History of Chile: 1808–1994.* Cambridge: Cambridge University Press.

Collins, Joseph, and John Lear. 1995. *Chile's Free-Market Miracle: A Second Look.* Monroe, OR: Food First Books.

Colloredo-Mansfeld, Rudi. 1999. *The Native Leisure Class: Consumption and Creativity in the Andes.* Chicago: University of Chicago Press.

———. 2002. An Ethnography of Neo-Liberalism: Understanding Competition in Artisan Economies. *Current Anthropology* 43 (1): 113–37.

Comaroff, John L. 1982. Dialectical Systems, History and Anthropology: Units of Study and Questions of Theory. *Journal of Southern African Studies* 8 (2): 143–72.

Comaroff, John, and Jean Comaroff. 1992. *Ethnography and the Historical Imagination.* Boulder, CO: Westview Press.

Comision Regional de Ganado Caprino. 1993. *Higiene de la Leche.* La Serena: Comision Regional de Ganado Caprino.

Conner, Walker. 1994. Ethnonationalism: The Quest for Understanding. Princeton: Princeton University Press.

Contreras T., David, and Juan Gasto C. 1986. Ecosistemas de Pastorero y su Organizacion Antropologica-Social. In *Ecosistemas Pastorales de la Zona Mediterranea Arida de Chile.* Vol. 1, *Estudio de las Comunidades Agricolas de Carquidano y Yerba Loca del Secano Costero de la Region de Coquimbo,* ed. David T. Conteras, Juan C. Gasto, and Fernadno G. Cosio. Montevideo: UNESCO-MAB, COMITE MAB-CHILE.

Cook, Scott, and Leigh Binford. 1990. *Obliging Need: Rural Petty Industry in Mexican Capitalism.* Austin: University of Texas Press.

Cooper, Frederick. 1993. Africa and the World Economy. In *Confronting Historical Paradigms: Peasants, Labor, and the Capitalist World System in Africa and Latin America,* ed. Frederick Cooper, Allen F. Isaacman, Florencia E. Mallon, William Roseberry, Steve J. Stern. Madison: University of Wisconsin Press.

Corrigan, Philip. 1975. On the Politics of Production. *Journal of Peasant Studies* 2 (3): 341–51.

Corrigan, Philip, and Derek Sayer. 1985. *The Great Arch: English State Formation as Cultural Revolution.* Oxford: Basil Blackwell.

Croll, Elisabeth, and David Parkin. 1992. Anthropology, the Environment and Development. In *Bush Base: Forest Farm; Culture, Environment, and Development,* ed. E. Croll and D. Parkin, 11–36. London: Routledge.

David, F. Jorge. 1993. *Trigo en Chile: Una Historia Desconocida.* Santiago: Ediciones Del Día.

de Janvry, Alain. 1981. *The Agrarian Question and Reformism in Latin America.* Baltimore: Johns Hopkins University Press.

de Janvry, Alain, and Ann Vandeman. 1987. Patterns of Proletarianization in Agriculture: An International Comparison. In *Household Economies and Their Transformations,* ed. M. Maclachlan. Lanham: University Press of America.

de la Peña, Guillermo. 1989. Commodity Production, Class Differentiation, and the Role of the State in the Morelos Highlands: An Historical Approach. In *State, Capital, and Rural Society,* ed. B. S. Orlove. Boulder, CO: Westview Press.

Descola, Philippe, and Gísli Pálsson. 1996. Introduction to *Nature and Society: Anthropological Perspectives,* ed. P. Descola and G. Pálsson, 1–21. London: Routledge.

DeWalt, Billie R. 1994. Using Indigenous Knowledge to Improve Agriculture and Natural Resource Management. *Human Organization* 53 (2): 123–31.

Diaz, Harry P. 1990. Proletarianisation and Marginality: The Modernisation of Chilean Agriculture. In *Neo-Liberal Agriculture in Rural Chile,* ed. David E. Hojman. London: Macmillan.

Djurfeldt, Goran. 1982. What Happened to the Agrarian Bourgeoisie and Rural Proletariat Under Monopoly Capitalism? In *Rural Development: Theories of Peasant Economy and Agrarian Change,* ed. John Harris. London: Hutchinson.

Douglas, Mary. 1966. *Purity and Danger: An Analysis of Concepts of Pollution and Taboo.* London: Routledge and Kegan Paul.

Dove, Michael R. 1996. Center, Periphery, and Biodiversity: A Paradox of Governance and a Developmental Challenge. In *Valuing Local Knowledge: Indigenous People and Intellectual Property Rights,* ed. S. B. Brush and D. Stabinsky, 41–67. Washington, DC: Island Press.

Durrenberger, E. Paul. 1984. Operationalizing Chayanov. In *Chayanov, Peasants, and Economic Anthropology,* ed. E. Durrenberger. New York: Academic Press.

Eagleton, Terry. 1991. *Ideology: An Introduction.* London: Verso.

Economist. 2001. What Help for the Temporeras? *Economist* 358 (8209): 41.

———. 2006. Doing It Her Way: Michelle Batchelet. *Economist* 378 (8461): 51.

Ellen, Roy F. 1982. *Environment, Subsistence and System: The Ecology of Small-Scale Social Formations.* Cambridge: Cambridge University Press.

El Día. 1998. Queso de Cabra, Repercusiones del Fin de la Prórroga. February 11, 1998, 16–17.

El Mercurio. 1997. El "Annus Horribilis" Del Norte Chico. October 16, 1997, C, 3.

Engels, Friedrich. 1890/1978. Letter to Joseph Bloch, Sept. 21–22, 1890. In *Marx-Engels Reader,* ed. Robert C. Tucker. 2nd ed. New York: W.W. Norton & Company.

Escobar, Arturo. 1995. *Encountering Development: The Making and Unmaking of the Third World.* Princeton: Princeton University Press.

Farley, John E. 2005. *Majority–Minority Relations.* 5th ed. Upper Saddle River, NJ: Prentice Hall.

Ferguson, James. 1990. *The Anti-politics Machine: "Development," Depoliticization, and Bureaucratic Power in Letsotho.* Cambridge: Cambridge University Press.

———. 1997. The Country and the City on the Copperbelt. In *Culture, Power, Place: Explorations in Critical Anthropology,* ed. Akhil Gupta and James Ferguson, 137–54. Durham, NC: Duke University Press.

Foster, George M. 1965. Peasant Society and the Image of the Limited Good. *American Anthropologist* 67: 293–314.

Foster-Carter, Aidan. 1978. Can We "Articulate" Articulation? In *The New Economic Anthropology,* ed. J. Clammer, 210–249. New York: St. Martin's Press.

Frank, Andre Gunder. 1967. *Capitalism and Underdevelopment in Latin America.* New York: Monthly Review Press.

Friedmann, Harriet 1986. Postscript: Small Commodity Production. *Labour, Capital, and Society* 19 (1): 36–69.

Friedman, Jonathan. 1974. Marxism, Structuralism, and Vulgar Materialism. *Man* 9 (3): 444–69.

Friedrich, Paul. 1977. *Agrarian Revolt in a Mexican Village.* 2nd ed. Chicago: University of Chicago Press.

Gallardo Fernández, Gloria L. 2002. *Communal Land Ownership in Chile: The Agricultural Communities in the Commune of Canela, Norte Chico (1600–1998).* Aldershot, UK: Ashgate Publishing.

Gastó, Juan, David Conteras, Fernando Cosio, and Rolando Demanet. 1990. Degradación y Rehabilitación de la Zona Mediterranea Árida de Chile. In *Terra Árida: Taller Interregional Africa/America Latina, MAB-UNESCO.* Coquimbo, Chile: Universidad de Chile Facultad de Ciencias Agrarias.

Geschiere, Peter, and Reini Raatgever 1985. Introduction to *Old Modes of Production and Capitalist Encroachment: Anthropological Explorations in Africa,* ed. Wim van Binsbergen and Peter Geschiere. London: KPI Ltd.

Ghani, Ashraf. 1995. Writing a History of Power: An Examination of Eric R. Wolf's Anthropological Quest. In *Articulating Hidden Histories: Exploring the Influence of Eric R. Wolf,* ed. Jane Schneider and Rayna Rapp. Berkeley: University of California Press.

Giddens, Anthony. 1999. Globalism. Part 1. British Broadcasting Corporation "Reef Lectures," April 10, 1999.

Godelier, Maurice. 1972. *Rationality and Irrationality in Economics.* New York: Monthly Review Press.

Gow, David. 1996. The Anthropology of Development: Discourse, Agency, and Culture. *Anthropological Quarterly* 69 (3): 165–73.

Gramsci, Antonio. 1971. *Selections from the Prison Notebooks.* New York: International Publishers

Greenberg, James E., and Thomas K. Park. 1994. Political Ecology. *Journal of Political Ecology* 1.

Grifo, Francesca T., and David R. Downes. 1996. Agreements to Collect Biodiversity for Pharmaceutical Research: Major Issues and Proposed Principles. In *Valuing Local Knowledge: Indigenous People and Intellectual Property Rights,* ed. S. B. Brush and D. Stabinsky, 281–304. Washington, DC: Island Press.

Gunderson, Lance H., and C. S. Holling eds. 2002. *Panarchy: Understanding Transformations in Human and Natural Systems.* Washington, DC: Island Press.

Gunderson, Lance H., and Lowell Pritchard, Jr., eds. 2002. Resilience and the Behavior of Large-Scale Systems. Washington DC: Island Press.

Gunderson, Lance H., C.S. Holling, Lowell PritchardJr., and Garry D. Peterson. 2002 Resilience of Large-Scale Resource Systems. In *Resilience and the Behavior of Large-Scale Systems.* Washington, DC: Island Press.

Gupta, Akhil, and James Ferguson, eds. 1997a. Culture, Power, Place: Ethnography at the End of an Era. In *Culture, Power, Place: Explorations in Cultural Anthropology*, 1–29. Durham, NC: Duke University Press.

———. 1997b. Beyond "Culture": Space, Identity, and the Politics of Difference. In *Culture, Power, Place: Explorations in Cultural Anthropology*, 33–51. Durham NC: Duke University Press.

Gwynne, Robert N. 1993. Outward Orientation and Marginal Environments: The Question of Sustainable Development in the Norte Chico, Chile. *Mountain Research and Development* 13 (3): 281–93.

Gwynne, Robert N., and Cristóbal Kay. 1997. Agrarian Change and the Democratic Transition in Chile: An Introduction. *Bulletin of Latin American Research* 16 (1): 3–10.

Gwynne, Robert N. and Claudio Meneses. 1994. Climate Change and Sustainable Development in the Norte Chico, Chile: Land, Water and the Commercialisation of Agriculture. University of Birmingham School of Geography Occasional Publication No. 34. Birmingham, UK.

Gwynne, Robert N., and Jorge Ortiz. 1997. Export Growth and Development in Poor Rural Regions: A Meso-Scale Analysis of the Upper Limarí. *Bulletin of Latin American Research* 16 (1): 25–41.

Hall, Stuart. 1988. The Toad in the Garden: Thatcherisms Among the Theorists. In *Marxism and the Interpreation of Culture*, ed. Carey Nelson and Laurence Grossberg. Urbana: University of Illinois Press.

Hannerz, Ulf. 1992. *Cultural Complexity*. New York: Columbia University Press.

Hardin, Garrett. 1968. The Tragedy of the Commons. *Science* 162:1243–48.

Harris, Marvin. 1977. *Cannibals and Kings*. New York: Random House.

Healy, Kevin. 2001. *Llamas, Weavings, and Organic Chocolate: Multicultural Grassroots Development in the Andes and Amazon of Bolivia*. Notre Dame, IN: University of Notre Dame Press.

Herring, Ronald J. 1984. Chayanovian versus Neoclassical Perspectives on Land Tenure and Productivity Interactions. In *Chayanov, Peasants, and Anthropology*, ed. E. Durrenberger. New York: Academic Press.

Hobsbawm, Eric. 1973. Peasants and Politics. *Journal of Peasant Studies* 1 (1): 3–21.

Hojman, David E. 1990. Introduction to *Neo-Liberal Agriculture in Rural Chile*, ed. David E. Hojman, London: Macmillan.

Holling, C. S. 1973. Resilience and stability of ecological systems. *Annual Review of Ecology and Systematics* 4:1–23.

———. 1996. Engineering Resilience versus Ecological Resilience. In *Engineering within Ecological Constraints*, ed. P. C. Schulze. Washington, DC: National Academy Press.

———. 2004. From Complex Regions to Complex Worlds. *Ecology and Society* 9 (1): 11. Online at http://www.ecologyandsociety.org/vol9/iss1/art11/ (accessed July 22, 2006).

Iannuzzi Mussuto, Rocco, and Victor Hug Salinas Hernandez. 1986. *Comunidades Agrícolas y Uso de los Recursos Territoriales en el Medio Semiárido*. Caso de Estudio: Comunidad Agrícola de Huentelauquen y Areas Aledanas. Memoria de Titulo. Santiago: Universidad de Chile Facultad de Urbanismo.

Ignold, Tim. 1992. Culture and the Perception of the Environment. In *Bush Base: Forest Farm; Culture, Environment, and Development*, ed. E. Croll and D. Parkin, 39–56. London: Routledge.

Instituto Nacional de Estadisticas (INE). 1996. Situacion Económica y Social de las Regiones de Chile. Santiago: INE. Instituto de Investigacion de Recursos Naturales para la Corporacion de Fomento de la Produccion (IREN-CORFO).

———. 1978. Estudio de las Comunidades Agricolas—IV Region. Informe Final Publicacion 20. Santiago: IREN-CORFO.

Intendencia IV Region—Coquimbo. 1996. Programa de Emergencia para la Sequia. La Serena: Intendencia IV Region—Coquimbo.

InternationalReports.net. 2002. President Ricardo Lagos Escobar: Socially Responsible Economic Growth. http://www.internationalreports.net/theamericas/chile/2002/presidentricardo.html. (accessed July 22, 2006).

Jarvis, Lovell S. 1985. *Chilean Agriculture under Military Rule.* Berkeley: Institute of International Studies, University of California.

Jay, Bruce. 2002. Chile Introduces New Rights for Farm Workers in Bid for US-Chile FTA. Summit of the Americas Amerciasnet Web site (March), http://www.americasnet.net/commentators/Bruce—Jay/jay—101.pdf. (accessed July 22, 2006).

Juventudes para el Desarrollo y la Produccion (JUNDEP). n.d. Una Breve Historia de las Comunidades Agrícolas. La Serena: JUNDEP.

———. 1988. Defensa de las Comunidades Agrícolas. La Serena: JUNDEP.

———. 1996. Principales Aspectos de la Ley de Comunidades Agricolas. La Serena: JUNDEP.

Kay, Cristobal. 1993. The Agrarian Policy of the Aylwin Government: Continuity or Change? In *Change in the Chilean Countryside,* ed. David E. Hojman. London: Macmillan.

———. 1997. Globalisation, Peasant Agriculture, and Reconversion. *Bulletin of Latin American Research* 16 (1): 11–24.

Kearney, Michael. 1986a. From the Invisible Hand to Visible Feet: Anthropological Studies of Migration and Development. *Annual Review of Anthropology* 15:331–61.

———. 1986b. Integration of the Mixteca and the Western U.S.–Mexico Region via Migratory Wage Labor. In *Regional Impacts of U.S.–Mexican Relations,* ed. I. Rosenthal-Urey, 71–102. San Diego: Center for U.S.-Mexican Studies, University of California.

———. 1996. *Reconceptualizing the Peasantry.* Boulder, CO: Westview Press.

Keyder, Calgar 1983. The Cycle of Sharecropping and the Consolidation of Small Peasant Ownership in Turkey. *Journal of Peasant Studies* 10 (2 & 3): 130–45.

Korovkin, Tanya. 1990. Neo-Liberal Counter-reform: Peasant Differentiation and Organisation in Tartaro, Central Chile. In *Neo-Liberal Agriculture in Rural Chile,* ed. David E. Hojman. London: Macmillan.

Kroeber, Alfred. 1948. *Anthropology.* New York: Harcourt Brace.

Laclau, Ernesto. 1971. Feudalism and Capitalism in Latin America. *New Left Review* 67:19–38.

Laclau, Ernesto, and Chantal Mouffe. 2001. *Hegemony and Socialist Strategy.* 2nd edition. London: Verso.

Lago, Tomas. 1953. *El Huaso.* Santiago: Ediciones de la Universidad de Chile.

Larrain, Jorge. 1989. *Theories of Development: Capitalism, Colonialism, and Dependency.* Cambridge, UK: Polity.

Lewellen, Ted C. 1983. *Political Anthropology: An Introduction.* South Hadley, MA: Bergin & Garvey Publishers.

Li, Tania Murray. 1996. Images of Community: Discourse and Strategy in Property Relations. *Development and Change* 27:501–27.

Livenais, Patrick, and Ximena Aranda. 2003. Sistema de Comundidea Agricolas. In *Dinámicas de los Sistemas Agrarios en Chile Árido: La Región de Coquimbo*, ed. Patrick Livenais and Ximena Aranda. Santiago: Universidad de Chile, Universidad de La Serena, Institut de Recherche pour le Développement.

Loveman, Brian. 1988. *Chile: The Legacy of Hispanic Capitalism.* 2nd ed. New York: Oxford University Press.

Martínez, Javier, and Alvaro Díaz. 1996. *Chile: The Great Transformation.* Washington, DC: Brookings Institution.

Marx, Karl, and Friedrich Engels. 2001. *The German Ideology.* Part 1. Ed. C. J. Arthur. London: Electric Book Company.

Marx, Karl. 1976. *Capital.* Vol. 1. London: Penguin Books.

———. 1989. *Readings from Karl Marx.* Ed. Derek Sayer. London: Routledge.

———. 1994. *The Eighteenth Brumaire of Louis Bonaparte.* New York: International Publishers.

McCay, Bonnie, and Svein Jentoft. 1998. Market or Community Failure? Critical Perspectives on Common Property Research. *Human Organization* 57 (1): 21–29.

McMichael, Philip. 2004. *Development and Social Change: A Global Perspective,* 3rd edition. Thousand Oaks, CA: Pineforge Press.

Medina, Laurie Kroshus. 1997. Development Policies and Identity Politics: Class and Collectivity in Belize. *American Ethnologist* 24 (1): 148–69.

Meillassoux, Claude. 1981. Maidens, Meals, and Money. Cambridge: Cambridge University Press.

Ministerio de Agricultura-Chile. 1995. Marco General de la Política Ambiental 1995: Sistema Medio Ambiental del Sector Silvoagropecuario. Santiago: Ministerio de Agricultura.

Ministerio de Bienes Nacionales. 1998. Características de las Comunidades Agrícolas. La Serena: Ministerio de Bienes Nacionales.

Ministerio de Obras Publicas, Direccion General de Aguas. 1997. Pronóstico de Disponibilidad de Agua Temporada de Riego, 1997–1998. Santiago: Ministerio de Obras Publicas.

Muñoz, Mélica. 1985. *Flores del Norte Chico.* La Serena, Chile: Dirección de Bibliotécas, Archivos y Museos, Munincipalidad de La Serena.

Nagengast, Carol, and Michael Kearney. 1990. Mixtec Ethnicity: Social Identity, Political Consciousness, and Political Activism. *Latin American Research Review* 25 (2): 61–91.

Nash, June. 1981. Ethnographic Aspects of the Modern World-System. *Annual Review of Anthropology* 10:393–423.

Nugent, Daniel. 1993. *Spent Cartridges of Revolution: An Anthropological History of Namiquipa, Chihuahua.* Chicago: University of Chicago Press.

———. 1994. Social Class and Labor Process in the Determination of a "Peasantry" in Northern Mexico. *Critique of Anthropology* 14 (3): 285–313.

Olson, Mancur. 1965. *The Logic of Collective Action: Public Goods and the Theory of Groups.* Cambridge, MA: Harvard University Press.

Ortner, Sherry. 1973. On Key Symbols. *American Anthropologist* 75 (5): 1338–46.

———. 1984. Theory in Anthropology since the Sixties. *Comparative Studies in Society and History* 26 (1): 126–66.

Paez, H., Manuel Orlando. 1991. Una Aproximacion al Analisis de la Sustentabilidad de la Produccion Caprina en un Sistema Predial Comunero de la Cuarta Region: Estudio de Caso. Dissertation, Universidad de Concepcion Facultad de Ciencias Agronomicos Veterinarias y orestales, Departamento de Medicina Veterinaria.

Paley, Julia. 2001. *Marketing Democracy: Power and Social Movements in Post-Dictatorship Chile.* Berkeley: University of California Press.

Pálsson, Gísli. 1996. Human-Environment Relations: Orientalism, Paternalism, Communalism. In *Nature and Society: Anthropological Perspectives,* ed. P. Descola and G. Pálsson, 63–81. London: Routledge.

Pederson, Leland. 1966. The Mining Industry of the Norte Chico, Chile. Evanston, IL: Northwestern University Studies in Geography, No. 11, Foreign Field Research Program, Report No. 29.

Peoples, James, and Garrick Bailey. 1988. *Humanity: An Introduction to Cultural Anthropology.* St. Paul, MN: West Publishing Company.

Petras, James, and Fernando Ignacio Leiva. 1994. *Democracy and Poverty in Chile: The Limits to Electoral Politics.* Boulder, CO: Westview Press.

Plattner, Stuart. 1989. Marxism. In *Economic Anthropology,* ed. Stuart Plattner. Stanford, CA: Stanford University Press.

Pollock, Alex. 1989. Sharecropping in the North Jordan Valley: Social Relations of Production. In *The Rural Middle East: Peasant Lives and Modes of Production,* ed. Kathy Glavanis and Pandeli Glavanis. London: Zed Books Ltd.

Portes, Alejandro. 2000. Neoliberalism and the Sociology of Development: Emerging Trends and Unanticipated Facts. In *From Modernization To Globalization: Perspectives on Development and Social Change,* ed. J. Timmons Roberts and Amy Hite, Malden MA: Blackwell, 353–372.

Post, Ken. 1978. *Arise, Ye Starvelings!* The Hague: Martinus Nijhoff.

PRODECOP (Proyecto de Desarrollo Ruralde Comunidades Campesinas y Pequeños Productoresde la IV Region). 1997. Memoria Annual 1997. La Serena: Chile: PRODECOP.

Ramírez Livingston, Martin Alberto. 1991. La Producción de Queso de Cabra (Capra Hircus) Análisis de Casos con Énfasis en una Comunidad Agrícolas de la Región de Coquimbo. Dissertation, Universidad Católica de Valparaíso, Facultad de Agronomía.

Reinhardt, Nola. 1988. *Our Daily Bread: The Peasant Question and Family Farming in the Colombia Andes.* Berkeley: University of California Press.

Resilience Alliance. Research on Resilience in Social-Ecological Systems: A Basis for Understanding Sustainability (homepage). http://www.resalliance.org/1.php (accessed July 22, 2006).

Rey, Pierre-Philippe. 1975. The Lineage Mode of Production. *Critique of Anthropology* 3:27–79.

Reyes Morales, Nira. 2002. Chile: No Future Without a Past. *La Monde Diplomatique* (November), http://mondediplo.com/2002/11/10chile (accessed July 22, 2006).

Rodgers, Susan. 1993. Batak Heritage and Indonesian State: Print Literacy and the Construction of Ethnic Cultures in Indonesia. In *Ethnicity and the State,* ed. Judith Toland. New Brunswick, NJ: Transcation Publications.

Roseberry, William. 1988. Domestic Modes, Domesticated Models. *Journal of Historical Sociology* 1 (4): 423–30.

———. 1989a. Peasants and the World. In *Economic Anthropology,* ed. S. Plattner. Stanford, CA: Stanford University Press.

———. 1989b. *Anthropologies and Histories: Essays in Culture, History, and Political Economy.* New Brunswick: Rutgers University Press.

———. 1991. Potatoes, Sacks, and Enclosures in Early Modern England. In *Golden Ages, Dark Ages: Imagining the Past in Anthropology and History*, ed. Jay O'Brien and William Roseberry. Berkeley: University of California Press.

Rosenfeld, Stephanie. 1993. Comunero Democracy Endures in Chile. *NACLA Report On The Americas* 27 (2): 29–34.

Rostow, W. W. 1960. *The Stages of Economic Growth: A Non-Communist Manifesto.* Cambridge: Cambridge University Press.

Russell, James W. 1989. *Modes of Production in World History.* London: Routledge.

Sahlins, Marshall. 1976. *Culture and Practical Reason.* Chicago: University of Chicago Press.

Santander Agapito M. 1992a. Comunidades Agrícolas IV Region: Proposición de una Estrategía para Tratar de Erradicar la Extrema Pobreza Aseguarando Protección y Conservación del edio Ambiente Perfiles de Planes y Programas de Desarrollo. Santaigo: CEDECOM (Centro de Desarrollo Comunitario Económico y Social).

———. 1992b. Comunidad Agrícola Peña Blanca: Principales Indicadores de Encuesta Técnico-Socio-Económica Realizada en 1991. Agraria—Desarrollo Campesino y Alimentario Proyecto Norte Árido—CEE IV Región (Ovalle).

———. 1993. Norte Chico (Chile). Contribución al Estudio del Impacto de la Economía Minero-Cuprifera en el Desmonte o Tala de la Vegetacion Arborea y Arbustiva, 1601–1900. Ovalle-Illapel.

——— 1994. Sequías en las Comunidades Agrícolas de la IV Región: Características y Impactos, Vulnerabilidad e Los Grupos Socio-Económicos la Acción del Estado Propuesta de una Estrategía de Lucha. Illapel.

———. 2003. Norte Chico (Chile). Consumo de Combustibles en el Procesamiento de los Minerales de Cobre y Su Impacto Sobre los Recursos Arbóreos y Arbustivos: 1601–1900. In *Dinámicas de los Sistemas Agrarios en Chile Árido: La Región de Coquimbo*, ed. Patrick Livenais and Ximena Aranda. Santiago: Universidad de Chile, Universidad de La Serena, Institut De Recherche Pour Le Developpement.

Saveedra, Mauricio. 1999. Chilean President Revives Labour Reforms in Bid to Win Votes. *World Socialist* web Site (Dec. 11), http://www.wsws.org/articles/1999/dec1999/chile-d11.shtml (accessed July 22, 2006).

Schneider, Hans. 1982. Drought, Demography, and Destitution: Crisis in the Norte Chico. *GeoJoural* 6 (2): 111–19.

Scott, Christopher D. 1990. Land Reform and Property Rights among Small Farmers in Chile, 1968–86. In *Neo-Liberal Agriculture in Rural Chile*, ed. David E. Hojman. London: Macmillan Press Ltd.

Shanin, Teodor. 1987. Introduction to *Peasants and Peasant Societies.* Ed. T. Shanin. London: Basil Blackwell.

Shiva, Vandana. 1993. *Monocultures of the Mind.* London: Zed Books.

Silva, Patricio. 1991. The Military Regime and Restructuring of Land Tenure. *Latin American Perspectives* 18 (1): 15–32.

Smith, Carol A. 1984. Does a Commodity Economy Enrich the Few While Ruining the Masses? Differentiation Among Petty Commodity Producers in Guatemala. *Journal of Peasant Studies* 11:60–95.

———. 1990. Class Position and Class Consciousness in an Indian Community: Totonicapán in the 1970s. In *Guatemalan Indians and the State: 1540–1988*, ed. Carol Smith. Austin: University of Texas Press.

Smith, M. Estellie. 1989. The Informal Economy. In *Economic Anthropology,* ed. Stuart Plattner. Stanford, CA: Stanford University Press.

Smith, Gavin 1989. *Livelihood and Resistance.* Berkeley: University of California Press.

So, Alvin Y. 1990. *Social Change and Development: Modernization, Dependency, and World-System Theories.* London: Sage Publications.

Solis de Ovando, Juan. 1992. Comunidad Agrícola Jimenez y Tapia: Documentos emanados del proceso de saneamiento. Santiago: Ministerio de Bienes Nacionales.

———. 1989. Normativa Legal de las Comunidades Agrícolas: Estudio Critico del D.F.L. No. 5 de 1967 del Ministerio de Agricultura con sus Modificaciones Posteriores. Santiago: JUNDEP.

Stavenhagen, Rodolfo. 1978. Capitalism and the Peasanty in Mexico. *Latin American Perspectives* 5 (3): 27–37.

Stern, Steve J. 1993. Feudalism, Capitalism, and the World-System in the Perspective of Latin America and the Caribbean. In *Confronting Historical Paradigms: Peasants, Labor, and the Capitalist World System in Africa and Latin America,* ed. Frederick Cooper, Allen F. Isaacman, Florencia E. Mallon, William Roseberry, and Steve J. Stern. Madison: University of Wisconsin Press.

———. 1987. New Approaches to the Study of Peasant Rebellion and Consciousness. In *Resistance, Rebellion, and Consciousness in the Andean Peasant World,* ed. Steve J. Stern. Madison: University of Wisconsin Press.

Stephen, Lynn. 2002. ¡Zapata Lives!: Histories and Cultural Politics in Southern Mexico Berkeley: University of California Press.

Toland, Judith. 1993. Introduction to *Ethnicity and the State,* ed. Judith Toland. New Brunswick, NJ: Transaction Publications.

Valdes, Juan G. 1995. *Pinochet's Economists: The Chicago School in Chile.* Cambridge: Cambridge University Press.

van den Berghe, Pierre L. 1990. *State Violence and Ethnicity.* Niwot: University Press of Colorado.

Vargas-Cetin, Gabriela. 2000. From Handicraft to Monocrop: The Production of Pecorino Cheese in Highland Sardinia. In *Commodities and Globalization: Anthropological Perspectives,* ed. Angelique Haugerud, M. Priscilla Stone, and Peter D. Little. Boston: Rowman and Littlefield.

Veidt, Heinz. 1993. Upper Quarternary Landscape and Climate Evolution in the Norte Chico: An Overview. *Mountain Research and Development* 13 (2): 138–44.

Wallerstein, Immanuel. 1974. *The Modern World System.* Vol. 1, *Capitalist Agriculture and the Origins of the European World-Economy in the Sixteenth Century.* New York: Academic Press.

Weaver, Thomas. 2001. Time, Space, and Articulation in the Economic Development of the U.S.-Mexico Border Region from 1940 to 1990. *Human Organization* 60 (2): 105–120.

——— 1996. Mapping the Policy Terrain: Political Economy, Policy Environment, and Forestry Production in Northern Mexico. *Journal of Political Ecology* 3:37–68.

Weaver, Thomas, William A. Shaw, and William L. Alexander. 1996. Problemas Encontrados en Bio-Prospectando de Plantas Medicinales. Actas del Segundo Congreso de Antropólogos Chilenos. Valdivia, Chile: Universidad de Chile.

———. 1999. Aspectos en la Bioprospección de Plantas Medicinales en Chile y Argentina. In *Aspectos Técnicos, Culturales, Políticos y Legales de la Bioprospección en*

Argentina, ed. E. Suarez, R. Fortunato, M. Elechosa, R. Casamiquela, and B. N. Timmermann. Buenos Aires: Latin American International Cooperative Biodiversity Groups Program—Argentina, Chile, and Mexico.

Wilk, Richard R. 1996. *Economies and Cultures: Foundations of Economic Anthropology.* Boulder, CO: Westview Press.

Williams, Brackette. 1989. A Class Act: Anthropology and the Race to Nation Across Ethnic Terrain. *Annual Review of Anthropology* 18:401–44.

Williams, Raymond. 1977. *Marxism and Literature.* Oxford: Oxford University Press.

Wolf, Eric. 1957. Closed Corporate Communities in Mesoamerica and Central Java. *Southwestern Journal of Anthropology* 13:1–18.

———. 1966. *Peasants.* Englewood Cliffs, NJ: Prentice-Hall.

———. 1982. *Europe and the People without History.* Berkeley: University of California Press.

Wolpe, Harold. 1980. Introduction to *The Articulation of Modes of Production*, ed. Harold Wolpe. London: Routledge and Paul Kegan.

Worsley, Peter. 1984. *The Three Worlds: Culture and World Development.* Chicago: University of Chicago Press.

Index

agrarian reform in Chile: 1965–1973, 77–78; counter-reform during dictatorship, 78–80

agribusiness: break up of estates, 79–80; export-oriented development of 52, 84–86, 95–96; expansion of wheat production, 75–76; mining and, 72; wage labor and, 77

Allende, Salvador (*Unidad Popular* government 1970–1973): agrarian reform and, 78–81, 83; support for rural communities and, 186–87

Alonso, Ana, 213

Althusser, Louis, 25, 45–47, 221. *See also* articulation of modes of production theory

Anderson, Benedict, 193, 194

anthropology: applied, 145; development, 51, 231; ethnographic research, 27, 29–30;

fieldwork, 23, 26, 231; neo-Marxist structuralist, 45–47; of peasant culture and rural communities, 24–28, 49

Appadurai, Arjun, 203–4

Argentina, 99, 147

articulation of modes of production theory, 25–26, 32, 41–49, 128, 184, 188, 191, 233. *See also* mode of production

"Asian Crisis" (1997–1998 financial crisis), 96–97

Aymara culture, 53, 66, 212

Balibar, Etienne, 45–46, 213

Bachelet, Michelle, 99

biodiversity: climate change and loss of, 240; international agreements on, 51–52; market value of, 237; and sustainable development, 229–32

bioprospecting, 51–52, 232

Bolivia, 209

"bounded community" concept, 24, 128, 234

Brazil, 99

Cancian, Frank 208

Castro Lucíc, Milka, 64, 67, 88–89, 96, 186

Chayanov, Alexander, 34–37, 188

coalition government in Chile (*Concertación*), 73: as "Third Way" Socialism, 97–99; during the "transition to democracy," 96

colonial era in Chile, 66–69, 74–75, 76. *See also* mining; wheat production

comunidades agrícolas ("agricultural communities"): 18; delimiting boundaries of and registering rights in, 76–77, 211; democracy in, 18, 21–22, 62–64, 82, 170–80, 235; historical origins of, 65–70; intercommunity relations between, 64–65; land privatization efforts (and resistance to), 82–84; land tenure system of, 21–22, 58–63, 232–33, 235; political organization of, 18, 63–64, 178–79, 183–84; persecution of during dictatorship, 73, 82, 152; post-dictatorship revitalization of, 215–17; regulation of land use in, 64, 182, 235; *vecinos* (non-comuneros) in, 63, 183; women's leadership in, 62–63, 216–17

comunero: title of, 21, 61–62, 130; image and identity of, 49, 70–71, 87, 128, 192, 205–7, 210–15

commodity fetishism, 204

communal land: 18, 102–3, 211, 233; for grazing (*campo común*), 60, 129–

communal land (*continued*)
39; for agriculture (*lluvias*), 60, 139–40
Comaroff, Jean and John, 213–14
Corrigan, Philip, 81, 194–95
copper. *See* mining
cowboy (*huaso*) culture, 65, 113–15, 117–19, 207
cultural materialism, 220–23

Day of the Dead (*El Día de los Difuntos*), 105–7
deJanvry, Alain, 38–39, 40, 78, 80, 83, 188. *See also* "functional dualism"
Dependency Theory: 41, 50; and "development of underdevelopment" thesis, 204
development agencies in Chile, 21–22: "Plan Punitaqui" (1964), 86–87; relationship with and projects in comunidades agrícolas, 87–89, 128–29, 150, 199–201, 215–18, 223–29, 236–37
Diaguita culture, 66–67, 211
Douglas, Mary 220

earthquake (October 14, 1997), 15–16, 18, 20, 104, 108, 121, 216
Ecuador, 209
El Mercurio (newspaper), 16
El Niño weather phenomenon (1997), 18
Engels, Friedrich, 194, 220, 221
environment and natural resources of Norte Chico, 16–18, 30, 52–58: deforestation, 75–76, 92, 212; drought, 16–17, 91–92, 186, 196–97, 216; economic livelihood and, 235–39; erosion, 17, 20, 52, 75, 94, 196; geology of arid land, 91–92; management of in communities, 235; protection of and public policy, 75, 237; reforestation projects, 196, 228–29
Escobar, Arturo, 222

Ferguson, James, 213, 214
formalist/substantivist debate in economic anthropology, 34–35
Foster, George, 180–81. *See also* "Image of Limited Good"
Foster-Carter, Aidan, 41–42
Frank, Andre Gunder, 41. *See also* Dependency Theory

Frei Montalva, Eduardo, 78–81, 86
frontier culture, 49, 70, 206–7. *See also* cowboy culture
"functional dualism," 38–39, 209

Gallardo-Fernández, Gloria, 69–70
Giddens, Anthony, 25
goats and goat cheese, 130–35: commercial production, 44–45, 148, 195–99, 215–16, 226–27; hygiene law regulating production of cheese, 31, 44–45, 195–97, 204–7, 212, 218, 223–26
Godelier, Maurice 153
Gunderson, Lance, 239–40. *See also* Resilience Theory
Gramsci, Antonio, 222–23
Guatemala, 209
Gupta, Akhil, 214

Hanerz, Ulf, 213
Hardin, Garrett, 181–82. *See also* "Tragedy of the Commons"
Harris, Marvin, 220. *See also* cultural materialism
hegemony: of the State, 193–95, 222–23
historical materialism, 44, 220–21
Hobsbawn, Eric, 80–81
Holling, Crawford Stanley, 239–40. *See also* Resilience Theory
horse races (*carreras*), 29, 70, 111, 119–21, 190, 207. *See also* mutual assistance

ideology: Althusser's notion of 45, 47, 221; development and the state, 223, 231–32; Marx on "ruling ideas," 220; neoliberal and development discourse, 23, 193, 212; peasant, 180; socialist and influence of mining labor unions, 72, 73, 82
identity. *See* comunero, image and identity of; cowboy culture; frontier culture; "Policy–Positioned Ascriptions of Ethnicity, Identity, and History"
"Image of Limited Good," 180–84
International Convention on Biodiversity (ICB) treaty (1992), 51. *See also* biodiversity

Kearney, Michael, 41, 48–49, 50, 188, 209, 214
Kroeber, Alfred, 207–8

labor unions, 48–49, 81–82, 212; influence in comunidades agrícolas, 72, 73, 82, 144
Lagos, Ricardo, 97–99
lamb production and sheep, 135–37
language, as marker of identity, 70, 206
Lenin, Vladmir (Ulyanov), 37–38
Levi-Strauss, Claude, 185
Loveman, Brian, 72

Mapuche culture, 53, 79, 206–7, 211, 212
Marx, Karl, 27, 37–38; *Capital,* 42–43, 204, 223; *The Eighteenth Brummaire of Louis Bonaparte,* 180, 221; *The German Ideology* 194, 220, 223
Meillassoux, Claude, 39–40, 188
Mexico, 29, 48–49, 77, 111, 209, 214
migration, wage labor, 21–22, 40, 42, 44, 48–49, 96–98, 188–90, 228, 232–34
military coup in Chile (September 11, 1973), 79, 82, 102
mining (copper) in Chile, 52, 73–75, 206; community articulation with via migration, 40, 73, 87, 184, 192, 221–22, 229, 233; comunero identity from, 192, 212; during colonial era, 67–68, 211, 221–22, 229, 233; environmental impact of, 75–76, 212; organized labor movement in, 72, 77, 81–82
Mistral, Gabriela (Lucila Godoy y Alcayaga), 71
mode of production, 77, 188–90, 213–14, 221–22, 230–31, 238
modernization, 49, 73, 81, 201–2, 204
"Mutable Mobile Modes of Resource Maximization," 31, 184, 227, 232–34, 241
mutual assistance: 18; "social forms of" in *comités* ("common good" community projects), 30, 103–8, 119–22, 183–84, 190, 224, 228, 233–34; "work-focused forms of" in shared labor, group production, and reciprocity, 30–31, 103, 122–27, 157, 173–78, 190, 224, 232–34

nationalism, 31, 116–19, 193–94, 212–14
neoliberalism in Chile: backlash against and anti-globalization movement, 99;

"Chilean Miracle," 96; during the dictatorship, 193, 229; export-orientation, 84–86; impact on poor 45, 96, 193, 227; rural development and, 226–29, 242; "Third Way Socialism" and 99; "Washington Consensus" and 99
Nugent, Daniel, 33, 46, 48, 50, 180, 188

Ortner, Sherry, 26–27

Paley, Julia, 203
pastoralism, 21–22, 58: expansion of grape production impact on, 85; migration during drought, 21, 143–51, 159–61, 186, 196–97, 233–34; overgrazing and, 22, 128, 192, 201; protection against overgrazing, 64, 182
peasantry and peasants: dual nature of 110–11, 128, 207–8, 238–39; "elimination of" theory, 29–30, 38–41, 73, 152, 179–80; expressions of identity, 48–49, 70, 116–19; petty commodities and, 45, 136, 190, 207–10, 227, 232; "persistence of" theory, 29–30, 34–38, 73, 153, 179, 241; rebellions and revolution, 80–81; views of development agents, 128
Peru, 66–68, 78
Pinochet dictatorship (1973–1990), 73, 78–79, 81, 96, 179, 181; social memory of, 186–88, 193
pisco, 67–71, 92, 205
"Policy-Positioned Ascriptions of Ethnicity, Identity, and History," 31, 49, 192, 210–15
political economy, 26, 31, 33, 44
political ecology, 27, 33
Portes, Alejandro, 79, 193
Post, Ken, 42, 47, 221
post-modernism, 27–28
poverty, 18, 31, 52, 96–99, 193, 227, 230, 232, 237; "Chile Solidario" program, 98
proletarianization, 38–39, 73, 95, 147, 180, 189, 208, 230–31

race and racism, 66, 205, 212–15. *See also* "Policy-Positioned Ascriptions of Ethnicity, Identity, and History"
reciprocity. *See* mutual assistance

Resilience Theory, 239–41; "adapt-
    ability" defined, 241; "panarchy"
    defined, 240; Resilience Alliance, 240;
    "resilience" defined, 241
Rey, Phillippe, 43, 45. *See also* articula-
    tion of modes of production theory
rodeo, 29, 70, 112–19, 207. *See also* mu-
    tual assistance
Roseberry, William, 24–25, 26, 41, 46,
    48, 50, 153, 208

Sahlins, Marshall, 26
Santander Marin, Agapito, 67–69, 75,
    88–89, 91
Sayer, Derek, 194–95
Shanin, Teodor, 34–36, 188
Shiva, Vandana, 237
spatialization of identity, 212–13
Stephen, Lynn 29
"Subsistence-Stewardship Approach to
    Productive Diversity," 31–32, 227,
    235–39, 241

"Tragedy of the Commons," 180–84

UFOs, 71
Uruguay, 99

Venezuela, 153

Wallerstein, Immanuel, 41. *See also*
    World System Theory
War of the Pacific (1879–1883), 66
water rights and markets, 92–96
Weaver, Thomas, 27, 52, 77, 192
wheat production: boom during seven-
    teenth and nineteenth centuries, 74,
    75–76, 221–22; ecological impact of,
    75–76; in Loma Seca, 22, 70, 102–4,
    107, 139–43, 124–27, 173–78, 224,
    233; persistence of in comunidades,
    64–65, 70
Williams, Brackette, 213
Williams, Raymond, 221
Wilk, Richard, 34–35
Wolf, Eric, 47, 48, 70–71, 214
Wolpe, Harold, 43, 46
World System Theory, 41, 50, 77

Zapatista rebellion, 29